THE OX ON THE ROOF

BY THE SAME AUTHOR

Saint-Saëns and His Circle
Sacha Guitry, The Last Boulevardier
The Duke of Wellington
Massenet
Rossini
The Astonishing Adventure of General Boulanger

Translation

Francis Poulenc: My Friends and Myself

JAMES HARDING

The Ox on the Roof

*Scenes from musical life in Paris
in the Twenties*

Macdonald · London

First published in Great Britain in 1972 by
Macdonald and Company (Publishers) Ltd,
St Giles House, 49 Poland Street, London W.1.

SBN 356 03967 6

Made and printed in Great Britain by
Tonbridge Printers Ltd, Peach Hall Works,
Shipbourne Road, Tonbridge, Kent

CONTENTS

ACKNOWLEDGEMENTS

IT is pleasant to acknowledge the kindness of Darius Milhaud and Louis Durey, two surviving members of 'les Six', who have been delightfully enthusiastic about this book and generous of their reminiscences. I am no less grateful for valuable help received from André Billy; René Clair; Marie Dormoy; Bengt Häger, of the Kereografiska Institutet in Stockholm; Marcel Jouhandeau ... and Élise; Paul Morand; Pascal Pia; and Graham Reynolds, Keeper of the Department of Prints and Drawings and Paintings, Victoria and Albert Museum. I owe, too, a very real debt to Mrs D. L. Mackay, of Duns, and to Mrs Stella Reed for her photographic skill. A final word of gratitude is due to Rollo Myers, who lived at the heart of the 'Ox on the Roof' period and who should really have written this book.

LIST OF ILLUSTRATIONS

Between pages 128–129

In Memory of
Francis Poulenc
Musicien de France

When will people get out of the habit of explaining everything?

FRANCIS PICABIA

ADVERTISEMENT

THE river known to Julius Caesar as the Sequana and to later generations as the Seine was, in neolithic times, a favourite watering place for thirsty mammoths. These specimens of *Elephas primigenius* dwelt up on the heights of today's Belleville, whence they were accustomed to lumber down each day to dip their nine-foot long tusks in the water. (Construction work in 1903 on the Métro near the Porte des Lilas unearthed one of their giant molars. At least one reason for the Métro's odorous atmosphere, one is tempted to think, may be the presence of elephant carcases as yet undiscovered.) Prehistorians have established that the march of the mammoths came into Paris by way of the rue Saint-Denis. A disrespectful chance makes it the traditional route followed by the kings and queens of France when they made their ceremonial entry for their coronation.

The Parisii tribe, centuries afterward, built an encampment on an island in the Sequana. The Romans called their settlement Lutetia. The French named it Paris. The subsequent history of that place is rich in marvels. Everyone knows how Saint Denis was decapitated by the Romans. He then bent down to pick up his head, and, tucking it beneath his arm, walked all the way up to Montmartre, the hill of the martyrs, accompanied by a sweet melody of angels. 'Monsieur,' said Madame du Deffand when an obliging cardinal told her the story, 'en de telles affaires il n'y a que le premier pas qui coûte.'

We know, too, how the miraculous Sainte Geneviève not only cured her mother of blindness but also preserved the city from Attila the Hun and saved it, yet again, from the besieging Childeric. The accounts of what Voltaire slyly called 'cette ville près de Gonesse' relate many other wondrous events. But since the time of the mammoths there has been little mention of animals. Until, that is, the 1920s.

During that period an ox was enthroned as a social and artistic symbol. *Le Boeuf sur le toit* was the title of a ballet devised by Jean Cocteau with music by Darius Milhaud. The name was given soon afterwards to a night club which prospered as a lively meeting place for all who were involved in the artistic movements which then made Paris a centre of experiment and exhilaration. The young Claude Mauriac was never to forget that solemn moment in the evening when his famous parent used to set off for the magic world where 'an enigmatic ox' grazed on the roof. The ox presided over the breakdown in social conventions brought on by the war. Its glassy eye watched unmoved the spectacle of women smoking cigarettes in public and of the arts invaded by anarchy. The benevolent animal was at home alike to 'flappers' and artists, to showmen and musicians, to dress designers and poets.

This book is about a movement that never was. It concerns the group of composers known as 'les Six' and their attendant spirits. With Jean Cocteau as their spokesman they helped to create the mood that set the ox on the roof. They were called 'les Six' because, as a journalist pointed out with Cartesian rigour, there were six of them. Their names were Georges Auric, Louis Durey, Arthur Honegger, Darius Milhaud, Francis Poulenc and Germaine Tailleferre. Honegger and Poulenc are dead. The others, indestructibly, remain.

The creation of the Six as a group was largely the work of Jean Cocteau. They had a mythopoeic quality as fleeting as the evanescent sparkle of his own brilliant conversation. He himself was later to admit that they were really little more than a gathering of people held together by friendship and social circumstance. If they did not found a school or stimulate disciples, they at least contributed something which made the flavour of the Twenties unique.

Many of that period's ideas have been taken up in our time and presented, with self-congratulation, as if they were new. Nothing, however, is new. In the seventeenth century La Bruyère was already observing: 'Tout est dit.' Every age rediscovers for itself. The Six brought to this act of rediscovery a spontaneous and informal gaiety that are no longer possible. Paris was still a city which had its own character and which made room for individuality and artistic innovation. Today it shares the fate of any other over-populated capital. The few remaining features that link it to the Paris of the Six include the defective telephone service, which even then was a source of exasperation, and the traffic problems which so annoyed Maurice Sachs in his time.

Some may look on the Six as belonging, with composers of other nationalities, to a sunset age that preceded the collapse of music into bankruptcy and charlatanry. Others may deplore in their work and their personalities a lack of that 'spirit of compulsory games' which, Sir Osbert Sitwell noted, so healthfully permeates the music of Elgar. There are those, also, who regret the absence of any preoccupation with the higher morality. Whatever the faults attributed to the Six, morality, it is pleasant to report, was never one of their interests, just as it is a topic which French music as a whole has always avoided with a refreshing grace.

For the purpose of this chronicle the Twenties begin with Satie's *Parade* in 1917 and end with Poulenc's *Aubade* in 1929, the moment of the Wall Street crash. That was the year when the ox came down from the roof. The period it represents is now as dead and distant as the age when the mammoths trooped over from Belleville. Together with the ox and François I's heraldic salamander, they form a little bestiary that has its place in the history of Paris.

J. H.

I

WAR–AND 'PARADE'

I

The Chemin des Dames is a pretty name. There is a ring of
gallantry to it, an air of deference. It suggests a readiness to
step aside and offer the ladies a road of their very own. In
1917 there were few ladies in the area except those unlucky
enough to have homes there, for the Chemin des Dames, which
runs over the ridges of the Aisne, was the scene of a bitter
collision between the French and German armies. The little
railway station of Vauxaillon, twenty minutes from Soissons on
the line that goes to Laon, was a heap of shattered stones.
From time to time a pile of rubble collapsed uneasily to the
jagged rhythm of distant mortar fire. On the slopes above the
railway line stood German blockhouses, well camouflaged and
robustly concreted.

Below and in front lay trenches and embankments dug by
the French. They were manned by colonials, rough and hearty
men, often drunk, fiercely patriotic, and generally tougher in
battle than recruits from the mother country. Their comrades
were Negro troops, magnificent African warriors who looked
even more unnerving in the dull rig of a poilu's uniform. An
officer, surprised by the peculiar smell that came from one of
their haversacks, ordered it to be opened. Inside it was the
decomposing head of an enemy soldier. The trophy had been
cut off by the huge machete that the blacks carried with
them.

In the freezing cold they waited, cursed, and anxiously inspected the state of their feet. Toes were the constant preoccupation of infantrymen. Frost-bite could penetrate the
thickest of boots and the warmest of socks. Chilblains flourished.
Trench-foot rotted luxuriantly. The turgid slime of a damp

foggy April sucked eagerly at the feet that stirred its muddy depths.

On the banks of the river Aisne tanks were drawn up in readiness. These novel machines, powered by engines that were alarmingly capricious, had never before accompanied a French army into battle. If the sheet iron which encased them was thin, the treads on which they moved were frailer still. Crossing a ditch was a major achievement. Climbing a slope represented a triumph. A stream was impassable. Within the carcase half a dozen men sweated in the stink of gun powder and unbearable heat. Here they guided, steered, fired and fought, and if they once opened the door for a breath of precious air they risked their lives. But the lumbering monsters, spitting fire and lurching inexorably towards their objective, would strike fear into the enemy and quickly demoralize them. That, at least, was the belief of their commander, an elegant, monocled and irrepressible artillery man. Old foot-soldiers thought otherwise. If they were to be fried alive, they preferred the event to take place in the open air.

The commander-in-chief of the armies of the North and North-East was General Robert Nivelle. A veteran of China and North Africa, he had distinguished himself at Verdun. As was to be expected from a brilliant product of the École Polytechnique, he had devised a carefully thought-out plan. This plan, a model of logic and clarity, was a textbook example of military thought at its most persuasive. It distilled the wisdom of many years' study and meditation. The Napoleonic principle of outflanking was skilfully adapted to the situation, and the aim of piercing the enemy's centre was outlined with immaculate reasoning. Only one slight flaw marred the smooth perfection of Nivelle's plan. This was that at Chemin des Dames the disobliging enemy presented neither a flank to be out-manoeuvred nor a centre that could be pierced. In every other respect the General's thinking was exemplary.

At six o'clock on the morning of 16 April 1917, the offensive began. The weather was appalling. Sleet lanced through icy fog and stung the faces of the infantrymen as they churned forward in the mud. They stumbled over slippery ground in a mist that obscured the light and cast a blank greyness on everything. After they had gone some two or three hundred yards they were met with criss-cross lines of machine-gun fire. The bullets seemed to come from every direction. Along the whole of the sector well-placed machine-gun posts raked the advancing French with a massive hail of fire. At each painful gain of a few yards new posts opened up from unexpected positions, and soon they were reinforced by heavy guns. Tank support was not so successful as had been hoped. The ungainly vehicles wallowed in mud and broke down. Others, through lack of cooperation between infantry and artillery, were left to wander off like lost children. Often they were hit by shells and turned into burning coffins whence human torches jumped out to roll in agony on the sodden earth. Nearly two hundred men were killed, crushed or burned alive in this way. When evening came a tiny portion of the enemy's first line of defence had been captured.

At four o'clock next morning, on a battlefield lit by rockets and gunfire that tore away the veil of smoke and fog, a moving barrage covered the French infantry on its advance towards the hills beyond. When dawn peered feebly through the drifts of mist that hung over trees and hovered close to the ground, it seemed that one of the hillocks was taken. By midday a new and strengthened barrage from the enemy showed that even this meagre gain was of dubious value. There could be no question now of pursuing the development of the offensive which had been so logically, so convincingly predicted in Nivelle's model plan of campaign.

It was a vain battle. Over 135,000 men had been lost. Nivelle refused to resign. He appeared before the cabinet, once more pointed out that by all the canons of strategy his plan had been unassailable, and concluded with a hearty tirade against the Minister of War. He was unwise. However divided the politicians may have been, this attack on one of their number quickly united them. When he again declined to offer his resignation, he was told, abruptly, that the shrewd and cautious Pétain had replaced him.

Only a little less fortunate than the people who lived in the places where battles raged were those who inhabited the areas throughout France occupied by the enemy. At first the occupant had guaranteed the safety of the inhabitants and their property. As the war continued the promise was forgotten. Harvests were seized and enormous taxes imposed. In the early months the form of these depradations was governed by chance. The

invaders' reputation for efficiency quickly asserted itself, however, and tribute soon came to be levied in a methodical fashion.
The residents of Saint-Quentin were relieved of their possessions by an imaginative piece of organization which was so
thorough that it even included provision for the collection of
footballs and corsets. For three years the town, like many others,
lived without eggs, meat, butter or milk. Appearances were
preserved with a Teutonic respect for form. It was pointed out
that the goods were always paid for. This interesting financial
operation was assured by plundering all the money and gold
available. The people of Lille were the unwilling contributors
of more than 180 million pre-war francs. In return, the Germans
issued paper vouchers as currency. By a further ingenious twist,
these same vouchers were taken back in the shape of new
contributions to the war effort and so ad infinitum.

Economic resources, of course, were not alone in catching
the invader's eye. There was human material as well. Every
man, woman and child between the ages of fourteen and sixty-
five appeared on the lists of available labour. They were
dragooned into workers' colonies liable to be sent off anywhere
at a moment's notice. Ill fed, ill kept, ill paid, they were sub-
jected to permanent supervision. Their employers took a
thoughtful pleasure in assigning the filthiest and roughest chores
to the youngest girls among them. Seven days a week, re-
gardless of weather, the delicate white hands were forced to
tear up beetroots, dig trenches and lay barbed wire. Another
favourite diversion was to round up all the women of a village.
Girls, old spinsters, mothers, nuns and prostitutes were stripped
naked and inspected, as if they were horses or cattle, before
being sent off to forced labour. Children also were found to
have their uses in the new regime dedicated to the virtues of
hard work. Despite the allowance of a hunk of bread every
three days, many of them were ungrateful enough to die from
hunger.

The next stage was wholesale deportation. Cart-loads of men
and women rattled through the empty streets of northern towns
bound for unknown destinations. Some were allowed the
healthier exercise of walking, and ragged processions guarded
by soldiers were observed from time to time as they plodded
blankly through the wind and the rain. Those who were lucky
enough to avoid deportation still lived in an atmosphere of

unease. They were often the unwilling hosts of the German soldiers billeted on them. Their guests, who had delicate tastes, often found that the furniture displeased their aesthetic sensibilities, in which case it had to be changed. The family waited on them at meals and afterwards, however many members it contained, dossed down in the single bare room which their guests allowed them. The restrictions placed on them in their own homes were complemented by others outside. Even the poorest linguists became thoroughly acquainted with the meaning of the word *verboten*. A fertile imagination created a multitude of punishable offences which were accompanied by a flexible system of penalties. The grades, neatly arranged in a series of rising importance, varied from a simple slap in the face, or a punch, to whipping, individual or collective fines, house arrest, prison, deportation, the taking of hostages, and execution by firing squad.

And so the people in the occupied areas lived out their existence of poverty and famine, of oppression and slavery. Their fellow countrymen who inhabited places on the battle-fields and who found themselves caught between 'curtains of iron and fire', as one of them said, either fled elsewhere as unwelcome refugees or stayed among buildings which were gradually being reduced to ruins. Reims, a town of fourteen thousand houses, became in 1918 a hamlet of only sixty or so. Little remained of the monuments and houses in Arras but piles of rubbish. Twice occupied and twice pillaged, Soissons lived under constant shelling for thirty-two months.

This tale of misery and destruction was the lot of civilians all along the firing line from Ypres to Belfort. Ypres was, indeed, to become a legend with all the nationalities who fought there, and to this day the name of Flanders remains a special, a symbolic word for Englishmen. It was in Flanders one evening that General Sir Douglas Haig put up at a local inn on his tour of the battlefield. The night was cold and foggy. Sheets of rain had been falling interminably, and ice stood on puddles. The innkeeper was in a state of nerves. After hours of preparation to welcome his distinguished guests, he had been forced, at a minute's notice, to take in a French ambulance unit staffed by civilians in uniform. They had ignored his protests and forced the door which he vainly attempted to close. Even now they were commandeering his best rooms and noisily quarrelling over the allowance of bath water.

One of them came down and reserved a table in the corner of the large dining-room. While he sipped his Dubonnet he watched, with curiosity, the entry of several high-ranking British officers. They were joined by others, and soon the whole of General Haig's H.Q. staff, some twenty or more, were tidily seated in their places. There were red bands on their caps. Their glossy Sam Brownes winked and glittered in the light. Some wore monocles. They all were resplendent in beautifully pressed uniforms and shining brass buttons. Stiff, reserved and taciturn, they were as punctilious in their deportment as if they had been sitting down to dinner at Windsor Castle rather than in the only tavern to remain open among miles of ruin and desolation. They were noble representatives of old England. The last to appear was Haig himself, and with British formality he escorted his wife to the top table.

Their conversation was suddenly interrupted. The quiet well-bred tones faltered into silence. Each hand put down its knife, each face turned up towards the top of the wide stairway that led down into the room. Eyebrows were raised and monocles fell from astonished eyes. At Omdurman Sir Douglas Haig, K.C.B., had ridden cavalry charges with inimitable dash. At Elandslaagte he had encompassed the defeat of the Boers. At the relief of Kimberley and the battle of Paardeberg he had behaved with icy valour. But at the vision which he and his staff now saw, his nerve gave way and he blanched.

Descending the stairs was an elegant person in black pyjamas. Behind him was another wearing pyjamas of a pinkish hue. The first walked nonchalantly with all the haughtiness of an aristocrat. The second trotted along with the look, said an observer, of a nymph surprised. The hypnotic silence was broken by the clink of the gold bracelets that each of them wore round their ankles. The comte Étienne de Beaumont, wealthy founder of an ambulance detachment, and Jean Cocteau, one of his auxiliaries, reached the final step and swayed elegantly through the cluster of tables to find their own. They were followed by colleagues attired with a similar daintiness. The assemblage of English officers and Parisian dandies ate their dinner in paralysed silence.

The two apparitions came, indeed, from another world, the

world of Paris. The people of Roubaix might be deported in their thousands, the citizens of Douai might be forced to pay taxes of fifty thousand gold francs, but Paris – ah, Paris was different. While the ten occupied departments of France laboured under a tyranny as harsh as it was efficient, the Parisians went to war piling sandbags around Carpeaux's bulbous statuary outside the Opéra and telling each other funny stories about the great siege of 1870. One of them which became a favourite in the hard days of 1917, when cake shops had to close two days a week, concerned a pet-lover who, driven by hunger, had his dog Médor killed and stewed. As he ate the meal and, by force of habit, put aside the bones, he said with tears in his eyes : 'What a pity Médor isn't here !'

There was, at one time, vague talk of rationing. Cards were issued for bread and sugar. Meat was rationed by the healthy operation of private enterprise which, by the end of the war, had tripled the price, as it did of most other supplies except for wine, a commodity which eventually reached five times its pre-war cost. In 1917 the Ministry of Food sowed the Parc de la Muette with potatoes and brought cows to pasture on the race track at Longchamp. Beans and carrots flourished in the Jardins du Luxembourg, and a plot at the rear of the Bibliothèque Nationale was said to produce the finest cabbages in Paris. At Versailles the stately park of the Trianon burst into a new splendour of turnips, lettuce, artichokes and swedes.

As if to remind Parisians of Arras, there were a few bombs from time to time. Eighteen fell on Ménilmontant in the third year of war, though casualties were hardly reassured by theories that the taubes, gothas, dirigibles and zeppelins which loomed in the skies above were mainly sent over for psychological effect. There were much more interesting problems to absorb the mind of a race which delights in the perpetual subtleties of intellectual argument. Should German music be banned? Suppose a patriotic musician who loves Wagner fights in the trenches and loses his right arm. He can no longer play *Tristan* for himself. In this case have people the right to deprive him of listening to Wagner played by an orchestra? Or what of the anguished fiancée whose betrothed is killed at the front? Should she re-marry? Should she remain a 'veuve blanche'?

The songs that distracted attention from such agonizing problems were varied and numerous. A famous one that gave

its name to an age was *la Madelon*. A ditty of period sauciness,
it was identified with a popular singer who went by the modest
name of Bach :

> Quand Madelon vient nous servir à boire
> Sous la tonnelle, on frôle son jupon.
> Et chacun lui raconte une histoire,
> Une histoire à sa façon.

If you wearied of touching up la Madelon's petticoats, you
could launch into the hearty advice which contrasted so sharply
with the respectable send-off given British troops as they departed from London : '*A nos poilus qui s'en vont sur le front,
qu'est-ce qu'il leur faut comme distraction? une femme . . . une
femme.*' There were shades of ribaldry in *Il était une
boulangère* which would hardly have pleased Mrs Asquith, and
though the refrain of *Les Boul'vards . . . les bell's Madames . . .*
had a pleasing nostalgia, it was not the sort of thing Lady Haig
much favoured. The rousing directness of *On les aura! On les
aura!* was to be preferred, along with the healthy strains of
la Brabançonne and *Tipperary*, or the gentle sentiments that
oozed from *Roses of Picardy*.

There was plenty of music and entertainment to be had. At
the Opéra-Comique the soprano Marthe Chenal draped her
ample contours in the tricolour flag and sang the *Marseillaise*
to an audience mad with enthusiasm. A rage for operetta
flooded theatres with the airy effusions of Vincent Scotto, author
of *la Tonkinoise*, and Raoul Moretti, whose *Tu m'plais* was
hummed everywhere at the Armistice. *Phi-Phi*, an operetta set
in classical times which owed its title to the hero Phidias,
brought to the Théâtre des Bouffes-Parisiens the unlikely
figures of Pericles and Aspasia, who trilled the sprightly
measures of Henry Christiné in settings of mock antiquity. It
ran for years, and the leading man played his role more than
four thousand times.

The music hall turned itself into a place of dazzling
spectacle. Never before had so much money been spent on so
little clothing. The Ba-Ta-Clan rivalled the Marigny in its
large promise of leg and thigh and ankle. Each claimed that
its girls wore less than the other and that their veils were the
thinner. The Casino de Paris re-opened in the last days of
1917 with a grand revue called *Laissez-les tomber!* The

patriotic understood the title as a challenge to German aircraft
to drop their bombs. Others less virtuously inclined read it as
a hopeful forecast of what the girls would do with their last
remaining clothes.

The most noticeable music-hall star was Polaire. Her oddly
slanting eyes and vast mouth earned her the title, which she
bore proudly, of the world's ugliest woman. She was the queen
of the suburban young men who adored her nightly at the
Bobino. Not the least of her extravagances was the Negro page-
boy whom she brought back from a visit to America. Around
his neck he wore a collar engraved with the words : 'I belong to
Polaire. Please send me back to her.' Her closest rival was
Gaby Deslys, who first knew fame as the mistress of King
Manoel of Portugal. Even Polaire could not outdo the froth
of plumes, muslin and ostrich feathers which cascaded around
her. Nor could Polaire imitate the huge hats in the shape of
aeroplane propellers and tropical birds which, in the height of
the most gorgeous bad taste, decorated Gaby's lovely head. Both,
however, were vanquished in the end by Mistinguett, who lived
on to cavort before the grandsons of men who applauded her
in 1917. The stubborn old creature never gave up, even when
the slim legs had become shrunken shanks and she had to be
helped on to the stage before tottering through her number in
a cracked, feeble voice. At the end of the war her star was in
the ascendant, and with Maurice Chevalier, a protégé who
soon became her lover, she triumphed in sumptuous revues at
the Casino de Paris.

And then, on 18 May 1917, a peculiar spectacle took place
at the Théâtre du Chatelet. There was something in it of the
music hall, and something of the circus, though regular patrons
of those entertainments would doubtless have been puzzled by
it. The work was entitled *Parade*, and the music was written
by an obscure alcoholic called Erik Satie.

II

On the day before *Parade* he had reached his fifty-first year.
He was a neat and tidy little man. In winter and summer
alike he wore a black bowler hat, an overcoat, and a suit and
waistcoat of sober tint. He always carried an umbrella. This

item was, for him, something of a talisman, since he detested the sunshine. At home he kept dozens of umbrellas, many of them still in their original wrappings. He adored wet weather, and the tradesmen in his district knew they could count on seeing Monsieur Satie take the air when rain fell. There was something about a cloudy day and drizzle which accorded with his melancholy temperament. The sharper the wind, the heavier the downpour, the more he was pleased.

Satie was born at Honfleur twelve years after the humorist Alphonse Allais, a friend and fellow Honfleurais whom he much resembled. A rue Alphonse Allais duly commemorates the writer, in the same way as a rue Delarue-Mardrus, a place Albert Sorel and a rue Eugène Boudin pay tribute to other natives of the town. Satie still awaits his street, as do Henri de Régnier and that enterprising mariner Pierre Berthelot, who, after becoming a bare-foot Carmelite and finding martyrdom in Sumatra, was later beatified. Is it the air of Honfleur that is responsible for breeding such independent characters? With Allais, Satie shared an impenetrable façade of quirky humour which expressed itself in puns and surrealistic word-play. Their wit has something desperate about it. You feel it is the reaction of lonely, over-sensitive men who seek to hide their nihilism with a display of anarchic jokes. The only true refuge they ever found was in drink.

Satie's grandfather was a shipbroker. He also served as captain (the strain of fantasy early declared itself) of the Honfleur fire brigade. He sent his two sons for an educational trip to England, where they lodged with a clergyman. Adrien, nicknamed 'Sea Bird', horrified the parish with his practical jokes, and, when forbidden to go out, passed the time in making improper suggestions to the housemaids. Alfred was quiet and studious. He married a Scottish girl and settled down to a respectable shipbroking career in Honfleur. They had three children, of whom Eric, later to change his name to Erik, was the oldest. The solitary boy, raised in a conventional home, came to feel more attracted to his eccentric uncle 'Sea Bird'. The latter had now given up business to follow his own whims. He built a superb carriage, so handsome that no one dared step into it for fear of causing damage. He also had a splendid boat constructed and sat in it for hours smoking his pipe. Very rarely would he take it out for a trip, and when he did he was accompanied by a single mate whose nickname was 'Mâchoire d'âne', or 'Ass's Jaw'. Eventually he bought a bookshop and ended his days studying horse breeding and seamanship.

Widowed six years after Erik's birth, his father left Honfleur and came to Paris where he found work as a translator and was caught up in the academic life. He married again and brought into the household a wife whose passion for music – music, that is, as understood by official establishments, by the Opéra and the Conservatoire – was enough to encourage Erik's feeling of revolt. He had acquired an interest in the piano, which, as he said, 'like money, is only pleasant to whoever touches it'. He allowed himself, with mixed feelings, to be hustled by his stepmother into taking piano lessons. In later years he used to say that a musical career had been imposed upon him. What is sure is that, despite his affection for the instrument, he was a worse pianist even than Ravel. He never played well. The piano in his bachelor lodgings was so decrepit as to be unplayable. Most of his music he wrote on café tables. When he wanted to try something out he would call on one of his friends, draw from his pocket the schoolboy's exercise books in which he noted his compositions, and ask if he might run over it on their piano.

At the Conservatoire, which he regarded as a variety of prison, he went through his course, a self-effacing shadow. He read a lot, especially the fairy tales of Hans Andersen who was to remain a favourite for life, and absorbed an orthodox admiration for Bach, Chopin and Schubert. More as an excuse for cutting short his musical education, he hastened to do his military service. The army proved as uncongenial as the Conservatoire. So he ensured a speedy discharge on health grounds by exposing his bare chest to the breezes of a cold winter night and contracting a serious attack of bronchitis.

While convalescing he discovered the writings of Joseph Péladan, a turbid mystagogue who expounded the doctrines of Rosicrucianism in prose of amiable lunacy. Satie had already composed a *Valse-ballet* and a *Fantaisie-Valse* that were recommended as eminently suitable for family music making, and a few songs which his father, in business now as stationer and publisher, brought out for him. He applied himself to the mysteries of the Rosy Cross, read long and laboriously in the literature relating to Gothic art, and meditated for hours in

Notre Dame. In 1891, at the age of twenty-five, he gilded some nonsense by Péladan, a play called *le Fils des Étoiles,* with three preludes. The spectacle was performed and received in an atmosphere of frozen incomprehension.

Earlier still he had written the *Sarabandes,* the *Gymnopédies* and the *Gnossiennes,* which, in their harmonies, anticipate innovations credited to the Debussysist group. The most original are the *Gymnopédies,* all three of which move in a bland line that slowly, sadly unrolls against a bass of monotonous chords with a hint of waltz rhythm. They give an impression of timelessness, of a melody that is perpetual and unhurried. The *Gnossiennes,* written without bar lines, announce a further characteristic, that of adding quaint or humorous remarks above the music. The pianist is advised to play 'without pride', or 'in a gleaming manner', or 'step by step'. The structure of the bare and simple melodies is such that the rhythm falls naturally into place without the need for bar lines. They show the effect of Satie's researches into Gregorian chant and of his visits to the Paris Exhibition of 1889, where Debussy, too, was fascinated by the performances of Oriental music.

Satie gravitated naturally towards Montmartre. There he be-friended his compatriot Alphonse Allais who was one of the personalities at the Chat Noir, a superior form of café-concert which specialized in topical songs of a higher quality than most. It had been founded by a group calling themselves 'les Hydropathes', a name inspired by their common resolve to employ water only for external use. (Their spiritual descendant was the immortal W.C. Fields, who once lamented that on his travels through some distant country : 'I had to live for days on nothing but food and water.') The leader was Rodolphe Salis, a painter of modest talent, who ran the place with flair and greeted his clients with an exaggerated politeness that bordered on insolence. He styled himself 'gentilhomme cabaretier' and dressed his waiters in the ceremonial uniform of the Académie Française. Only once did his aplomb desert him. This was when the Prince of Wales, later Edward VII, arrived incognito and unannounced. 'Your Highness,' stammered Salis, 'what an honour . . . for myself . . . for my colleagues . . . for the Chat Noir.' After which, pulling himself together : 'And how's your Mum, then?'

It was through Allais, known to his friends as 'Alphi', that

Satie was taken on at the Chat Noir as second pianist. These two exponents of the straight-faced humour described as 'pince sans rire' got on well together. The characters with whom Allais peopled his stories and the monologues he delivered at the Chat Noir have their whimsical counterparts in the prose that decorates Satie's music. A Paris omnibus route inspired Allais to create the 'vicomte O. d'Éon Clichy'. There was a classic flavour to the Greek lady 'Dona Ferentes' and her compatriot 'le général Timéo Danaos'. His clerics had names like 'l'abbé Tumaine à Hettu (près Monvieux)', his aristocrats were such people as 'Sir John Loofock' and 'Sir Cordon Sonnet'. Little ingenuity is needed to appreciate the name of the business firm called 'Jean Passe et Desmeilleurs', or the shameful figure called 'Jean Rougy de Ontt'.*

Neither Allais nor Satie confined fantasy to their art. One afternoon, on a café terrace, Allais said to his friends : 'Would you like me to perform my trapeze number?' He leapt up at the iron bars which supported the canvas and swung for a moment. Everything collapsed. Tables overturned, glasses smashed, customers and waiters vanished beneath a sea of squirming canvas. Allais' voice was heard : 'Of course, I didn't say I could do it . . .' Satie, too, was a fantasist in real life. He grew tired of a mistress with whom he had associated and wished to end the affair. His solution to this perennial dilemma had an admirable logic about it. He complained to the police that the voracious female was molesting him, and when she next came to visit her capricious lover she found herself turned away by a gendarme.

At the Chat Noir Satie obediently tinkled away as accompanist to the shadow plays and the irreverent choruses chanted by Salis and his clients. One of the singers he accompanied was Vincent Hyspa, a chansonnier whose southern accent was so strong that Salis always raised a laugh by introducing him as a Belgian. Hyspa did not find his pianist the most reliable of colleagues. Satie himself admitted that the singer often had to lock him up during the day to ensure that he would be sober enough to play the piano by evening. (As 'Alphi' used to tell him with impressive gravity, drinking all day in a café was enough to ruin a marriage.) He was on better terms with

* A fuller account of Alphonse Allais will be found in the present author's *Sacha Guitry, The Last Boulevardier*, Methuen, 1968.

Paulette Darty, a blonde whose proportions delighted an age which appraised sex appeal in terms of avoirdupois. She had a pleasant voice and exquisite diction. Her speciality made her known as the 'Queen of the Slow Waltz', and she sang her numbers in a way that entranced her listeners. Satie dedicated to her his waltz 'Je te veux', and there is no doubt that her personality invested the facile nostalgia of this trifle with a charm that stirred the bosoms of the midinettes and clerks who were her keenest admirers. She died in 1940 at the age of sixty-nine after a long retirement, unaware that her shy little pianist was to have his place of honour as a pioneer in the history of modern music.*

Satie did not stay long at the Chat Noir. It was said by Willy, otherwise Henri Gauthier-Villars, the much-ghosted novelist and music critic who undertook the formidable role of Colette's first husband, that he had been sacked by Rodolphe Salis because 'he played too badly and drank too much.' He soon found another job at the Auberge du Clou, where in 1891 he improved the acquaintance of Debussy whom he appears to have met a year before. Amid the clatter of glasses and haze of cigar smoke they talked together about opera. Satie suggested Debussy take a subject from Maeterlinck, thus being partly responsible for the creation of *Pelléas et Mélisande*. Their friendship was an uneasy affair. Satie went regularly to Debussy's house, played his piano and stayed to lunch. He was made welcome for the sake of his amusing conversation and his stimulating judgements. That there was affection between them is shown by the inscription Debussy wrote on a presentation copy of his *Cinq poèmes de Baudelaire:* 'Pour Erik Satie, musicien médiéval et doux, égaré dans ce siècle pour la joie de son bien amical Claude Debussy.' But the gentle medieval musician had an irascible strain in his character, and beneath the relationship there flowed an undercurrent of resentment on Satie's part, a feeling perhaps of jealousy. The peculiar titles he gave to his piano pieces – *Heures séculaires et instantanées, Vieux séquins et vieilles cuirasses* – may be seen in one way as mockery of the 'poetic' names Debussy bestowed on some of his preludes.

* She was also the dedicatee of 'Sur un casque', the third of his *Descriptions automatiques*. What on earth she made of it must, like the song the sirens sang, remain a field for pleasing conjecture.

Satie in the late 1890s had taken a room in the suburb of
Arcueil. The district was not, and is not still, a place for
luxurious living. The names given to the streets there – Lenin,
Jaurès, Robespierre, Stalingrad, Pierre Curie, Voltaire – show
the political sympathies of a poor working-class populace.
(Satie today has joined this distinguished list : his name has
been bestowed, most appropriately, on a dead end.) From
Montmartre he trundled a hand cart bearing his meagre
possessions to the barrack-like building that was to be his home
for many years. His neighbours, impressed by the grey corduroy
suit he affected, took him for an artist. A small legacy from his
father enabled him to buy a dozen suits in the material and
hundreds of stiff collars which he never wore. Gradually he
was accepted by the local people. He joined the Radical
Socialist Committee, wrote for the Arcueil newspaper, organized
concerts and took bands of schoolchildren out for treats.
The worthy citizen even received an award of the Palmes
Académiques.

At the same time he went on playing in Montmartre cabarets.
He would come home to Arcueil through deserted streets in
the early hours of the morning, arriving after his long walk
with only just a little time left before he had to go back again.
On his lonely promenades he would carry a large hammer in
his pocket in order to defend himself against possible marauders.
On other occasions the inhabitants of Arcueil would note with
alarm the presence in that pocket of a lighted clay pipe whose
stem reached up to his ear. Much of his time he spent writing
music in local cafés. The notes were traced in a delicate
calligraphy and the manuscripts embellished with fanciful little
drawings. Here, too, he conducted his correspondence – a note
to the director of the Opéra challenging him to a duel, a letter
card insulting the critics he detested, designs for aeroplanes and
dirigibles – all executed with maniacal precision and rich in a
Gothic imagery as striking as Victor Hugo's, though more
amusing. He was an accepted figure in the glum atmosphere
of Arcueil among its peeling walls and desolate waste-grounds.
It is impossible to think of him in the lofty surroundings of the
Institut de France. Yet three times had he offered, with cold
effrontery, his candidature for that establishment, and three
times had he been refused. On the failure of his attempt to
succeed Gounod he addressed to Saint-Saëns, the arch-

academician, an open letter of dignified remonstrance. It ended : 'I forgive you in Jesus Christ and embrace you in the mercy of God.'

There does not seem to have been much room for women in Satie's life. His only known liaison was with Suzanne Valadon, herself an artist and the mother of Utrillo. She was said to have profited twice over from Renoir, Degas and Puvis de Chavannes, both as model and as mistress. They were grateful enough to buy her pictures when she set up as a artist on her own. Her brief life with Satie was punctuated by noisy quarrels. When she annoyed him more than usual, he would draw up in his meticulous lettering a proclamation which cast grave doubt on her virtue and tabulated her faults in a wealth of detail. This document he would display prominently in a window overlooking the busiest part of the street. 'Biqui', as he called her in absent-minded moments of affection, did two portraits of him and vanished out of his existence. Nothing is known of his adventures after this. It is doubtful if there were any. He allowed no one into his room and never spoke of his private life. His shyness, his irony, and his total unworldliness were not guaranteed to endear him. He once remarked that he did not marry because he was afraid of being cuckolded. He favoured, perhaps, that opinion held by the fathers of the early Christian church who believed women to be unclean creatures.

By 1905 he had composed a bizarre mixture of Rosicrucian music and café-concert pieces of the type sung by Paulette Darty. Among this novel output are several items which show that he was not just a practical joker. The pantomime ballet *Jack in the Box*, discovered after his death in the heaps of dusty rubbish which he lovingly hoarded, has a perky appeal merging into child-like wistfulness that Milhaud's later orchestration beautifully preserves. The *Messe des pauvres* goes beyond objectivity and creates an unforgettable atmosphere of isolation. The most important of these works, however, are the two sets of *Pièces froides*. In the first set, uninvitingly baptized 'Airs à faire fuir', the pieces which open and close the proceedings offer unexpected gleams of warmth peeping through the strands of desolation. The middle piece takes a simple tune of the nursery type and subjects it to a number of disturbing harmonies from which it emerges with its innocence unscathed. The second set, 'Danses de travers', is laid out in a series of broken chords almost, but not quite, like the figurations so characteristic of Fauré.

In his fortieth year Satie decided to go to school again. Did he regret not having studied seriously at the Conservatoire? Had he at last made up his mind that the musical career into which he drifted should be properly developed? His choice of the Schola Cantorum, that rigorous establishment founded by the austere Vincent d'Indy, shows intentness of purpose. At first his teacher, Albert Roussel, a younger man than Satie, tried to persuade him that on the evidence of his published works he had nothing more to learn. The mature student politely disagreed. For the next three years he did his home-work punctually and assiduously. The exercises he handed in were written with exemplary tidiness and augmented with commentaries in red ink. He was, said his teacher, profoundly musical. He absorbed himself in counterpoint, analysis and orchestration. Graduating with a diploma for counterpoint with the mention 'Très bien', he was to pass the years between 1908 and 1917 in writing the piano pieces on which a large part of his fame, or notoriety, now depends.

The earliest of these were the *Aperçus désagréables* for piano duet. The suite bears all the traces of the fugal disciplines to which he had recently submitted himself at the Schola. So does *En habit de cheval*. Then came the *Véritables préludes flasques* (*pour un chien*) which set the stage for his famous mannerisms – mock pedantry, facetious remarks and an obsession with the figure three. The preludes are, in fact, the opposite of *flasques,* being taut, lean excursions with a marked contrapuntal bias. The *Descriptions automatiques,* heavily overlaid with Satiste quips, comprise another trio of miniatures that serve to exemplify his mature manner. 'Sur un vaisseau' proceeds in leisurely tango rhythm, suggestive of a ship rocking on the waves, and hints slyly at a popular song of the day. 'Sur une lanterne' is equally deft in wedding a music-hall chorus to the basic scheme of the piece. In 'Sur un casque' the listener is gratified with a faux-naïf evocation of a 14 July celebration: the soldiers march past, the Spahis trot by at a pas redoublé, the drums rattle, the trumpets squawk, the *Carmagnole* darts fleetingly for a moment, and the women are overwhelmed with admiration for the handsome troopers.

The piano pieces range from satire – 'Españaña' in the

Croquis et agaceries d'un gros bonhomme en bois laughs at
Chabrier in bits marked 'Plaza Clichy' and 'Rue de Madrid' –
to the eerie portrait of a miser in *Vieux séquins et vieilles
cuirasses*. They also embrace the music for children, *Menus
propos enfantins, Enfantillages pittoresques* and *Peccadilles
importunes*. These, unlike most works in the genre, are not
written by an adult who is watching the little tots from outside,
but by a man who had a mind genuinely attuned to children's
imagination.

Satie's techniques, his unique flavour and his originality, are
summed up in the *Sports et divertissements* of 1914. Stravinsky
having demanded too large a sum to illustrate with music an
album of drawings, the publishers decided to give Satie the
commission. He, less shrewd than Stravinsky, was bitterly
offended at the fee they proposed to him and considered it
much too high. Being accustomed to draw as little as seventy-
six centimes a quarter in royalties, he was astonished at the
notion of earning money from his music. In the end he agreed
and produced twenty little pieces which depict blind man's
buff, puss in the corner, fishing, yachting, swimming, a picnic,
a carnival, racing, and so forth. They are prefaced by a
'Choral inappétissant' which lives up to Satie's direction:
'rébarbatif et hargneux'. All are much embroidered with a
delirium of dotty remarks which can be ignored if necessary,
though the elaborate combination of text with music is, like
Apollinaire's experiments with typography, of interest to
historians. The point is that each of these pieces, whether
classified as snapshots or miniatures, is complete in itself. They
are neither fragments nor sketches, but fully worked-out models
of concision. None takes up more than a single page, and the
most appropriate comparison is with the Japanese form of
Haiku. Within the tiny compass of thirty seconds he pictures,
for example, the vast expanse of the sea and the surge of waves
coming forward to die on the shore ('Le bain de mer'); a
handful of staccato notes and a few slurred phrases are enough
to show a teasing cat-and-mouse game ('Les quatre coins'); a
cascade of fireworks glitters momentarily to leave a vivid impression on the retina ('Le feu d'artifice'); a tweedy colonel,
accompanied by a distorted prediction of 'Tea for Two', comes
on to the links and sees his club shiver into pieces ('Le golf').
Whether Satie re-creates the pounding of horses on a race-

track or the cool flittering depths of a river well stocked with fish ('La pêche'), he does so with a genius for concentrating into a minute area all the essentials of what he has observed with the crystal acuteness of a microscope.

The publication of *Sports et divertissements* coincided with the outbreak of the First World War. Satie's legend assumed its definitive shape. He no longer wore corduroy suits or the floppy hat Suzanne Valadon showed in her portrait of him. His raiment was dark, with a respectable hint of wing collars. The beard was clipped to the decent proportions associated with a provincial schoolmaster under the Third Republic. You might have taken him for a minor bank official. Only the derisive glitter of malice behind the pince-nez suggested that the appearance was deceptive. When he spoke, the effect was even more disconcerting. A deep, lazy voice told an admirer: 'I never take a bath! You can only wash properly in little bits! I use pumice stone on my skin. It goes further than soap, dear lady.' The remarks were often accompanied by rumbles of suppressed laughter as he spread his left hand fan-wise over his face. His drollery was unchanged since the time when, as a young man, he would regularly meet the incoming trains from Normandy. Picking on a likely arrival, he would address him: 'Good morning, cousin. Did my aunt give you the parcel she said she was sending in her last letter?' While the traveller stammered in confusion, Satie went on chatting about the family, guided his companion's steps to a nearby restaurant, and helpfully recommended the quality of the fare. The long-lost 'relative' usually found himself treating his 'cousin' to a free meal.

The war had little effect on Satie. He became a corporal in the militia and performed duties of baffling vagueness in Arcueil. During one of the heaviest bombardments of the war a friend discovered him crouching at the foot of the obelisk in the place de la Concorde. 'I know it's mad and I'm not under cover,' he explained, 'but that thing up in the air there gives me a feeling of safety. I'm composing some music for the obelisk. Actually it's for the Pharaoh's wife who's buried down below. Nobody ever thinks of her...' It was also his pleasant habit, when the air raids were at their height, to join the occupants of shelters and to remark, in grave tones: 'Good evening, I have come to die with you.'

In the second year of the war Satie made the acquaintance of Jean Cocteau. The latter was twenty-six years old and already a notable Parisian figure. Launched by Maurice Barrès in a flattering article, admired by Anna de Noailles and cherished by Proust, he achieved a reputation even before his major works had been published. His home was in the rue d'Anjou where he lived in the company of a widowed mother, next door to an equally wayward talent, the young Sacha Guitry. A winding stair led up to the flat beneath a candelabrum of monumental size which Apollinaire once described as the eighth wonder of the world: it hung from the ceiling of the top floor and shed its pallid light from globes hanging on brass arms at every landing. The door was opened by Cyprien, the Cocteau family's manservant. His wife, who was the cook, devoted all her spare time to mysterious writings. Were they memoirs, novels, letters, or simply the kitchen accounts? No one ever knew.

Madame Cocteau lived in a drawing room to the left of the hall, her feet encased in a muff, her knees wrapped in a plaid shawl of the type Mallarmé wore. She went daily to Mass and viewed with Christian resignation the frivolities of her gifted son. Her hair was snow-white, her simple dress was black. Cocteau's room gave the impression of having been furnished by a magpie of bizarre instincts. Among the chaos of objects which assaulted the eye it was possible to distinguish a crystal ball, a blackboard, cubes of crystal, files stuffed with drawings, meerschaum pipes, a skull, jewellery, ceramics, postcards, preserved flowers ... and practically everywhere on the walls photographs and pictures ranging from odd depictions of unknown persons to sketches by Picasso and Chirico. This variety of objects, their owner used to say, enabled him to judge the 'chemical reaction' of his visitors. By noting whatever attracted their special attention he could sum up the sort of people who called.

An admirer who came to see him heard a sharp, brittle voice call from a neighbouring room: 'Come in, come in and settle down! I'll be with you immediately!' The telephone rang. 'Pierre, mon petit,' crackled the voice, 'be an angel, will you answer? Say I'm ill, I can't talk. Yes, ask who's speaking. ... No, I don't want to talk to anyone. ... Who? ... oh, it's Valentine ... of *course* I'll speak to her ... hold on, I'm coming.' And into the room trotted a figure wearing a white dressing gown knotted with a black silk cord. The face was invisible, for it was covered by a red and yellow silk hand-kerchief which, kept in place by a battered old felt hat, hung down to the chest. The apparition advanced hesitantly, as if playing hide-and-seek, the hands with their long angular fingers fluttering gracefully in the air.

The telephone, once grasped, became the confidant of a long monologue: 'Mais ma chérie ... how could you believe that for a moment? It's madness ... lunacy. How can she have said such a thing about me?' The conversation, punctuated with many a reproachful 'ma chérie', continued until the master of the house, replacing the receiver, sighed to his audience: 'Mes pauvres enfants, you can see what a life I lead. It's impossible, awful. I'm going to shave – wait for me.' Still invisible, he draped the handkerchief over a saucepan of boiling water, dipped his face in the steam, and at last emerged with his beard conveniently softened for the razor. He disappeared next door and returned a few minutes later, a blue ribbon tightly wound round his neck, cheek-bones prominent, eyes shining with a steely glance. Opium was hospitably proffered. Cocteau's day had begun.

When he met Satie he was working on a version of *A Midsummer Night's Dream*. The fairy wood became a circus ring, and Oberon was to perform to the air of *It's a Long Way to Tipperary*. The project was tailor-made for incidental music by Satie. The idea lapsed and all that remained of it were the *Cinq grimaces* which he wrote at Cocteau's invitation. The following year Diaghilev asked Cocteau to prepare a ballet. Satie was again invoked. Cocteau outlined to him an idea that had struck him while listening to a performance of the *Trois morceaux en forme de poire*. He returned to those ambulance duties in the course of which he had so disturbed General Haig, and left Satie with a bundle of notes. The setting was a fairground, the characters included a Chinaman, an American girl and an acrobat, and the scenes were divided into music-hall numbers. Since the word 'parade' can signify the brief turns given outside a fairground booth to attract an audience for the main show, it seemed a natural title for the ballet.

While Satie was writing his score, Picasso designed the set

and costumes. His sketches suggested to Cocteau the addition of extra characters, the 'Managers', who, by their superhuman nature, would reduce the dancers to the stature of puppets. Satie stayed peaceably at Arcueil and Cocteau went off to Rome to join Diaghilev and his company. There Picasso's designs were fitted to Massine's choreography. 'We created *Parade* in a cellar in Rome known as the 'Taglioni cellar' where the troupe practised,' wrote Cocteau. 'We went for walks in the moonlight with the ballerinas, we visited Naples and Pompeii.' The date of the new production was fixed and a theatre engaged in Paris.

III

A month before *Parade* exploded in Paris the French army threw itself into the disastrous offensive at Chemin des Dames. Pétain took over from the discredited Nivelle and was faced immediately with problems of demoralization and mutiny. Behind the lines an embattled government faced widespread strikes.

The grand ladies who came to the first night at the Théâtre du Châtelet stepped out of their de luxe 'torpedos' with feelings of guilt. Their expensive dresses, they said, had been bought for the next visit from 'the lads' on leave. Instead of eau de Cologne, with its German undertones, they wore eau de Pologne and eau de Louvain. They found their strongest justification in the purpose of the evening's entertainment, which was to benefit war charities. The various committees involved in this edifying occasion were, moreover, chaired by some of the capital's most distinguished noblewomen. Countesses abounded, and there were few occupants of the dearer seats who lacked a nobiliary particle.

The audience settled down to read its programme. A few days ago in that theatre they had applauded the easy charm of ballets with music by Scarlatti and Liadov. They remembered that Cocteau, the poet of *Parade*, once collaborated with Reynaldo Hahn on an after-dinner ballet called *le Dieu bleu*. Those who looked beyond the names of the dancers found themselves reading a programme note by Guillaume Apollinaire. Just back from the front, where he had undergone a delicate trepanning operation for a shell splinter in his right temple, he presented 'the first Cubist spectacle'.

Parade [said Apollinaire] brings together Satie's first piece of orchestral writing, Picasso's first stage designs, Massine's first choreography, and the first attempt, for a poet, to express himself on several different levels.

Massine and Picasso have realized this ballet by perfecting, for the first time, that alliance of painting and the dance, of the plastic and the mimic arts, which symbolizes the advent of an art complete in itself. We hope that the public will look on *Parade* as a work that hides poetry beneath its crude Punch and Judy wrapping.

In a further discussion of *Parade*, Apollinaire made use of a newly created word : *le surréalisme*.

Against a drop curtain by Picasso showing a circus horse, a bare-back rider and clowns, the orchestra launched into *la Marseillaise*. Then they played the *Song of the Volga Boatmen* in a new orchestration which Diaghilev had commissioned from Stravinsky. The 'ballet réaliste', as it was described, opened with a short 'Choral' whose acrid chords must have warned the audience what to expect. This was followed by the 'Prélude du Rideau rouge', a sombre fugal piece, and the entry of the first 'Manager', or barker. Like his fellow Manager, he wore a towering Cubist contraption made of cardboard in the shape of skyscrapers and balconies. The two Managers' roles were exhausting ones, for while bearing the heavy weight of their costumes they had at certain given times to stamp rhythmically – an idea, it is said, of Diaghilev, who had a favourite theory about 'pure' rhythm as opposed to music. The two men who danced the third Manager had no less an uncomfortable task, since they were immured between the hot, sweaty confines of a pantomime horse.

The Managers' busy theme gave way to the entry of the Chinese conjuror danced by Massine in a costume which Diaghilev so admired that he later used the design as an emblem for the Ballets Russes. The already large orchestra was now augmented with a variety of drums, tambourine, cymbals, gong, lottery wheel and ship's siren. The conjuror produced an egg from his wig, swallowed it, ate fire and showered sparks. The second Manager burst in with another attempt to beat up custom. The bait this time was the little American girl who

pirouetted on in a whirling cascade of violin phrases. She wore
a pale blue and white costume. In her efforts to attract the
crowd she pretended to ride a bicycle, boxed, fired a pistol
(duly written in the score), imitated Charlie Chaplin, and
danced a lugubrious rag-time which Satie, characteristically,
had marked 'triste'. Next came the acrobat, who, supported by
a lurching waltz-tune that alternated between heaviness and
sudden darts of aerial grace, performed gymnastics. But the
customers did not appear, and the Managers, in a last
thundrous *tutti*, collapsed in exhaustion. The performers tried
to explain that the real show was being held inside . . . and
trooped slowly out of the empty fairground as the orchestra
completed the 'Prélude du Rideau rouge' with which the ballet
opened.

Satie's score was a precisely conceived montage in which little
phrases were juxtaposed one with another to build up an im-
placable mosaic of sound. It is possible to find, in such passages
as the fugal writing or in the machine-like interjections of the
brass during the Chinese conjuror's number, evidence of
Satie's refusal to display softer emotions. On the other hand,
there are several themes – among them the questing melody
that floats over the orchestra during the conjuror's turn –
which show genuine feeling. Again, the handling of the tuba
part in the rag-time section suggests that grotesquerie is serving
as a mask for sentiment. Satie himself termed his contribution
'a background to certain noises which Cocteau thought indispensable to define the atmosphere of his characters'. This,
as Cocteau replied, was too modest. The score of *Parade* is as
unique in orchestral writing as *Sports et divertissements* are in
the repertory of the piano.* Georges Auric has captured the
essence of the music in his remark : '. . . all the sorrow of the
travelling circus is here – the nostalgia of the barrel organ which
will never play Bach fugues.'

For most of the audience who sat through *Parade* the only
normal thing about it was the unmistakable chord of C major

---

* As with Satie's piano works, *Parade* contains diverting instructions to
the players – 'Trembler comme une feuille', etc. – some of which might
have been suitable for the choreography. Since he had many arguments
with Cocteau during rehearsals, it is unlikely that they were adopted.
There is, incidentally, an interesting foretaste of *Mercure* ('Signes du
zodiaque') in bars 59–62 of the Petite fille Américaine.

with which it ended. Long before that time, however, the music was being heard intermittently through howls of protest, and the conductor, Ernest Ansermet, occasionally could not hear his players for the uproar. The spectators grew restive at the American girl's turn. Their anger was released by the entry of the pantomime horse. From then on shouts of 'Dagoes!', 'Boches!', 'à Berlin!' and piercing whistles added to the liveliness of the spectacle. Top hats were crushed and walking sticks brandished. A lady screamed the supreme insult: 'Opium smokers!' An indignant matron hissed: 'If I'd known it was so silly I'd have brought the children.'

'But for Apollinaire,' wrote Cocteau, 'his uniform, his shaven skull, his temple marked with a scar and the bandage round his head, women armed with hat pins would have gouged out our eyes!' Cocteau stood with his fellow conspirators and watched the unruly scene. He wore grey spats, tight trousers, and a colourful scarf at his neck. Picasso, dreaming of Olga Khoklova, the ballerina he was soon to marry, stood negligently by in his open-necked shirt, sweater and corduroys. The composer of *Parade* sat squarely in his seat. Beside him, on a chair, his bowler hat and grey silk gloves were neatly laid out. He gazed at the raging audience with an eye that was 'limpid, blue and pitiless'.

The battle continued for days in newspaper columns. The chief concern of the majority of writers was to establish the exact degree of idiocy which *Parade* represented. For some, it was a compound of Picasso's stupidity and Satie's banality. Others argued that the chief sin was to have inflicted a practical joke on a theatre audience in the wrong place and at the wrong time. A leading voice in the chorus of outrage belonged to the music critic Jean Poueigh. He himself, under the prudent veil of a pseudonym, composed music that was rarely performed and still more rarely published. As an assailant of better-known composers' work he wrote in a tone that was notably sharp. Monsieur Erik Satie, he declared, had tried to impress by writing a few pitiable bits of fugue, and had sought to conceal his lack of invention by putting rattles and type-writers into his score. Immediately after the curtain dropped on *Parade*, however, Poueigh had congratulated Satie on his music. This abrupt defection enraged the composer. He sent Poueigh one of his famous postcards bearing a message whose crudity was all the more glaring in that the script was exquisite. The critic, duly annoyed at being addressed as a fundament, replied with legal action.

A fortnight later Satie, Cocteau and their turbulent supporters crowded into a Paris court-room for the battle. Poueigh's lawyer claimed that the postcard, being open to all, exposed his client to the ridicule of his concierge and to the jeers of the street. He went on to develop an interesting thesis in which Picasso, Derain, Braque and Apollinaire were to be classified as 'Boches', and he arraigned them, with incisive eloquence, as the gravediggers of civilization. The judge was little interested in aesthetic discussion, but he was certainly annoyed by the row Satie's unruly band created. He awarded a sentence of one week's prison, a hundred francs fine, and damages of a thousand francs to the critic.

Cocteau went pale with rage under his make-up. In the passage leading from the court-room he threw himself on Poueigh's lawyer and slapped his face. Two policemen managed to drag away the infuriated poet, tumbled him downstairs to a cell, and there beat him up with that vigorous devotion to their work for which the Paris constabulary is noted. He emerged with swollen eyes, bloodied face and torn clothes. Satie meanwhile foundered in despair. Poueigh now had the right to distrain on his belongings, on his scores! How would Satie's music ever be performed in a government-subsidized theatre again? (Up to now it never had been and there was no likelihood of such a revolutionary event occurring.) And what disgrace for a respectable musician to have a police record! He appealed against the judgement. A lenient judge waived the damages. Things were so arranged, even, that he never saw the inside of a prison, where, we may be sure, he would have turned out to be a model and punctilious tenant.

A month or so after *Parade* came that joyous outburst of Apollinaire, *les Mamelles de Tirésias*. Its reception was stormy. Satie thought of collaborating with Apollinaire on a work for the stage, but they could find no common ground. Seven years were to pass before Satie produced another ballet, and for *Mercure*, as it was called, he turned again to Cocteau. It was true that at the moment there was need for him to write something that would keep him in the public eye, since *Parade* had brought him notoriety for a life-time – except, of course, in England, where a first performance of the work was received by the phlegmatic British as 'amusing' and little else. But together with the execrations *Parade* earned him there came also the admiration of younger composers. The earliest of these included a youth who, at the age of eighteen, had been a fiery advocate of Satie at the battle of *Parade* and one of those whose protests had most annoyed the judge at the subsequent court proceedings. His name was Georges Auric.

2

THE GATHERING OF THE SIX

I

I T is fitting that one of the most Parisian of composers should have been born hundreds of miles away from the capital and at the other end of France. If illustrious Londoners are often found to hail from the provinces, even more so do typical Parisians choose to come into the world anywhere but in Paris. Georges Auric's native town was Lodève in the Hérault. He is therefore a 'Lutévain'. (The inhabitants of nearby Saint-Affrique happily style themselves 'Saint-Affricains'.)

He soon showed musical gifts. An old lady, starched and ringleted in the tradition of provincial music mistresses, introduced him to the piano. From her he escaped to the conservatoire in Montpellier, where a sympathetic teacher, who disturbed everyone by an unhealthy interest in modern music, put him in touch with that picturesque southerner Déodat de Séverac, whose wanderings in the rustic paths of folklore caused him to style himself as a 'peasant-musician'. He surely looked the part with his black curly hair, waxed moustache, and capacious Panama hat.

Another attraction in Montpellier was the big library which Auric's teacher opened up to him. The boy read everything – and remembered, unusually, most of what he read. At the age of fifteen, said Poulenc, he was discussing sociology with Léon Bloy and theology with Maritain. At the age of seventeen Apollinaire was reading to him *les Mamelles de Tirésias* and asking his opinion. At the age of ten he started composing, and a year later had written his first orchestral piece. Montpellier was then the home of Charles Bordes, who, with Vincent d'Indy, founded the Schola Cantorum. In that town Bordes organized concerts where Auric heard a deal of good

of good music. Auric's talent was so promising that his family
was persuaded to send him to Paris. A letter from Séverac
ensured a friendly meeting with Florent Schmitt, the testy
composer of monumental works little heard these days. Albert
Roussel, the sailor turned composer, was another to be impressed by Auric. (Only a few years before his pupils had
included Satie. His capacity to be surprised had revived since
then.)

Through Roussel Auric obtained a first hearing in Paris.
His group of songs, *Trois interludes*, to prose poems by René
Chalupt, was sung at a concert when the composer was fifteen
years old. With adult irony he points up a text (*le Tilbury*) in
which the poet evokes Constantin Guys and his pictures of
fashionable folk driving out in their tilburys, and of *cocodettes*
toying with ice-creams on cafe terraces ... but alas, says the
poet, he has not Guys' talent, so he must rest content with
looking at his prints in art-dealers' windows. This trio of
Second Empire vignettes, all crinolines and strutting dandies,
is completed with *le Pouf* and *le Gloxinia*. Had it been written
by a mature composer there would not have been much to
remark. Coming from a musician scarcely into his teens it was
arresting. As Florent Schmitt grunted unwillingly to him:
'When I don't like music I make a point of listening to it more
closely.'

The young prodigy was invited out and put on show.
Awkward, shy, he stood nervously in drawing rooms, shifted
his weight from one foot to the other, and tangled his hands
into knots. Only his eyes, sharp and searching, betrayed the
unusual talent that was his. When he sat at the piano he
played with the assurance of an experienced artist. His musical
fate had been decided the day he came across one of the
Sarabandes by Erik Satie. In 1913, at the home of his parents
who now lived in Montmartre, he had his first meeting with
Satie. The older musician treated him as an equal, and, while
he gave him advice, was always willing to hear with deference
the counsels offered him in return by a composer more than
thirty years his junior.

Perhaps it was Satie's example that led Auric to take
composition lessons in Vincert d'Indy's class at the Schola
Cantorum. This he did after working his way through the
Conservatoire. While studying there he made the acquaintance

of a student called Germaine Tailleferre. In three successive years, from 1913 to 1915, she carried off first prizes in harmony, in counterpoint and in accompaniment. She had more than her just share of gifts. The talent which enabled her to play the piano at five and to transpose, at the age of seven, a Mozart sonata before she really knew her notes, was partnered by physical beauty, a fair complexion and lovely blonde hair.

She was born and brought up a few miles outside Paris. Her ancestors were Norman by descent and had been farmers for generations. Monsieur Tailleferre disapproved of her musical ambitions, and her childhood was punctuated by arguments between him and her mother over whether she should be allowed to fulfil them. The mother won. Although Germaine soon proved her skill as an instrumentalist during her training, it was composition that attracted her most. Where Satie, Stravinsky and Chabrier were Auric's models, Ravel, at least in the early years, was her ideal.

'Take some piano pieces and orchestrate them in different ways,' Ravel used to tell her. 'It's a wonderful exercise.'

She was a frequent visitor at le Belvédère, Ravel's house in the village of Montfort l'Amaury. She shared his delight in the fake ornaments and knicknacks which filled a little room – the musical box with a nightingale that opened its beak and waggled real feathers, the doll in a glass jar, the miniature sailing boat that rocked over painted paper waves in obedience to the turning of a handle. The reserved little dandy proudly showed her his 'Japanese room', where everything, from the 'Japanese' prints to the 'Japanese' flowers in ground glass, was imitation. 'Mais c'est du faux!' he would cry maliciously to those who showed polite admiration.

His friendship with her was sealed when she gave him a tiny white sofa made of porcelain, delicately escalloped. The seat opened up like a box. That day they went out on the terrace, crossed the ornamental garden with its dwarf trees and elaborate fountain, and went for a long walk in the forest of Rambouillet. He showed her his favourite pool, where the blue sky turned to green in the reflection of its leaden waters. Every path, every glade was known to him. He could imitate the song of birds with accurate intonation and reproduce the rhythm perfectly. When they returned to the house, Ravel's

wiry legs untired by miles of walking, Germaine Tailleferre
showed she was his equal for energy. She sat down at the
piano and played, from memory, the whole of *Petrouchka*
while he listened appreciatively, cloaked in the harsh fumes of
his eternal Caporal cigarette.

The influence of Ravel was challenged by her fellow students
at the Conservatoire. Auric was there to urge the example of
Satie. From Darius Milhaud came praise for Stravinsky.
Milhaud was almost her exact contemporary in age. His origin
and beliefs he stated unequivocally: 'I am a Frenchman from
Provence and Jewish by religion.' His great-grandfather helped
found the synagogue of Aix-en-Provence in 1840. His mother
descended from the Sephardic Jews established for centuries in
Italy. The child Darius, untypically named after the Persian
warrior king, grew up in an old house at the centre of Aix.
From his window he could watch the sunlit street filled with
mule-drawn carts and blue-bloused peasants who, as in a
Cézanne picture, drank and played cards in cafés. Far off, he
he could glimpse the trees that bordered the road to Marseille,
and on the horizon the curve of hills that stood out in the
setting sun. Up from the courtyard drifted scraps of Provençal
dialect, the gentle clump of fruit tumbling into baskets, the
rumble of carts, and the steady murmur of the employees who
worked for his father, the proprietor of an old-established
almond business.

At 'l'Enclos', the family's country house, the sounds were
different. By night a chorus of frogs chanted sturdily. Sometimes
a mysterious click, sharp like the sudden snip of a pair of
secateurs, cut through the air. A nightingale launched into
prolonged modulations that plagued the boy's ear until a quick
trill resolved the suspense. An owl lamented in the garden.
Dawn brought a medley of crowing cocks, strident cicadas, and
convent bells, one of which tolled a chord in the major sixth
that vibrated endlessly.

Milhaud was a frail little boy. A keen sensitivity to noise
formed part of a nervous system that was highly strung. Before
he reached the age of three he picked out, on a piano, the
tune of 'Funiculi Funicula' which he had heard played by some
Italian street musicians. A year or so later he was attacking
four-handed duets with his father. He took violin lessons. His
sympathetic family prepared for the emergence of a virtuoso.

They even acquiesced in his impatient departure from a theatre in the middle of the first act of *Samson et Dalila,* a treat which they had been anticipating for some time. His judgement of Massenet was quite as severe, and only politeness to his hosts kept him squirming reluctantly on his seat through a performance of *Manon.* Debussy meant a great deal more to him, and the string quartet which he had played with his friends led him on to the revelation of *Pelléas et Mélisande.*

He was an only child. Though Milhaud senior could have wished him to succeed in the family business, no obstacle was put in the way of a musical career. His father's only stipulation was that he should pass his Baccalauréat. This he did and at last came to Paris for good. Here he went to all the concerts and operas that Aix had lacked. For a performance of Wagner's *Ring* he reverently booked a seat in the stalls rather than his usual place in the humble gallery. He was bored to death. Perseverance in the attempt to understand Wagner found him once again in the church-like atmosphere which invaded the Opéra with *Parsifal.* And once again he felt 'the impression of a Latin heart which could not adapt to the musico-philosophical gibberish, the mystico-harmonic tin-plating of an art that was essentially pompous and whose very "leitmotiven", a sort of musical Baedeker that made the audience drunk with pride because they always "knew where they were", seemed to me a childish technique. I deplored, too, the music's influence on our own.'

The Conservatoire provided Milhaud with alternating phases of enchantment and boredom. He went to the orchestral classes given by Paul Dukas. That severe self-critic had already composed a massive piano sonata, the over-played *Apprenti sorcier,* the sumptuous opera *Ariane et Barb-Bleue,* and the tone poem *la Péri.* At the time when Milhaud first knew him he had more or less stopped publishing his music. Between 1912 and 1935, the date of his death, he brought out only two brief piano pieces. The rest of his compositions he destroyed without mercy. This relentless quest for perfection induced, maybe, a certain diffidence in his personal relations. He was a poor conductor and unimpressive at rehearsals. His students did not respect him. His classes were often disorderly and inconclusive. Only Milhaud and one or two others showed indignation at their comrades' attitude towards a great musician.

It must have been a touching surprise for Dukas when Milhaud asked him to autograph a copy of *Ariane*.

Milhaud was already composing voluminously. In Aix during the holidays he had written six hundred pages of an opera, as well as a violin sonata. He tried, with not much success, to interest Xavier Leroux, his harmony teacher. The fiercely moustachioed Leroux, purveyor to Opéra-Comique audiences of such fragrant bagatelles as *William Ratcliff* and *la Fille de Figaro*, took evasive action. He knew that Milhaud was an unwilling student with little taste for the traditional harmony he taught. Milhaud persisted. Leroux gave way and agreed to listen to the violin sonata. After hearing the first bars his face lit up. He began to sing the violin part and to play it on the piano. 'What on earth are you doing here?' he cried enthusiastically. 'You're trying to learn a conventional language, whereas you already have one of your own. Leave the class. Resign.'

Milhaud was advised to study with André Gédalge. Having started life as a bookseller, Gédalge became professor of fugue and counterpoint at the Conservatoire and an outstanding teacher of the day. The young musician was told to call on him at midday. He found the pedagogue at lunch. A beret on his head and a napkin tucked round his neck, Gédalge was busy eating a chop. 'Play me something,' he ordered between mouthfuls. Milhaud nervously started on one of his pieces.

'Why have you got a D sharp seventeen times in the first page?' interrupted Gédalge. 'You don't know how to construct a tune. What do you want to do: learn your job or win a prize?'

'Learn my job,' Milhaud promptly replied. Under Gédalge's vigorous tuition that is what he did.

Soon he deserted the violin entirely for composition. A wish to set *la Brebis égarée* by Francis Jammes led him and a friend to Orthez, the poet's sun-splashed retreat among the hills of the Basses Pyrénées. It was here that Jammes wrote most of his work – poems of rustic life, evocations of the scents and colours of nature, with, at times, nostalgic forays into distant lands. In supple verse he told the romances of beautiful girls long dead, of Clara d'Ellebeuse, of Almaïde d'Etremont, of Guadalupe de Alcaraz. The patriarchal Jammes stroked his long white beard, gazed benevolently at Milhaud from behind his pince-nez, and recited some of his poetry. He spoke with a strong Pyrenean accent, lingering over the final syllables of words and prolonging the resonance. Then it was Milhaud's turn to perform. The poet's piano was virtually derelict, so they went to Jammes' elderly spinster cousins. The instrument there, chastely draped with thick velvet, was in tune. Weak tea and dry biscuits were served in a drawing room much encumbered with delicate china, little tables enveloped in tasteful embroidery, and heavy fringed curtains. For over an hour Milhaud played and sang, at the top of his lungs, the first act of his setting of *la Brebis égarée*. The cousins, too polite to express an opinion, sat primly by and wondered within themselves at the nature of the young lunatic bellowing in their parlour. Francis Jammes, not quite so set in his ways, listened with interested approval.

Jammes was responsible for bringing Milhaud and Paul Claudel together. The friendship between the exuberant, meridional Jew and the severe Catholic of granite-like faith was on the surface an improbable one. Milhaud has never ceased to regard his meeting with Claudel as a turning point in his life. They immediately felt in sympathy. Milhaud played him some settings of *Poèmes de la Connaissance de l'Est*, in which he had attempted to match the ruggedness of the verse with robust music. 'Vous êtes un mâle!' roared Claudel, flapping the sleeves of his Chinese dressing gown. The secret of their relationship lies perhaps in this remark. For Milhaud's music, while it shows a strain of sweet sensitiveness, is also given to unexpected bursts of violence. His collaboration with the poet was to produce some of his best works. In 1917 Claudel, then a member of the diplomatic service, was posted to Brazil. He asked Milhaud, who was unfit for military service, to accompany him as secretary. So began the wanderings that have characterized Milhaud's life ever since. When he returned to Paris the war had ended. He brought back with him a medley of Brazilian impressions that coloured his music and stamped it with a restless exoticism.

II

Milhaud, Auric and Tailleferre had already met each other at the Conservatoire. Auric astonished Milhaud with his wide culture and sharp intelligence. His compositions showed a spontaneity already disciplined by a mature control. The mixture of tenderness and clear sightedness impressed Milhaud. The three young musicians were joined, around 1911, by a fourth called Arthur Honegger. Reinforced by this new comrade they scandalized their composition teacher, the charming and sociable Widor, with their determined dissonances. 'The worst of it is that one gets used to them!' sighed Widor.

Honegger came from le Havre where his parents, Swiss by origin, had been settled for some time. He never forgot the atmosphere of the busy old port. As a child he knew everything about square-rigging, stowing, dunnage and trimming. The models of sailing boats he made showed an intimate familiarity with all the refinements of three-masters and brigs, of schooners and fore-and-aft vessels. He was fascinated, too by railway engines. His appreciation of the steaming monsters he saw flash through stations was based on a precise knowledge of wheels, axles and boiler gauges. In le Havre, at the age of nine, he saw *Faust* and *les Huguenots*. His passion for boats and engines was transferred to opera. He wrote one himself, seventy-seven pages in a school exercise book covering three whole acts and four tableaux. Soon after learning the rudiments of music he was turning out page upon page of oratorio, sonata and lieder. They were all written in the key of G. His mother, a musician herself, obliged by sight-reading them for him at the piano and tactfully refrained from questioning his faithful attachment to the ever-recurring key.

One afternoon towards his sixteenth birthday he heard some Bach cantatas in the Protestant church at le Havre. This was a vital experience. He had found the model that was to serve him for life. His excitement gave way to a long study of Bach. He thought now in terms of the architecture of music, of bold lines and of sweeping frescoes. Soon after this he had to choose a career. It was obviously going to be music. His father, like Milhaud's, did not insist on his entering the family business. While the family were on holiday in Zurich some of his compositions were shown to the director of the Conservatoire. The verdict was favourable and he was sent to Paris. Every week, for two years, he travelled between le Havre and Paris. (He rarely failed to cast an expert eye over the engine that drew his carriage.) At the end of this period his family decided to go back to Zurich. Arthur was left in Paris. He took up quarters in the rue Say, just off the avenue Trudaine in the Opéra district. It was, at that time, a quiet street and only a few métro stations away from the rue de Madrid and the Conservatoire.

As a 'timid little provincial' Honegger was at first dazzled by the Parisian atmosphere. 'I arrived in Paris at the age of nineteen,' he said later. 'I'd been brought up on the Classics and the Romantics, and I was mad about Richard Strauss and Max Reger. The latter was completely unknown in Paris. In exchange I found, not the school, but the flowering of Debussy's influence. I was introduced to d'Indy and Fauré. I took a long time to get through to the personality of Fauré, whom I considered for some time as a salon composer. Once I'd passed through that stage I gave myself up with pleasure to his example. So far as my own aesthetic and sensibility are concerned, Debussy and Fauré acted as a very useful counterbalance to the Classics and Wagner.'

He flourished on the discipline Gédalge imposed at the Conservatoire. Whenever he brought to his teacher a piece into which he'd introduced a few 'daring' novelties, Gédalge would comment sardonically : 'It's not really difficult to do. Whereas in Bach, or Mozart ... take a look at them ...' Music haunted the young student. At the dentist's one day he lay back in the chair working out, in his mind, a passage of counterpoint. When the dentist stood aside for the filling to dry, Honegger seized pencil and paper, and, his mouth still open, scribbled down the crucial bars.

Mobilized in 1914, Honegger went on writing music. In between training recruits he found time to compose a few songs heavily Debussyst in manner. Posted back to Paris, he reappeared at the Conservatoire. His explorations into Bach continued. While his friends, disconcerted by his unfashionable preferences – unfashionable, that is, among young French musicians of the period – urged him back to Debussy or even Mussorgsky, he persisted with the German Romantics : Brahms, Strauss, and later Schoenberg. The only contemporary French composer to attract him was Florent Schmitt, in whom he admired a taste for big orchestral effects.

From the rue Say he moved to the rue Duperré, a neighbourhood that seemed not at all in sympathy with his character.

It runs into the place Pigalle, with its garish electric lights, noisy crowds and busy traffic. The clatter of the fair and its sideshows could be heard a long way off. Yet Honegger did not share with the group of musicians, whom he was soon to join, one of their most striking characteristics. 'I've no enthusiasm for fairs or music halls,' he said. 'On the contrary, I admire chamber music and symphonic music in everything they have that's most serious and austere.' As if to underline the paradox of his choice of district, the flat he lived in had once belonged to Olivier Métra, the popular composer of innumerable best-selling waltzes, polkas, mazurkas and quadrilles.

He had friendly arguments with Darius Milhaud. The clash between Milhaud's Latin preferences and Honegger's more Northern tastes was already there. It did not spoil their relationship. Satie, whom Milhaud and Auric so admired, was for Honegger without interest. Honegger's passion for Strauss and Wagner left his two friends indifferent. They agreed, with the best of humour, to leave it at that. 'Darius Milhaud,' said Honegger with his usual modesty, 'is the most gifted of us.' Germaine Tailleferre remembers their time together with affection : 'We spent long days in Milhaud's flat since classes were empty because of the war. He initiated us into Stravinsky, Magnard, Debussy, etc., in short, everything the Conservatoire despised and rejected! everything that delighted us! Arthur was divinely handsome, extremely witty, the great sportsman of the company. There was a remarkably calm, balanced atmosphere about him. His kindness and his modesty always remained with him when he became famous. In spite of the years of suffering which later transfigured him, it is still Arthur's handsome, genial face in the years of our youth that I prefer to remember.'

Among the girls who noticed Honegger's good looks, the thick black hair and the firm profile, was a pianist called Andrée Vaurabourg. She gave, in 1916, the first public performance of an instrumental work by him. This was the *Toccata et variations*. It was the first of many occasions when she was to bring to the performance of Honegger's work the sympathy of an expert interpreter. And she was, in addition, to become one of the most important women in his life.

A year after the war began Milhaud was on holiday in Aix. The post brought him a letter from a boy asking for an autograph. 'I shall be back in Paris in September . . .' replied Milhaud. He had heard, he added, 'that you write music, and you know how interested I am in what people younger than myself are doing'. The venerable Milhaud was twenty-three years old. His correspondent, Francis Poulenc, was sixteen.

Poulenc was born in the heart of Paris, a few steps away from the Madeleine and the palais de l'Élysée. His father belonged to an old Aveyron family of strong Catholic beliefs. There was even a great-great uncle who had been an abbé. The father, with two brothers, ran the chemical firm which is today the huge enterprise known as Rhône-Poulenc. Poulenc's mother had an entirely Parisian ancestry. So there was, from the very beginning, that combination in Poulenc of religious devotion on the one hand, and light-heartedness on the other, which was often to perplex in later years.

The family circle was rich and comfortable. It was also musical. Poulenc's father, though playing no instrument, was a patron of fashionable concerts and opera. His favourite composers were Beethoven, Berlioz, Franck and Massenet. The son did not follow him in his musical taste, and leaned rather to that of his mother. She was an excellent pianist and had studied with one of Liszt's pupils. To her son she transmitted a love of Mozart – whom he set above all others – Schubert and Chopin. There was also a maternal uncle nicknamed 'Papoum', so called from Poulenc's childish attempt to pronounce the word 'parrain'. He was a type long since vanished, the leisured, cultured boulevardier who lived well and divided his time between club, concert, theatre and opera. He also painted, for his own pleasure, execrable pictures in the style of Toulouse-Lautrec. His roomy flat overlooking the Jardins du Luxembourg was crammed with Japanese bibelots and objets d'art for which the Goncourt brothers, twenty years earlier, had set the rage. When uncle Papoum came to see Madame Poulenc, the boy, ostensibly playing with his model railway, would sit under the table spellbound at the sophisticated talk about a magic world of the stage and actors and art galleries.

Summer holidays were spent at the home of Poulenc's grandmother in Nogent-sur-Marne. Although the little town is only a few miles outside the capital, for the Parisian members of his family it represented the heart of the countryside. Nogent is at the eastern end of the bois de Vincennes. It lies on a slope overlooking the right bank of the Marne, where in hot months pleasure boats run and bathers gaily splash. The river's edge is lively with restaurants and flags. There are beer gardens and festoons of coloured lights. The chatter of accordions playing for popular dances floats out over the water to the île de Beauté in mid-river. It is very cheerful and common. If Poulenc's childhood holidays in Nogent were to endow him with a strain of suburban vulgarity, it is worth remembering that here also the elegant painter Watteau, who was another influence on him, lived and died.

There is somewhere a photograph of Poulenc at the age of three. Wearing a little dress and a round straw hat with a ribbon, he sits before a tiny piano. The miniature instrument is lacquered in white and has cherries painted on it. He would pretend to sight-read at it department store catalogues and old railway time-tables. As far back as he could remember music was his passion. At the age of fifteen he had composed a grand 'Processional for the Cremation of a Mandarin' inspired by Stravinsky. Only much later did he pay direct tribute to the Nogent of his early years with a valse-musette for two pianos. It evokes 'the Nogent pleasure gardens with their bantering, sentimental accordions', and, in its title *l'Embarquement pour Cythère*, his admired Watteau.

Unlike Milhaud, Tailleferre, Auric and Honegger, Poulenc never studied at the Conservatoire. His mother began teaching him the piano when he was five. She was succeeded by a female pedagogue who left behind an impression of huge spangled hats and mediocre instruction. He was then taken on by a niece of César Franck who taught him so well that by the time he was fourteen he could play, quite respectably, not only Debussy, Ravel and Stravinsky, but also Bartok and Schoenberg. His mother would have sent him to the Conservatoire. His father, despite his own love of music, preferred the boy to pass the usual school exams first. By the time Poulenc had done as he was told, the war had begun and military service intervened. It was not until 1921 that he started composing seriously and with method.

After the war Darius Milhaud put him in touch with Charles Koechlin for counterpoint lessons. Koechlin was an interesting composer who is today unfairly neglected. His major pieces are the big symphonic poems whose subjects he found in Kipling, Gide, H. G. Wells and Romain Rolland. He was an independent sort of man who wrote with integrity and bore hostile criticism with good humour. Most people remember him as the orchestrator of Fauré's *Pelléas et Mélisande* incidental music. Such work, he modestly observed, taught him a lot. His alertness to modern trends involved him early on in film music : among the large-scale works based on Kipling's *Jungle Book*, the copious instrumental pieces and the ballets, there is a *Seven Stars Symphony*. It pictures, among others, Douglas Fairbanks, Greta Garbo, Marlene Dietrich and Charlie Chaplin. He also wrote *Danses pour Ginger*, which are respectfully sub-titled 'en hommage à Ginger Rogers'. His appearance bore out a lively and curious personality. A capacious beard gave him the look of a genial river god, and a large black cloak flapped at his heels. When he travelled abroad he wrapped his belongings in a brown paper parcel since he never in his life owned a suitcase. He was often to be seen padding the streets in shabby but comfortable carpet slippers.

Poulenc found him a sympathetic teacher who had a gift for adapting to pupils. Another mentor was Ricardo Viñes, noted as being the only virtuoso of the time to play Debussy and Ravel. 'He was a delightful man,' Poulenc remembered. 'A kind of exotic Hidalgo with enormous moustaches, a flat-topped sombrero in the purest Spanish style, and button boots with which he used to rap my shins when I didn't vary the pedalling enough.' Though he could have built a glittering career for himself, Viñes chose to devote his ample gifts to such unpopular composers as Mompou and Satie. He made no concessions to celebrity and would rather introduce new talent than follow the path of the conventional virtuoso. It was Viñes who gave the first performance of Poulenc's early piano works. They could have had no better advocate.

Through Viñes Poulenc was introduced to Satie. The older man was at first suspicious of the youth from a rich middle-class background. Then an incident occurred which engaged Satie's friendship. Before Poulenc studied under Koechlin he had gone in search of lessons from one Paul Vidal. The latter, who presided over the Opéra-Comique, was also the composer of ballets and operettas much prized by undemanding audiences. He received Poulenc in his office and glanced at the manuscript his visitor put before him. It was the larkish *Rapsodie négre.* Vidal flew into a high rage. He spluttered, red-faced, that Poulenc was a practical joker and threatened to put his boot up a tender spot if the composer did not leave immediately. The news of Vidal's reaction so delighted Satie that he wrote a warm letter to Poulenc. From that moment on their friendship was close.

Round about this time Poulenc was composing his *Bestiaire,* a setting of six poems by Apollinaire. He knew the poet only briefly, for Apollinaire died in 1918, barely a year after their first meeting. His chief memory was of Apollinaire's gentle voice, half-ironic, half-melancholy. Suddenly a great roar of laughter would shake his plump girth, and a stream of fantasy would pour from the tiny mouth set in the large, moon-like face. The quatrains Poulenc chose from the *Bestiaire* were those featuring the dromedary, the Tibetan goat, the grasshopper, the dolphin, the crab and the carp. Each is very short, and the concision is paralleled by the music. There is no irony, no tongue-in-the-cheek roguery about these utterly sincere pieces. Each syllable, for example, of that magnificent name 'Don Pedro d'Alfaroubeira' is lovingly enunciated with the grave pomposity which the owner of the dromedaries would doubtless have assumed when introducing himself. The charm of that endearing creature the dolphin is caught with sparkling play-fulness, while by contrast the music for the carp shimmers in mysterious depths. The *Bestiaire* was the first of many Poulenc settings of Apollinaire, with whom, he declared, he felt a 'strong and mysterious bond'.

No sooner had Poulenc finished his work than he was stupified to learn that a musician called Louis Durey was also setting the *Bestiaire* – and, moreover, was including all twenty-six of the poems it comprised. He went to meet Durey while on leave from the army. They both took the situation very well. 'Immediately,' wrote Poulenc, 'I dedicated *my Bestiaire* to him.'

Louis Durey was already in his thirties. He had, like Poulenc, come to music by a circuitous route which avoided the Con-servatoire. His father was a partner in a prosperous foundry which had developed from a small business that printed visiting cards by hand. Louis studied at the École des Hautes Études Commerciales and emerged with a diploma in languages and accountancy. He entered the foundry and proved to be an efficient book-keeper. There also he learned enough about typography to be able later to design the covers for editions of his own music.

An early attempt to interest him in music had failed. When the family invited the eight-year-old boy to learn the piano he stubbornly refused. The piano, he said, was suitable for girls, as were cooking and dress-making. But for boys. . . ! Much later, when he was nineteen, he started going to the opera. Gradually he absorbed the current repertory. Then he heard *Pelléas et Mélisande* for the first time, and until war came he attended every performance of it that was given in Paris. Hearing music no longer satisfied him. He wanted to write it. Private lessons from a teacher at the Schola Cantorum gave him the technical knowledge he lacked. Orchestration he taught himself by studying text books and the classic works.

His early songs were, inevitably, Debussyst, and flagrantly so. Schoenberg was to change all that for him. In 1914 he came across an extract from the *Buch der hängenden Gärten*. Schoenberg, said Durey, offered him a means of liberation and the possibility of expressing himself in the way best adapted to his own character. The result of the discovery was *l'Offrande lyrique*, a song cycle taken from poems by Rabindranath Tagore in André Gide's translation. It is probably the first example of a French composer using atonal techniques. Since the work has never been published, the composer's own opinion is of interest: 'In spite of its imperfections which are due to inexperience, [it] marks a decisive step.' Those who heard it when first played in 1919, five years after its composition, remarked on 'a genuine poetic talent'. Also unpublished is the *Voyage d'Urien*, a setting of prose by André Gide. Roland Manuel, a reliable judge, says that it represents a further evolution in that it is more personal, more daring. The *Voyage d'Urien*, written in 1916, was not publicly performed until 1965, nearly half a century later.

In August 1914, Durey became an unwilling soldier. The stupidities of military life, the horror of war and the excesses of jingoism appalled him. With deliberate ostentation he began to write an opera based on a German play – and this, at a time of noisy patriotism, demanded bravery of a sort. He avidly read articles written by the socialist Jean Jaurès in *l'Humanité*. During the war he was a regular subscriber to *la Guerre sociale* and *le Bonnet rouge*. Already he was set on the way that led him in later years to write such pieces as *Quatre Chants de Lutte pour l'Union de la Jeunesse Républicaine de France*, to set poems by Mao Tse Tung and Ho Chi Minh, and to find in the Communist party those ideals which he cherished as a young man.

With the addition of Louis Durey the group that was to be known as 'les Six' becomes complete. While Auric, Milhaud, Tailleferre and Honegger were doing their best to storm the embattled establishment of French musical life, Poulenc and Durey, coming in from the periphery, hastened to join them. And in the background, smiling at their youth, encouraging their audacities, floated the impenitent shadow of Erik Satie.

3

THE SIX ARE BAPTIZED

I

ALTHOUGH he survived lustily into the 1940s to become a war correspondent and did not, in fact, reluctantly give up the ghost until 1961, Blaise Cendrars remained an archetypal figure of the Twenties. A full account of his life would be as exhausting as a perusal of his complete works. You cannot just say he was a writer. He was by turn an explorer who wrote novels, an anthropologist who wrote poetry, a bee-keeper who threw off plays, a diamond dealer who produced film scripts, a lorry driver who translated books into French, and a musicologist who wrote art criticism. At one point in his career he turned up as a juggler in a London music hall where he shared the bill, and a room, with a Jewish comedian who read Schopenhauer between the acts and who was called Charlie Chaplin.

His mother was Scottish, his father Swiss, and he spent his childhood in Egypt before travelling, with an English tutor, to Naples and Sicily, where he attended a German school. When his family came to Switzerland he decided to go off on his own travels. At the age of fifteen he ran away and toured Europe by train, never setting foot outside railway stations, until he exhausted his funds in Munich. There a Polish Jew, a travelling merchant, took him on as assistant. For three years they wandered over Russia, China, Armenia and Persia. They sold alarm clocks at the fair of Nijni-Novgorod, bartered gramophones for jewels in Ispahan, and haggled over diamonds in Bombay. 'I like danger,' Cendrars confessed. 'I'm not a man for the study. I've never been able to resist the appeal of the unknown. Writing is the thing most contrary to my temperament, and I suffer like the damned from having to stay shut

57

up within four walls blackening paper when life is teeming outside and I can hear car horns on the road, the whistle of railway engines, the siren of the steamboat . . .'

He claimed to have made, and lost, fortunes. At one moment he lived in luxurious hotels. At others he starved. In 1915 a machine-gun bullet shattered his hand. The right arm had to be amputated. With typical defiance he refused the offer of a false limb and made himself play, and excel at, the most violent sports. He drove his racing car in a way that made people wonder if he was a fool or a hero. After the war, a crumpled Caporal stuck permanently in the middle of his battered features, he tore off to Africa and came back with the *Anthologie nègre*. Artists were fascinated by his revelations of African folklore and sculptures.

When in Paris he usually stayed with painter friends. They introduced him to Apollinaire. Later, Cendrars claimed that Apollinaire had plagiarized him in the *Calligrammes*. This was a charge he brought against several people at one time or another. Perhaps it was the penalty he paid for being so spendthrift of his own ideas. Apollinaire's greatness as a poet, roared the wounded Blaise, ended in 1911, seven years before his death. He let it be understood, without modesty, that after that date another man deserved the title of France's greatest poet. A less controversial link between the two rivals was their generous support of new art. Cendrars was an early champion of Léger, Picasso and Chagall. None other than Braque designed the coachwork of the Alfa Romeo sports car that Cendrars piloted for thousands of hair-raising miles through South America. In music, too, Cendrars was a pioneer. Stravinsky and Honegger benefited from his enthusiasm. Erik Satie was encouraged by him. Cendrars was prominent at most of the 'scandalous' musical events of the time. At the first night of *Petrouchka* he was attacked by a protesting member of the audience who wrenched a folding seat from its bearings and crowned him with it. He spent the rest of the evening in Montmartre drinking champagne with Stravinksy and Diaghilev, the seat hanging round his neck like a grotesque horse collar, his face bleeding with scratches.

Early in 1916 Cendrars became involved with a group of artists who held exhibitions in a studio at 6 rue Huyghens, a little street off the boulevard du Montparnasse. Originally in-

B

tended for use as an art school, the studio was turned during
the war into an informal concert hall. Poetry readings and
music were given there to raise funds for starving artists. A
society called 'Lyre et Palette' was formed and organized
recitals of Debussy, Satie and Ravel. There were exhibitions of
paintings by Modigliani, Kisling, Matisse and the ubiquitous
Picasso. Cendrars and Cocteau appeared on the scene to read
their poems before a crowded audience sitting on chairs
borrowed from a sympathetic attendant in the Jardins du
Luxembourg. The place was uncomfortable, and, except for
Cubist pictures on the wall, stark. If spectators did not freeze
in the icy draughts, they were roasted by a monstrous stove
and choked by its fumes. Despite all this, the studio in the rue
Huyghens soon acquired chic. Smart cars drew up outside and
delivered well-dressed ladies to mingle with artists wearing
sweaters and smoking foul pipes.

On 6 June 1917, Cendrars organized a concert there to
mark the first performance a few weeks before of *Parade*.
Auric arrived with a newly composed *Trio*. Plump and beaming, he looked, said an alert observer, as if he had been blown
up like a ball for a joke, so that he could hardly link together
the dimpled hands at the end of his short arms. His close
friend Louis Laloy, a critic and poet steeped in Chinese
literature, had absorbed into his gaunt frame something of a
Chinese appearance also.* When seen together, which was
often, they resembled the Buddha and his high priest. Honegger
was there too, with his deep-toned laugh and vigorous gestures.
His contribution included some Apollinaire settings. Louis
Durey joined them, thin-featured and bird-like behind fragile
spectacles. He brought with him *Carillons*, a fluttery impressionistic piece for two pianos which was performed by Auric
and a young musician called Juliette Meerowitch. Finally there
was Satie himself, who, with Mademoiselle Meerowitch, played
a four-handed arrangement of *Parade*. After the concert Satie
was driven home in a friend's car. As usual, he asked the
car to stop some distance from his flat. Then he vanished
into the night and returned alone to that wretched dwell-
ing where he allowed none but himself to enter for thirty
years.

* Laloy had also absorbed opium, a delicacy to which he introduced
Cocteau and Poulenc.

C

Thanks to Cendrars, half of the group soon to be known as
'les Six' had now made their public debut. The names of Auric,
Durey and Honegger appeared for the first time together on
the rue Huyghens programme. Though nothing by Germaine
Tailleferre was played on that occasion, she was an active
member of the group. Poulenc was about to compress his lanky
figure into soldier's uniform and to write wistful letters to Paris
from dreary barracks in a dismal hamlet. Milhaud toured
Brazil with Claudel, admiring the bay of Rio and its palm
trees, and going on trips into the forest where he slept under
arches of liana and orchids. He was not to be reunited with
'les Nouveaux Jeunes', as Satie baptized his friends in the rue
Huyghens, until the following year.

Poulenc's turn, however, was not long in coming. Before he
joined the army he had already composed the *Rapsodie nègre*
which so outraged, as we have seen, the conventional Paul
Vidal. In a bookshop one day he found a volume called *les
Poésies de Makoko Kangourou*. The publication was a
practical joke inspired by the current rage for African art, and
the gifted 'Makoko Kangourou', claiming to be a Liberian
Negro, wrote his work in a mysterious dialect which owed more
to the boulevards of Paris than to the streets of Monrovia.
Enchanted with his discovery, the composer started work on
the earliest of those pieces which were later to be described as
'leg-Poulenc'. He scored it for piano, string quartet, flute and
clarinet, with a vocal interlude for baritone voice.

The first performance was given on 11 December 1917, at
the Théâtre du Vieux-Colombier, in one of a series organized
by Jane Bathori. In the absence of Jacques Copeau, who gave
her the use of the theatre while he was away, she seized the
opportunity of encouraging the contemporary music that was
her chief interest in life. She was a brilliant singer and in her
time introduced nearly all the songs of Debussy, Ravel, Satie,
Roussel and Milhaud, often accompanying herself on the piano.
Denied an outlet for her energy during the 1939–45 war, she
took herself off to Buenos Aires and organized the music section
of the French Institute there. When she retired from the concert platform she continued her evangelism by lecturing, teaching and broadcasting. 'Dear Jane Bathori,' said Poulenc, 'what
hasn't she done for modern music !'

The *Rapsodie nègre* is dedicated to Satie, and this was

enough to infuriate Vidal when he inspected the score. 'I see you've joined that gang of Stravinsky, Satie and Company,' he shouted. 'Very well then, you can clear off!' The audience at the Vieux-Colombier did not appear to share his indignation. They listened quietly enough to the *Prelude*, a lazy, ambling movement with an occasional reminiscence of Ravel's *Introduction et Allegro*. (Poulenc already had the characteristic of dropping sly quotations into his own music with an immovably straight face.) The *Ronde* that follows, breathless and pulsating, is a Parisian's version of a primitive tribal dance. The vocal interlude, *Honouloulou*, provided the greatest surprise of the evening. At the last minute the singer who had been engaged changed his mind and refused to be associated with the proceedings. So Poulenc, wearing military uniform, stepped up behind a music desk and bawled 'Makoko's' three verses himself. The first of these gems is as follows :–

> Honouloulou, poti lama!
> Honouloulou, Honouloulou,
> Kati moko, mosi bolou
> Ratakou sira, polama!

The lines are set to a monotonous descending figure of maddening repetitiousness. As though to rest the listener's ears, a *Pastorale* now unwinds its gentle length. But the *Final*, alive with flickering tremolos and percussive intrusions by the piano, rushes helter-skelter to its end via the 'Honouloulou' theme, which is quickly repeated, and a brusque pizzicato.

The humour of the piece, its originality and individual orchestration made Poulenc's name well-known in Parisian music circles. 'How gifted he is,' said Ravel, 'provided he works hard.' Stravinsky offered congratulation and introduced him to the English publishers J. & W. Chester. Soon afterwards, with Stravinsky's approval, Poulenc was playing one of the four pianos in the first performances of *les Noces*. (Another of the pianists was Auric.) Stravinksy, said Poulenc, treated him like a son. 'I adorrrrre him!'

The *Rapsodie nègre* soon came up for another airing, since people were keen to acquaint themselves with this latest novelty. It was played again next month at a Vieux-Colombier concert, where Jane Bathori gave some Honegger songs and Durey's *Carillons* made a reappearance. This time Germaine

Tailleferre was represented by a *Sonatine* for string quartet, and Auric by a piano suite, *Gaspard et Zoé*. The latter, sub-titled 'Afternoon in a park', was originally written for a magic lantern show. It depicted the adventures of two children as they play in a sand-pit, catch frogs, and flirt with the gardener's son until Nanny comes to take them home. Among the individual items are a Stravinskian polka, a café concert waltz and a mazurka imitated from Chopin, who is one of Auric's idols.

Throughout the rest of 1918 'les Nouveaux Jeunes' dominated events in the rue Huyghens and at the Théâtre du Vieux-Colombier. An important song cycle by Louis Durey, the *Images à Crusoë*, was heard for the first time in the salle Huyghens. It is a setting of poems by Saint-John Perse, or Saint-Léger Léger, as he is known in the diplomatic service. There was an obvious affinity between him and Durey. Totally independent and isolated from current literary movements, Saint-John Perse both as man and poet appealed to Durey's taste for keeping a distance between himself and others. The *Images à Crusoë*, fluctuating between the tonal, the polytonal and the atonal, develop an austere lyricism on the theme of loneliness, of regret and of lost horizons. The music is un-compromising. One is not surprised that Jean Cocteau, who was rapidly becoming the spokesman of 'les Nouveaux Jeunes', should have been a little puzzled by Durey's reserve. He who was the natural impresario of every group in which he found himself could not wholly sympathize with Durey's retiring nature. 'The lonely one' was the epithet he applied to Durey, and he remarked that the theme was wholly suitable to him. The *Trois poèmes de Pétrone* created a similar impression of reserve by drawing its inspiration from antiquity. On the differences between Durey's version of the *Bestiaire* and Poulenc's, Cocteau was more at ease: 'Where Poulenc frolics on puppy paws,' he wrote, 'Durey treads with the step of a doe. Both are wholly natural. That is why one appreciates them with the same enjoyment.'

Durey's piano trio, which Auric helped to launch in the salle Huyghens, had a fate typical of the ambiguity which sur-rounds this composer and his work. The manuscript was lost by one of the players, and in the absence of notes or sketches there was no way of reconstructing it. The *Scènes de cirque* also remain unpublished. They were commissioned by the pianist Marcelle Meyer after she heard the first performance of *Carillons*, and they form a suite of three pieces for piano – 'Prélude', 'Entrée des clowns', and 'Les soeurs Rodolphe gracieuses gymnastes'. Durey judged them to be poor in technique and hastily put together, so he withdrew them.

As all the world knows, Poulenc was more successful with his piano works. During 1918, while engaged on military duties that took him from the provinces at last back to Paris, where he worked as a typist in the Ministry of Aviation, he wrote the *Mouvements perpétuels*. Composed at an old schoolroom piano, they were first played in the salle Huyghens by Ricardo Viñes. Since then they have never lost their original popularity. They combined the urbanity of drawing-room music with audacities discreet enough not to frighten traditionally-minded listeners of the 1920s, but real enough to add an ironic savour. The widespread success of the *Mouvements perpétuels* gave Poulenc some of the qualms he felt about his later 'Pastourelle'. The celebrity this composition achieved often exasperated him. More deserving of attention was the four-handed piano sonata which he wrote at the same time. Each of the three movements is based on the slimmest of material which is used with notable economy. The parodistic references are in the line of Satie, the transparent texture comes from Stravinsky, but the middle movement, 'Rustique', is undeniably Poulenc's. His Sonata for two clarinets, the third piece he wrote during the year, has the tartness of an acid drop.

Other members of the 'Nouveaux Jeunes' continued that year to produce new work. Germaine Tailleferre's *Jeux de plein air* for two pianos amused listeners in the salle Huyghens with its verve and dashing technique. The two sections, 'La Tirelitontaine' and 'Cache-Cache Mitoula', took as their starting point children's songs and wove them into a framework of controlled spontaneity. Honegger was encouraged by Jane Bathori to make his first venture into music for the stage, which he did with *le Dit des Jeux du Monde*, a play she produced at the Vieux-Colombier. He wrote for a small orchestra including the 'bouteillophone' beloved of Erik Satie, though he later (intriguing decision) replaced it with a triangle. Even so, his score was unusual enough to arouse disagreement in the audience, and his admission that it was written under the influence of Schoenberg and Stravinsky did nothing to please his critics. (Among them was the maid he employed in his flat. When he played in the percussion section himself, she told his parents that their Arthur seemed to spend much of his time banging on saucepans.) Strangely enough, a work he wrote in the previous year was much more personal in tone. This was *le Chant de Nigamon*, a symphonic poem on the martyrdom of an Iroquois chief in the days of the early Canadian settlers. It had those qualities of ruggedness and breadth that were more characteristic of him.

Auric's next offering was *Chandelles romaines*, an extract from a full-length but unpublished ballet. 'Fireworks in the country,' wrote Cocteau breathlessly. 'Firemen arrive. Everyone goes home. Next day the crackers are picked up in the grass.' Auric's song, *la Fête du duc*, was encored in the salle Huyghens. Some of the audience's enthusiasm was due to the singer Pierre Bertin, whose association with the group made him an honorary member of it. Originally trained as a doctor, Bertin turned to acting and became a protégé of Antoine, then director of the Odéon. Often he would have to rush away from the dissecting room to be in time for an afternoon matinée. He did not regret keeping up his medical studies. Medicine, he explained, gave direct experience of pain and suffering, all of which was useful to the actor whose main concern was observing human psychology. Once, when a member of the audience at the Odéon sprained her ankle, she emerged from her faint to see bending over her a man wearing the pointed hat and black robe of a seventeenth-century doctor. It was Pierre Bertin, who had jumped from the cast of *le Médecin malgre lui* to give her a twentieth-century injection. In 1917 he was deputed by Copeau to organize talks and literary evenings at the Théâtre du Vieux-Colombier. There he met Jane Bathori, who looked after the musical side, and through her the 'Nouveaux Jeunes'. As a performer of versatile achievement he fitted well into their ranks.

Milhaud so far had had little performed either in the salle Huyghens or at the Vieux-Colombier. By the end of 1918, however, he had reached his opus 53 and given evidence of an industriousness which even Auric, for all his prolific though unpublished activity, could scarcely rival. At the age of twenty-six Milhaud had written a full-length opera, two symphonies, four string quartets, five sonatas for various instruments, a ballet, a quantity of incidental music and many choral pieces. An indication of his wide interests is that while he chose to set, as one would expect, poems by Jammes and Rimbaud and Mallarmé, he found his texts also in Rabindranath Tagore, as had Durey, and went farther afield with verse by Christina Rossetti, Alice Meynell and Coventry Patmore. He was soon to add his own special brand of effervescence to the 'Nouveaux Jeunes'.

II

Before the year was out Jean Cocteau had made himself the standard-bearer of the group. The Éditions de la Sirène, which he founded with Blaise Cendrars, brought out as its first publication *le Coq et l'Arlequin*. That slim collection of epigram and aphorism gave the 'Nouveaux Jeunes', whether they wanted it or not, an aesthetic doctrine. The situation was rather like that where a clever advertising man creates a campaign which reveals to a delighted manufacturer all sorts of dazzling qualities in his product which the latter had never before suspected. Cocteau's gift for assimilation and for tinselled paradox codified all sorts of notions which composers had only vaguely thought about. *Le Coq et l'Arlequin* is very much the work of a young man. 'The essential tact in daring,' announced Cocteau, 'is to know *to what extent one can go too far.*' The young were warned not to invest in gilt-edged securities. When a work of art seemed in advance of its time, this was simply because its time was behind it. Thus, the public only adopted yesterday's works of art as a weapon to strike at today's. If an artist gave way to the public's blandishments, he was doomed. His duty was to be a living man and a posthumous artist.

Music, said Cocteau, must beware of the insidious charms of Debussy, Stravinsky and Wagner. If Debussy avoided the German ambush, he did not succeed in escaping the Russian trap. Though he played in French he used a Russian pedal. *Pelléas et Mélisande* was the sort of music you listened to with your face in your hands. Such music was suspect. Though you could not lose youself in Debussy's mist as you did in Wagner's fog, the experience was no less harmful. Even

Stravinsky was tainted. Did not his masterpiece, *le Sacre du printemps*, create among its hearers a sort of religious complicity between adepts, a hypnotism as at Bayreuth? It was visceral music, it contained the mysticism of the theatre . . . and it was, again, music you listened to with your face in your hands. As for Wagner, he was the great enemy. There existed long operas which were short, but Wagner's were really long because boredom had seemed to that heavy old god a useful drug with which to bemuse the faithful. Then, with an amusing somersault of the type that in his final years was to land him in the ultra-respectable Académie Française, Cocteau lined himself up in agreement with the aged Saint-Saëns, a diehard representative of the old guard who viewed Cocteau with the most venomous suspicion on all other points. 'To defend Wagner because Saint-Saëns attacks him is too simple,' Cocteau gleefully declared. 'We must shout "Down with Wagner!" in Saint-Saëns' company. That is genuine bravery.'

What Cocteau wanted was for French music to be true to itself. It must strip off the incrustations of foreign influence. 'Enough of clouds, waves, aquariums, water sprites and night scents; we need down-to-earth music, everyday music.' Away with gondolas and garlands! Of course, the public was sure to be disconcerted by an art reduced to its bare essentials. The public does not like to be surprised. So the artist is wise to cultivate in his work that element of which the public disapproves, since therein he can be sure lies the best of himself. For the artist is the truly rich man. He travels in a private car. The public lags behind in a bus. Why should one be astonished that it follows him at a distance?

Music must be cured of its present ills, said Cocteau. 'A poet always has too many words in his vocabulary, a painter too many colours on his palette, a musician too many notes on his keyboard.' The need was for a constant paring down. Where better was this to be found than in the work of Erik Satie? The master of Arcueil had evaded the greedy octopus arms of Wagner, Stravinsky and Debussy. He taught the greatest audacity of the age: he dared to be simple. That was why musicians of the Impressionist school had believed, quite wrongly, that the orchestration of *Parade* was poor. It was, on the contrary, an architectural masterpiece from beginning to end. Ears accustomed to vagueness and subtlety could not understand it. Satie had voluntarily deprived himself of flourishes and conjurer's tricks in his quest for simplicity. But the general public, sighed Cocteau, detested frankness.

Satie was the hero of *le Coq et l'Arlequin*. He was the figure Cocteau put forward to combat the harmful urges which were stifling French music. The fact that every piece of music he composed was, in Cocteau's phrase, a renunciation, made him an ideal example of the new aesthetic. *Parade*, it will be remembered, took place in a music-hall setting. It is to the music hall that Cocteau turns to elaborate his theory of a pure art created by economy of means. He does not imply, as people sometimes thought, that the music played there should be taken as model. What he advocated was the technique of the music hall, a technique where every gesture of the acrobat or of the tight-rope dancer was only allowed because it was a necessary part of the whole and complete in itself. There was no room for fantasy. The art of the music hall was objective. It therefore, by contrast with impressionism, offered an ideal of purity to be admired. Another source Cocteau suggested was the café-concert: 'The café-concert is often pure; the theatre is always corrupt.' Despite encroaching influences from elsewhere, it had preserved a certain tradition which would enable young composers to pick up again the thread that had been lost in the Germano-Slavic labyrinth. Cocteau looked forward to an orchestra that replaced the gentle caress of strings with the harder tones of brass, woodwind and percussion. (There still resounded in his ears the strumming of banjoes at the Casino de Paris accompanying Harry Pilcer and Gaby Deslys in their frenetic dance number.)

Le Coq et l'Arlequin, sub-titled 'Notes autour de la musique', was dedicated to Georges Auric whom Cocteau praised for having 'escaped from Germany'. He chose Auric because

a musician of your age proclaims the wealth and grace of a generation that no longer grimaces, puts on a mask, shirks or hides itself away, but fears neither to love nor to defend what it loves. Paradox and eclecticism are repugnant to this generation. It despises their smile and their faded elegance. It distrusts the colossal. That is what I mean when I talk about 'escaping from Germany'. Long live the Cock! Down with Harlequin!

The pamphlet was followed by four broadsheets also called 'Le Coq et l'Arlequin' which were published at irregular in-

tervals on coloured poster-paper. In one of them Satie made
his famous gibe about Ravel: 'M. Ravel has refused the
Légion d'honneur but all his music accepts it.' In another,
Auric heaped more abuse on the unfortunate Ravel, who in
his eyes was tarred with the same brush as Debussy. *Daphnis
et Chloé*, said Auric, used a wind-machine – there was no
reason for surprise, therefore, if one fine day younger composers
should bring on a machine to blow the wind away. The
seductive charm of Debussy and the gracefulness of Ravel were
a tragic quicksand. Crudeness and stridency were needed to
sound an urgent warning against them.

A few months after *le Coq et l'Arlequin* loosed off its opening shots, people were filing through the dark courtyard that
led into the salle Huyghens for another concert by the
'Nouveaux Jeunes'. It was a Saturday evening, 5 April 1919.
The atmosphere now was one of old friends who met regularly.
Members of the audience came up to help performers shift
the piano and arrange the chairs. The stove, as usual, refused
to work, and despairing musicians with coal-blackened hands
sought to charm the pot-bellied bulk into activity. It looked
like being a typical evening.

The programme included all six names of the 'Nouveaux
Jeunes', for Milhaud was back among them now, his head
filled with the sounds of the Brazilian forest and the rhythms
of the tango. His fourth string quartet figured among the works
played that evening. It contained one of his earliest experiments
in polytonality, a subject that had interested him since the
time he discovered a Bach duet which,

written in canon at the fifth, created a genuine impression of two
separate keys following each other and then becoming superimposed and contrasted, although of course the harmonic texture
remained tonal.... I began to study every possible combination
of two keys superimposed and the chords that resulted. I also
experimented to see what inverting them could produce.... I
came to know some of these chords quite well. They satisfied my
ear more than normal ones, for a polytonal chord is more subtle
in its sweetness, more violent in its power.

Also on the programme were Durey's *Images à Crusoë* which
were given in an accompaniment the composer had orchestrated from the original piano version. Ricardo Viñes, the
'fairy-fingered' as an admirer called him, played the *Mouve-*

ments perpétuets of Poulenc. Other items came from Auric, Honegger and Tailleferre. It was a concert much like any other that had been given over the past few years in the cramped quarters of the salle Huyghens. On that occasion, however, the music critic Henri Collet was among the audience. The review he wrote afterwards was entitled 'les Cinq Russes, les Six Français et Satie'. He followed it up with another which was headlined 'les Six Français'. His journalist's instinct led him to christen the six French composers on the analogy of the Russian group – Balakiref, Cui, Borodin, Mussorgsky and Rimsky-Korsakov – who were loosely known as 'the Five'.

Rather to their surprise, 'les Nouveaux Jeunes' became, overnight, 'les Six'. Yet their instant notoriety contradicted the real state of affairs. They were even less closely-knit than the five Russians who had inspired the nickname. The links that bound them were purely those of friendship, time and circumstance. Their tastes and inclinations were wholly different. Honegger's models were the German Romantics. Milhaud drew upon southern lyricism. Durey persisted in his attachment to Ravel and Debussy. Auric and Poulenc alone were whole-hearted in their support of Cocteau's ideas, while Germaine Tailleferre, with feminine discretion, was ready to adopt whatever seemed to be the prevailing tone.

Still, if the public insisted on calling them 'les Six', they were ready to oblige by keeping up the game. On Saturday evenings they would gather at Milhaud's home. Paul Morand, whose novels contain the very essence of the 1920s, mixed there cocktails of fiery excellence. If Milhaud happened to be away on one of his frequent journeys, the meetings took place at Germaine Tailleferre's flat. They were joined by writers, painters, singers and pianists. Then they would go to le Petit Bessonneau, a restaurant at the end of the rue Blanche which lived up to its name by providing a room so small that the Six and their friends filled it to overflowing. After dinner they strolled through the fair in Montmartre and mingled with the crowds who watched the steam-driven roundabouts, listened to the harsh music ground out by mechanical organs, and tried their luck in the shooting galleries. Sometimes they went to the Cirque Médrano, where Cocteau pointed out for their admiration the brilliant technique the Fratellini brothers displayed in their clowning routines. At the end of the evening

they returned to Milhaud's flat. Auric would present his latest
composition with bland ingenuity. Poulenc hunched his awkward frame over the keyboard and played a favourite piece,
singing all the parts himself and entertaining them with his
mimicry. Poets declaimed their verse and painters argued about
the construction of a cube.

On 14 July, the date set for the great Victory Parade,
Milhaud, Honegger and Durey set off at dawn to see the
spectacle. They forced their way through the immense crowds
and found a place where they could look out over the heads
of the multitude. People were everywhere. Each tree, each roof,
each balcony, was festooned with humanity. The long march
past began, sweeping by in front of them the faces of Joffre,
Haig and Foch which they had only known in jerky newsreels.
The English passed in a sea of banners, the Americans to the
vigorous step of *Over There.* 'Everything,' said Milhaud,
'seemed big with promise for a new age of peace.'

Soon after this Milhaud went down as usual to Aix for the
summer holiday. Cocteau and Durey were staying in a nearby
hotel. The establishment was conducted on original lines. The
proprietor dealt in antiques which he stored in the bedrooms
and which he removed when he had made a sale. A guest
would often return to find that the handsome Louis XIV chest
of drawers which graced his surroundings the night before had
vanished. The personal belongings he had put in it were likely
to be heaped carelessly on the floor. Another distinctive feature
of the hotel was the opera performances that were held in the
grounds. Milhaud decided he would add to these with a first
performance of a musical setting he had made of a Cocteau
poem. Brass instruments and a big drum were hired from the
local town band. Friends were recruited to perform. Cocteau
read his poem. Durey ministered to the percussion. A passing
Marquise was enlisted to play the triangle. The tableau was
characteristic. There they were on the terrace in that hot
summer of 1919, Cocteau reciting, Durey percussing, and the
flustered Marquise attempting to come in at the right moment
with her triangle. Had a camera been there it might have
frozen that typical moment for ever by catching the spirit of
improvisation, of light-heartedness and of informality which
was the hallmark of the Six.

4

THE OX GOES UP ON THE ROOF

I

THE opening weeks of 1920 brought a new President of the Third Republic in the person of Paul Deschanel. This dapper little man, whose suave manner had been polished by long frequentation of high-toned drawing rooms where he pursued his other ambition of attaining the Académie Française, owed his success to party manoeuvres designed to keep Clemenceau from the post. Unfortunately he did not enjoy for long the triumph he had coveted from his earliest days. Soon after his election officials at the Élysée were perturbed by his behaviour. On a presidential tour at Nice, when his congratulatory remarks to the townsfolk were much applauded, he struck a theatrical attitude and repeated them, like an actor who has been encored. In Menton he picked up flowers that had been thrown towards him and flung them back, blowing kisses at the cheering crowd. One May evening the presidential train ran through Montargis. Just before midnight a railway worker discerned a pyjama-clad figure staggering on bare feet along the line.

'My friend,' announced the wanderer, 'I'm going to surprise you. You won't believe me. I am the President of the Republic!'

The railwayman did not believe him at first, although his wife was more trusting. 'I could see he was a gentleman,' she said, 'because his feet were so clean . . .'

He was, indeed, the unhappy President Deschanel, and the momentary aberration which had made him fall from his carriage was one sign among many of his worsening mental state. Six months after he became President he resigned and went into a clinic. He ended his days in senatorial obscurity,

71

though not before the cruel chansonniers of Montmartre had
sung :

> Il n'a pas oublié son pyjama.
> C'est épatant mais c'est comme ça.

The pathetic presidency of Monsieur Deschanel chanced to
coincide with an age when old ideas of dignity and tradition
were swept aside. Young girls now frequented swimming pools,
tennis courts and theatres far from the eyes of mothers or
chaperons. They smoked cigarettes and wore make-up. They
went to cabarets and danced in night-clubs where the lavatory
attendants were former ladies in waiting to the Tsarina. They
observed, with youthful zeal, Freud's advice to get rid of
inhibitions. The disappearance of the *grandes cocottes* of the
1900s was explained by the new freedom of married women
to grant their favours to lovers. The delinquencies of wives and
mistresses were viewed sympathetically by husbands. Had not
Paul Morand declared that love was becoming so boring that
the more people joined in an affair the more interesting it
would be?

Trains went faster, cruisers became more luxurious and
motor cars more efficient. There was competition to buy the
smartest Hispano-Suiza and the latest Bugatti. Money cir-
culated freely between countries and the 'tourist' came into his
own. The titles of popular books written at this time – Paul
Morand's *Ouvert la nuit* and *l'Europe galante*, and Maurice
Dekobra's *la Madone des sleepings* – are enough to indicate the
mass of literature that sprang up around the modernity of life :
luxury cruises, sleeping cars, and holiday resorts of which
Deauville, under the guiding hand of the owner of Maxim's
restaurant, was the most baroque example.

New words flowed into the language. A 'nurse' was the
female you employed to look after your children. In the afternoon you went to a 'tea-room' for your 'five o'clock'. Later in
the evening, amidst your 'modern-style' furnishings, you offered
'un cocktail' (not an *apéritif*), which you poured from 'un
shaker' and called perhaps 'Bosom caresser' in your eagerness
to keep 'up-to-date'. Then you might go on to 'un dancing',
where 'un jazz-band' discoursed 'one-step' and 'shimmy'. At
the Folies-Bergère you could watch the Negress Josephine
Baker throw herself into a frantic 'Charleston'. Her compatriots

were everwhere on the Paris stage in the 1920s. Where
African art attracted Cendrars and Apollinaire, revues starring
Florence Mills drew the crowds. In night-clubs and cellars 'le
jazz hot' announced the arrival of Louis Armstrong and Bessie
Smith.

Even what once was known as 'le gratin' did not escape the
fever of extravagance that infected the lower ranks of society.
The manager of a hotel at Marienbad was surprised one day
to see a head waiter arranging a long line of screens down the
stairs all the way to the dining room. He learned it was being
done on the orders of the comtesse de Greffulhe who was
travelling incognito. On her return home she gave her husband
a bill for sixty thousand pre-war gold francs. 'How do you expect
me to know what money is?' she murmured in reply to his
protests. 'I've never had any.'

The comtesse de Greffulhe belonged to one of the few remaining families who occupied large private houses as grand
families had done before the war. Others included Lady Mendl,
Mrs Reginald Fellowes, the comtesse de la Rochefoucauld,
whose staff wore red livery and violet breeches, and the
princesse de la Tour d'Auvergne, whose domestics paraded in
silver froggings. They were among the exceptions. Not many
people now left visiting cards as they had up to 1914. Worse
still, young persons were marrying for love rather than wealth
and position. Some of the old rakes lingered on. The most
unrepentant was Boni de Castellane, owner of one of the oldest
titles in the aristocracy. His marriage to the American heiress
Anna Gould had made notorious headlines. She was hideous
but enormously rich. 'My wife will never know how much I
loved her for her money,' he remarked after their inevitable
divorce. And when, still hungry for the romance of nobility,
she re-married, this time the duc de Talleyrand, Boni replied
to questions as to whether he knew him : 'Yes, I know him very
well. We have served in the same corps.' (The pun is more
amusing in French, since *corps* also means body.)

Throughout the twenties he kept his head above water by
dealing, like so many of his friends, in antiques, and by designing schemes of interior decoration. He never lost his haughty
superiority. He anticipated Syrie Maugham and created, for a
rich foreign client, a room all in white. A few months later he
revisited it : 'What an odd idea to live in a dairy !' he said with

languid cunning. His client commissioned him to do it up again at even greater expense. To a hostess who apologized for not putting him on her right, he remarked: 'The seat where a Castellane sits is always best.' Invited to a costume ball, he asked a well-known parvenu to lend him some diamonds to wear. The latter obliged by sending only a brooch and explaining that his other stones were family jewels. 'I knew,' answered the marquis de Castellane, 'that you had jewels, but I didn't know you had a family.'

The costume ball that Boni thought to honour with his presence was a typical feature of the twenties. These functions were often held for charity. The Bal des Petits Lits Blancs was in aid of hospitals. The Bal des Trois Couleurs celebrated the army. The Bal de l'Opéra, which called for no excuse, took place among huge garlands: cockatoos balanced on the creepers and monkeys gambolled in a vast cage. The Duchess of Aosta moved through a glitter of golden dresses wearing a Venetian mask with an eagle's beak in diamonds. She symbolized the spirit of an era which, after four years of suffering and self-denial, plunged into a mood of spendthrift hysteria. Sacha Guitry put the matter very simply. 'We've had enough of privations!' he cried, and ordered himself a bath coated in gold.

Against this background where a President of the Republic wandered through the night in pyjamas, where a girl wrote to the murderer Landru (he killed at least ten women and burned their corpses in a stove): 'I'm yours, all yours till the furnace!' and where Surrealists shouted 'Down with France!', members of the Six prepared their first concerted effort. Or rather, as usual, it would be more correct to say that Jean Cocteau decided to put on a joint spectacle and bustled around the group exhorting them to give him something with which he could startle the conventional. The post-war vogue of silent films had inspired Milhaud, always eager for novelty, with the idea of writing some incidental music. 'Still haunted by memories of Brazil,' he said, 'I amused myself by putting together a few popular melodies, tangoes, maxixes, sambas and even a Portuguese fado, and transcribed them with a theme that recurred between each of them like a rondo. I called this fantasia *le Boeuf sur le toit*, which was the title of a Brazilian popular song. I thought that the character of the music would make it suitable as an accompaniment for one of Charlie Chaplin's films.' Cocteau immediately saw the piece as a ballet and improvised a scenario.

No sooner had Cocteau sketched out the main lines of his idea than he went to see the immensely rich comte Étienne de Beaumont. Beaumont had financed *Parade* from resources which, as artists of the twenties had cause to know, seemed bottomless. He lived with his wife in a large house in the boulevard des Invalides. Around him gathered musicians, poets, artists, actors, whom from time to time he would royally command to put on some lavish spectacle or other. For all this, however, he was not a creator and he lacked the impresario gifts of a Cocteau. Though not particularly cultured he loved literature with an impeccable taste. Unpractised in art or music, he was able to distinguish the good qualities of a picture and the merits of an opera. His strength lay in his practical knowledge of men. He knew how to handle them, how to play on their good points, and how to turn circumstances to advantage. He knew, moreover, how to look after Cocteau, and that in itself was no small talent. When Cocteau joined the ambulance detachment which the count organized during the war, there were several occasions when Beaumont stepped in to save him from awkward situations.

Étienne de Beaumont had a long sharp nose and a long thin upper lip. His eyes were slightly hooded and there were shadows beneath them. His greying hair was so immaculate that is looked as if it had been painted on his skull. He was tall and a little given to plumpness. His voice sounded rather precious. It had something of a lisp in it, a mincing quality that was not unpleasing and which was graced by frequent chuckles. He was a sympathetic man.

Beaumont agreed without hesitation to underwrite the new ballet. When Cocteau showed him the seating plan of the theatre he reserved, at a high price, the boxes and first rows of stalls. A few days later the whole theatre was sold out. Interest was so great that the Shah of Persia was ready to pay ten thousand francs for a seat. He could see nothing from it, but since he himself was in full view of everyone else he was satisfied. The financial success of the ballet was guaranteed. All that remained was to produce it.

There are several suggested origins for the title. Milhaud

said *le Boeuf sur le toit* was the name of a Brazilian song.
Others say it was taken from the sign-board of a tavern. A
third explanation comes from Parisian legend. There was once
a man who lived on the top floor of an apartment building
where he kept dozens of birds. When the people below complained of the smell he took no notice. More, he added to his
collection a small calf. Eventually his neighbours started legal
action against him. What with the law's delay, it was some
time before the court ordered him to dispose of his menagerie.
When police arrived to enforce the judgement they found the
calf had now become a full-grown ox. It would have been impossible to get it down to ground level without demolishing doors
and passages. So it remained in solitary glory, the ox on the
roof. Needless to say, whatever the reason for the title, it had
nothing at all to do with the story-line of a ballet pantomime
which was inspired by what Cocteau had seen of popular
American films.

Sub-titled, in Gallic English, 'The Nothing Happens Bar',
le Boeuf sur le toit had costumes designed by the artist Guy
Paul Fauconnet. He was one of the entourage who joined the
Six on their Saturday evenings. From Cocteau's descriptions
he drew the various characters who were to appear – the
Barman, the Red-Headed Lady, the Fashionable Lady, the
Policeman, the Negro Boxer, the Bookmaker, the Gentleman
in Evening Dress, and the Billiard Player Piccaninny. Perhaps
the effect of these fantasies was too much for him. He suffered
from an enlarged heart and suddenly died among his designs.
His place was taken by Raoul Dufy, who agreed to do the
scenery. Dufy was then far from the celebrity that later made
him, with van Dongen, a typical artist of the Twenties. Although
he had already painted those famous pictures of Deauville and
Honfleur and had illustrated Apollinaire's *Bestiaire* with some
ravishing woodcuts, he depended for his living on the designs
he made under contract to a Lyon silk manufacturer. The art
dealer Bernheim who took him up could only offer him 150
francs for a water-colour. Advised by the silk manufacturer to
go to Auteuil race-course and study the effect of the dresses
being presented there at fashion shows, Dufy instead found
himself absorbed by the sight of the jockeys, the crowds and
the galloping horses. The result was his series of race-course
pictures.

Soon afterwards Dufy made an important discovery. On the beach at Honfleur he watched a little girl in red playing on the sand. He noticed that when she moved the area of red stayed momentarily in the same place and did not fill in her outline. In other words, line moved more quickly than colour. Concluding that form and tone did not always coincide exactly, from then on he made a habit of painting shapes a little out of true and gave to pictures already filled with sunshine and happiness a distinctive air of movement and lightness. Dufy never lost his enjoyment of life. He always looked, said those who knew him, like an amazed cherub. The colourful naïveté he brought to the set of *le Boeuf sur le toit* helped to make his reputation in the little world of avant-garde collectors.

The action of what Constant Lambert once called 'the most amusing of the highbrow music-hall ballets' is pleasantly devoid of all meaning. The Negro Boxer finds that his cigar is drawing badly so the Barman cuts it for him with a pistol shot. The bullet strikes down the Piccaninny Billiard Player. The rest of the company enter and throw dice. The Bookmaker, annoyed by the attentions the Boxer is paying to the Red-Headed Lady, knocks him down and joins the ladies for a triumphant tango. A police whistle sounds. The Barman hastily puts up a notice: 'Milk only is served here,' and hides bottles and glasses. A giant Policeman enters, and, after smelling everyone's breath and tasting the milk, dances a genial ballet. The Barman presses a button. A ventilator comes down from the ceiling and cuts off the Policeman's head. He staggers, tries to put it on again, and falls dead. No one is concerned. One of the ladies takes the head and, like Salome, dances with it. The company departs. Alone again, the Barman pours a bottle of gin into the Policeman's body and puts the head back on his shoulders. The Policeman comes to, and the Barman unrolls in front of him a bill three yards long. Throughout the ballet all the characters, who wear cardboard heads three times life-size, have danced in slow motion, like deep-sea divers moving against the current.

The music makes little attempt at development, and, when heard on its own, becomes monotonous. It burbles cheerfully on for some fifteen minutes and ends as it began. But Milhaud never intended his 'Cinema-symphony on South American melodies' to be anything more than a modest accompaniment, the sort of thing one listens to with half an ear while watching Charlie Chaplin's antics on the screen. It was Cocteau, irresistible and unscrupulous, who seized on the little piece of music and blew it up into a ballet that became a natural topic of conversation at cocktail-time. The music probably fitted in very well with the comic evolutions of the Fratellini brothers who clowned, *en travesti*, the peculiar ladies who frequented the 'Nothing Happens Bar'. Milhaud was rueful about his contribution. He, a serious composer, who intended only a gay little divertissement, was now being regarded by the public as a figure of fun, a musician of the fairground. He had Cocteau to thank for that. He was even abused by Cendrars, who, ever ready with charges of plagiarism, accused him of stealing the principal refrain from a Brazilian composer with whom he, Cendrars, was on terms of friendship.

A full house applauded *le Boeuf sur le toit* on its first performance at the Comédie des Champs Élysées on 21 February 1920. Some saw it as an ingenious adaptation of the old Commedia dell'Arte, with Harlequin and Colombine replaced by equally traditional types from American films. Others looked on it as a practical demonstration of the new aesthetic of the music hall. Many enjoyed or disliked it simply as a joke. The ballet formed the second half of the programme. Before the interval a small orchestra played an overture by Poulenc. This seems to have been its only performance since it has remained unpublished. The next item was a foxtrot called *Adieu, New-York!* written by Georges Auric and featuring the clown 'Foottit'. It was a straightforward pastiche of the dance already known as 'un fox' to patrons of *bals publics*. Satie had done the same sort of thing with his 'Ragtime du Paquebot' in *Parade*, and so had Milhaud in the 'shimmy' he wrote and entitled *Caramel Mou*. Auric's foxtrot was an example of artistic slumming, and apart from proving yet again the group's interest in jazz its significance was mainly limited to the 'Adieu' of the title. For, in a current number of *le Coq et l'Arlequin*, Auric pointed out that the jazz band was one of the elements which had played its part in the musical reawakening. Its work was done: 'Let's stop up our ears so as to hear it no more.' 'Stop Press' in the same issue announced: 'Founding of the Anti-Modern League. Return to poetry. Disappearance of the skyscraper. Reappearance of the rose.'

After *Adieu, New-York!* came Poulenc's setting of three Cocteau poems. They were, said Poulenc, influenced by Stravinsky, though in the score for violin, cornet, trombone, big drum and triangle one can also detect the manner of Satie. *Cocardes* is the title, and they are described as 'Petites pièces plaisantes'. The technique is one of free association. As Poulenc observed, the words 'fly like a bird from one branch to another'. Each poem strings together a medley of what seem to be random phrases until one realizes that, taken as a whole, they create a particular atmosphere: the Médrano circus of the Twenties, pre-1914 Paris and so on. The word 'cocarde' means a cockade or rosette, and for one member of the audience who heard the songs for the first time they represented 'Parisian patriotism', or the Parisian's love for his city. Just as the national flag awoke the idea of 'country' more vividly than by speaking the word, so did Cocteau's lines evoke Paris without mentioning its name. Poulenc classified the music he wrote for them as belonging to his 'oeuvres de Nogent', the works that expressed his taste for the high-spirited vulgarity of that suburban resort. Finally, the instrumental part of the concert was completed by Satie's *Trois petites pièces montées*. Supposedly illustrating scenes from Rabelais, they were, like *Cocardes*, a boisterously 'popular' trinity.

Six months later *le Boeuf sur le toit* emigrated to London and found a home at the Coliseum. Milhaud and Cocteau travelled with it to supervise rehearsals. These were held at the Baroness d'Erlanger's house in Piccadilly which had once been Byron's home. With some apprehension, Milhaud watched the dancers – weird creatures, he said, who looked as if they'd come from the depths of Whitechapel – manoeuvring uncertainly about the valuable pieces of furniture scattered around the luxurious room. At the theatre the ventilator, an important prop in the show, was only fixed up at the last minute. Happily it functioned without accident during the performance. The ladies of the orchestra, unaccustomed to Milhaud's music, provided a sore test of his natural geniality. They made up for it afterwards by showing him snapshots of their babies which he admired with polite enthusiasm. 'The Nothing Doing Bar', as it was Englished for the Coliseum, came on between a number performed by Japanese acrobats and a sketch by Ruth Draper. It was warmly received – so warmly that the Coliseum management decided to take it on tour and asked Milhaud to write something for next season – and the first performance drew five encores. The press was generally good except for *The Times*, which, Milhaud saw delightedly, carried a violent attack on him that made for excellent publicity.

From his temporary flat in Lennox Gardens Milhaud ventured out to the exotic reaches of Hammersmith. In the Palais de Danse there his round and energetic figure moved through the 'taxi girls' and 'taxi boys' who, on payment of sixpence, were ready to act as partners in tangoes, one-steps, paso dobles and foxtrots. He spent hours sitting beside the American Billy Arnold and his jazz band. Here he made a prolonged study of jazz. He found it a subtle contrast with the treacly gipsy music of before the war and the crude combinations of the *bal-musette*. The different timbres fascinated him : the clarinet often straying into the upper register, the trumpet veering from langorous to dramatic, the trombone pealing off quarter tones while the piano moulded them together and the complex rhythm of the drums supplied the vital pulse. Satie's 'Ragtime du Paquebot' and Auric's *Adieu, New-York!* had been simple adaptations of dance music that used conventional orchestras. Milhaud wanted to go deeper. He decided, amid the novel sonorities that blared through the Hammersmith Palais, to get to grips with this new technique and to incorporate it in a piece of chamber-music.

The consequences of *le Boeuf sur le toit* extended as well to the social scene. It was an age of cafés, night-clubs and cabarets. In Montparnasse, from the apéritif hour until late in the morning afterwards, crowds gathered, drank and gossiped at the Dôme, the Rotonde and the Coupole. There were 'boîtes à musique' like the Jockey, at the corner of the rue Chevreuse and the boulevard Montparnasse, and the Jungle. The queen of the Jockey was undoubtedly a lady known as 'Kiki de Montparnasse'. She modelled for pictures by Modigliani, Soutine and Kisling. Her favours she distributed with whole-hearted generosity. Born Alice Prin, the daughter of a matron who had five other children, each by different fathers unknown, Kiki started life in a baker's shop. As a girl she was of handsome proportions and would display, on payment of five francs, a magnificient bust that was the admiration of the neighbourhood. (Clients she liked the look of were only charged two francs.) After the war the streets of Montparnasse became her kingdom. Her nearest rival was the English painter Nina Hamnet, who enthralled customers at the Dôme with uncensored renderings of 'She was poor but she was honest', and 'Rollicking Bill the sailor'. These were of immaculate decency compared with the ditties Kiki used to bellow. At the Jockey, where a Negro pianist thumped out jazz and a Cherokee barman poured the drinks, Kiki would chant, indulging in a wealth of gesture which called for no linguistic ability to understand, a hearty tribute to the girls of Camaret :

> Les filles de Camaret se disent toutes vierges (bis)
> > Mais quand elles sont dans mon lit
> > Elles préfèrent tenir ma vis
> Qu'un cierge – qu'un cierge – qu'un cier-er-ge.

> Mon mari s'en est allé à la pêche en Espagne (bis)
> > Il m'a laissé sans un sou
> > Mais avec mon p'tit trou
> J'en gagne – j'en gagne – j'en gagn-gagn-e.

Later she took up painting and held successful one-man shows. It was inevitable that she should open her own cabaret, 'Chez Kiki'.*

The passion for night-clubs did not confine itself to the wilder shores of Montparnasse. One of the liveliest places had been established near the place de la Concorde, in the rue Duphot which begins its select course in the rue Saint Honoré and ends in the boulevard de la Madeleine. Le Gaya was minute, and the walls, covered in white tiles, gave the impression of a lavatory or a Métro station. Some of its reputation derived from the resident pianist, a composer called Jean Wiéner. Times were hard, there was a family to support, and he played the night-club piano to earn a living. At the Gaya his bespectacled features, ascetic and high-domed, loomed over a keyboard from which he produced the strains of 'Lady be good' and 'Please do it again'. His own compositions, including

---

* Soon after 1945 she reappeared, having worked in the Resistance. Her body was thick and coarse, her face was caked in dusty make-up, and she reeked of alcohol. She died penniless and her funeral was paid for by a collection taken in Montparnasse cafés. Several people still remember her with affection – and with love.

a *Concerto franco-américain* and an accordion concerto, gave
evidence of his interest in jazz. While he tinkled out Gershwin
melodies with a feathery touch, he was also responsible for
concerts which introduced to Paris new music by Schoenberg,
Stravinsky and Webern.

Wiéner was a friend of Milhaud. They had lost touch during
the war, and when they saw each other again Milhaud was
delighted with the Gaya and its surroundings. He told Cocteau:
'I've got a bar for you!' The place became a rendezvous for
the Six and their friends, who now held their Saturday meetings within its crowded walls. They were followed by everyone who prided himself on being 'up-to-date – modern style'.
The Gaya was as full each night as the tube during rush-hour.
Its greatest glory came one evening when the Prince of Wales,
Artur Rubinstein and Princess Murat listened to Jean Cocteau
playing the drums while a mass of disappointed guests clamoured
outside for entry.

The proprietor, Louis Moysès, had a gold-mine on his hands.
He was tall and fair-haired. He came from Charleville,
Rimbaud's home town, where his father was a bar-keeper.
Realizing the potentialities for wealth that lay in society's crav-
ing for expensive discomfort, he looked around for new
premises. The right ones turned up on the ground floor of a
property at 28 rue Boissy d'Anglas, just off the place de la
Concorde. Moysès was a shrewd man. He asked if he might
call it 'le Boeuf sur le toit'. Cocteau, thrilled over Moysès'
remark that as a boy he had lived in a room once tenanted by
Rimbaud, jumped at the idea.

The 'Boeuf' opened on the 15 December 1921. New Year's
Eve found the duchesse d'Uzès there smoking a clay-pipe over
a bottle of Bordeaux and showing rank disloyalty to the Veuve-
Cliquot champagne on which the family fortune was based;
the singer Marthe Chenal, whose taste for Bohemianism
assorted oddly with her background of the Opera; the art
dealer Ambroise Vollard; and Cocteau, perched behind the
drums to warm up an atmosphere which always reached its
zenith between eleven o'clock and two in the morning.* At that

---

* The Public Orator at Oxford did not forget Cocteau's sponsorship of
the 'Bovem in Tegulis' when conferring an honorary degree on him in
1956. He also reminded his hearers that Sergius Diaghileff had once said to
Joannem Cocteau: 'fac stupeam.' (Learned contribution from Rollo Myers.)

time, in any season, the names of the diners there sounded like a roll call of everyone connected with the social, artistic and literary worlds of Paris. Word soon spread that the only place to meet celebrities was at the 'Boeuf'. People wore evening dress or grey flannels. High society mingled with artists in jerseys. Businessmen talked with writers. Everyone knew everyone else. Gay conversations went on from table to table. The unique mixture of elegance and wit, of informality and good manners, was expertly tended by Moysès. He knew exactly which guest to seat where and how to arrange everything with the utmost tact. His staff were on friendly terms with all. The lady who superintended the washroom with such finesse was heard respectfully by her customers when, in the autumn, she spoke of her pilgrimage to Lourdes and displayed the religious medallions she had brought back. Field marshals and kings frequented the 'Boeuf'. No evening was complete that had not been rounded off by a visit there. The accolade was bestowed when Proust himself stepped over the threshold. 'I wish,' he had said, 'I was well enough to go once to the cinema and to the "Boeuf sur le toit".' Supported by friends he made a wan appearance. The chicken he ordered was, he thought, excellent. The service, though, was not as good as at the Ritz. (His waiter was hideously ugly.)

The food was surprisingly good for a night-club of snob repute. A guide book of 1925 spoke of the 'Boeuf' as symbolizing 'the wildest fantasy within the finest of established traditions', and praised the Alsatian specialities and Rhine wines that Moysès served. You could eat very well for twenty-five francs – if, that is, your digestion stood up to the sight of a monstrous picture which hung over the mahogany bar. It was called 'l'oeil cacodylate', a cacodyl being liquid of a revolting smell which flames up on exposure to air.* The artist was Francis Picabia, a Dada personality of whom more will be heard later. The linen canvas, bearing a few cut-out pictures of friends stuck on haphazard, was mainly covered with scrawled inscriptions: 'My name has been DADA since 1892,' wrote Milhaud. 'I like salad,' was Poulenc's contribution, punning on the word 'salade' which also means disorder. 'Isadora loves Picabia with all her heart,' added a hand whose

* The canvas now perfumes the air of Gallery 31 on the first floor of the Musée National d'Art Moderne in Paris.

identity it is not hard to recognize. Altogether there were about fifty autographs. Next to this picture, with its stylized representation of a glaring eye, hung another. It was encrusted with various objects : an empty matchbox, a piece of string, an out-of-date invitation to a party given by Marthe Chenal. A startling legend ran across it : 'Merde pour celui qui le regarde.' Here Cocteau received his guests with the blandness of a reigning monarch.

The music was provided by Jean Wiéner and his friend, the Belgian Clément Doucet. They played on two upright pianos put back to back. Wiéner's father had a colleague who owned the patent of a bizarre new instrument, rather like a harmonium, which was guaranteed to reproduce the sounds of the violin, piano, organ, flute and suchlike. When nearly a hundred models had been sold, the exasperated purchasers found they were unable to make it work. The only person ever known to play it successfully had been the demonstrator, plump, slow-moving Doucet. He was something of a genius at the piano. His technique of tracing the melody with the thumb of his right hand, while his others fingers spread over the keys in rigid precision and his left hand marked the rhythm unfalteringly, astonished musicians who came to the 'Boeuf'. To his right stood a glass of beer which he steadily engulfed between numbers. If he were not talking to a customer he would read a detective novel while playing, turning the pages with his left hand and never missing a note. His eyes looking everywhere but at the keyboard, he wandered idly through 'Ain't she sweet?', 'Sometimes I'm happy', and 'Breezin' along with the breeze'. When he played Gershwin's 'The man I love', composers at the 'Boeuf' acclaimed its high musical quality – an opinion they shared with so dissimilar a musician as John Ireland.

Later on, when for some reason the 'Boeuf' moved to the rue de Penthièvre, the magic vanished. The atmosphere of such a place is created no one knows how. It is liable to evaporate with mysterious rapidity. While the 'Boeuf' stayed in the rue Boissy d'Anglas it attracted a famous clientèle – the champions of art movements like Dadaism and Surrealism, diplomatists, English dukes, music hall artists like Maurice Chevalier and Mistinguett, Diaghilev, and the flamboyant André Citroën of the car firm. In the rue de Penthièvre the 'Boeuf' drew only tourists curious for the personalities who had by then deserted it. Afterwards Moysès set up other night-clubs. *Le Grand Écart* and *les Enfants terribles* were both named after Cocteau novels in an attempt to repeat the success of the 'Boeuf'. None of them recaptured its unique ambience. But all that was in later years. For the time being the ox was well and truly up on the roof.

5

SOCRATES – A PRODIGY – THE
WEDDING ON THE EIFFEL TOWER

I

In the year the 'Boeuf' was founded Satie brought out a work
that was unusual even for him. He began to write it soon after
Parade. Having made a sensation with that ballet, he turned,
in a spirit of contrariness or independence, to the composition
of a chamber oratorio as far removed from the vivacity of
Parade as it would be possible to imagine. At the 'Boeuf',
where he sat among the younger musicians, he had the air of
a latter-day Socrates. It amused him to act the part of a
favourite uncle imparting dangerous advice to the young.
There was, though, a more serious element to this. Whether
or not he voluntarily fostered the passing resemblance to
Socrates, he felt genuinely attracted to the Greek philosopher.

His opportunity to express this in music arose when the
princesse Edmond de Polignac commissioned a new work from
him. She was born in America as Wennaretta Singer, the
daughter of the sewing-machine millionaire. Brought up in
Paris and London, she married the prince Edmond de
Polignac, holder of a Vatican title dating from 1820. This
union of American wealth and French nobility produced a
famous salon of the Twenties. The prince died soon after the
marriage and his princess devoted herself to encouraging the
arts with generous hospitality and, still more laudably, with
hard cash. Fauré benefited from her practical kindness. She
was the friend of Chabrier and of Richard Strauss. Falla, Ravel
and Stravinsky wrote music for her, and so did various members
of the Six. The Palazzo Polignac in Venice had vast drawing
rooms plentifully supplied with grand pianos where her
favourite composers were invited to play. Satie was only one
of many to enjoy her patronage.

The result of the Polignac commission was *Socrate*, a 'drame symphonique en trois parties'. Satie used Victor Cousin's French translation of three of the Socratic dialogues, the Symposium, Phaedrus and Phaedo, which he adapted and abridged for his purpose. The first part is a dialogue between Socrates and Alcibiades. The second features Socrates and Phaedrus on the banks of the Ilyssus. The third, for solo voice, narrates the death of Socrates. *Socrate* was first heard in the princesse de Polignac's salon. A second performance followed in Sylvia Beach's bookshop at the sign of 'Shakespeare & Co.', another famous meeting place for intellectuals. A public performance in the full orchestral version spread alarm, confusion and annoyance among all right-thinking people. The critics were generally bored by its apparent monotony and irritated by its unexpectedness. There were boos and titters. This was enough for the Six to rally in support and adopt it as their mascot.

Socrate is a wholly serious work. The only touches of humour Satie allowed himself were a jest that Plato was an easy-going collaborator to work with, and the exhortation : 'Those who do not understand are asked to assume an attitude of submissiveness and inferiority.' At a first hearing the music seems bereft of all movement. It ends as it began, without climax or traditional development. The listener has a feeling that he is overhearing something that started long before he came within range and that will continue long after he has departed. The vocal line is unemphatic and follows the rhythms of everyday speech, a point which deceived critics into thinking that Satie was imitating the technique of *Pelléas et Mélisande*. An accompaniment of woodwind, cor anglais, horn, trumpet, harp and strings goes blandly on its way as if to proclaim its independence of the four sopranos who are singing the text.

One may believe that in *Socrate* the composer achieved the most complete and satisfying expression of his artistic ideas. Here he produces music that is free of associations and reduced to the barest of essentials. Themes do not grow in the conventional way, and the effect of motion is created by a series of ostinato phrases. These are repeated and occasionally varied to a small degree, but they are never developed. The notes flow along to present an immaculate and unbroken sheen. By denying himself the usual devices of composition, Satie evokes a rare impression of unbounded space. Tune is supplanted by continuous melody. It is true that *Socrate* demands concentration from its listeners. The effort once made brings its reward in appreciation of the wonderfully pellucid texture, the timelessness of its Greek spirit, and the rarefied emotion of Socrates' death.

The audience at the performance in Sylvia Beach's shop included André Gide, who sat enveloped in his cape, eyes lowered and sniffing nervously from time to time. Gide was conventional in his musical tastes and loved Chopin and the Viennese classics. He made polite remarks after *Socrate* had ended, but no one knew what he really thought. When Milhaud played him a setting of some Tagore poems Gide had translated, the author was happier when the composer afterwards switched to Mendelssohn. He was no more enthusiastic about Milhaud's version of his *Retour de l'enfant prodigue*. Milhaud's suite *Alissa,* taken from the novel *la Porte étroite,* inspired the sibylline remark : 'Thank you for making my prose seem so beautiful.' Another literary man at *Socrate* was Paul Claudel, whose relations with Milhaud were much more sympathetic. He sat, rather grimly, on his own. Then, on being drawn into the conversation, he rose and spoke over the heads of his listeners as if reciting a passage from one of his plays, sumptuously rhetorical and exalted in image.

After the strange beauty of *Socrate,* a piece of music hall buffoonery entitled *la Belle Excentrique* showed that Satie had not lost his taste for unpredictability. The little suite of four numbers – 'Grande Ritournelle', 'Marche Franco-Lunaire', 'Valse du Mystérieux baiser dans l'oeil', and 'Cancan Grand Mondain' – starts off with a fussy pitter-patter that recalls, of all people, Percy Grainger. It is irresistibly comic, and, despite echoes of *Parade*, it is rooted in Satie's earlier café-concert period. The dancer who introduced it was known as Caryathis. A poster by Léon Bakst shows her poised in a dramatic stance and trailing a wealth of drapes while her own exiguous costume barely conceals her undoubted charms.* She was admirably suited to the music, for she was herself both beautiful and eccentric – beautiful enough to have had many lovers including Charles Dullin, and eccentric enough to marry the writer

* The poster now hangs in the Jouhandeau home at Malmaison, where it practically covers a whole wall.

Marcel Jouhandeau. Once again Cocteau played the part of impresario. He was responsible for persuading them to marry, thus giving Jouhandeau an inexhaustible source for the numerous books he was to write about his life with the majestic, the insufferable, the unbelievable 'Élise'. In her dancing days she was noted for her qualities of mimicry and a kind of bizarre genius. Her version of *la Belle Excentrique* was a satire on dance routines. In the same programme she did Auric's *Paris-Sport*, a little thing by Poulenc called *le Jongleur*, a Granados item, and, indefatigable creature, Ravel's *Rapsodie espagnole*.

A few months after *Socrate*, on 8 March, there was a concert at the Galerie Barbazange which inaugurated yet another Satiesque venture to puzzle respectable folk. On the analogy of furniture to which one pays little attention though it undoubtedly exists, Satie inquired why there should not be music of a similar nature. Just as the eye saw wallpaper patterns, cornices and looking-glass frames without being fully aware of them, the ear was capable of picking up background music that could be varied like the furniture in the room where it was played. So, in the Galerie Barbazange, which at that time housed an exhibition of children's paintings, a session of 'musique d'ameublement', or furnishing music, was arranged. Auric and Poulenc did not think much of the idea, but Milhaud was ready to experiment. During the interval Pierre Bertin came forward and announced that 'musique d'ameublement' would now be played. He asked the audience not to place the slightest importance on it and to talk and act as if it did not exist.

There were three clarinet players, each stationed in three different corners of the room, with a pianist in the fourth and a trombonist higher up. The intention was to have music coming from all sides at once. (The unusual nature of the combination was dictated by instruments called for in the items, including Stravinsky's *Berceuses du chat*, on the rest of the programme.) An endless chain of ritornellos embodying scraps from the *Danse macabre* and *Mignon*, together with single phrases monotonously repeated, began to chatter away in the hall. People stopped talking. They sat down and prepared to listen. This was the last thing Satie wanted. He erupted among them saying: 'Talk! Go on talking! Move about. Whatever you do, don't listen!' But they were too polite. The first conscious example of 'musique d'ameublement' was spoilt.

Since then, of course, the more unwelcome aspect of Satie's experiment has succeeded. He wanted, he said, to establish a type of music designed to fill 'useful' needs. It was to be music that played the same part as lighting and heating. Banks, offices, houses, marriage ceremonies even, called for furnishing music. Today his half-serious plea has been granted. From undertakers' parlours to aeroplanes there are few public places where the oleaginous drool of musical sounds is not heard. On the other hand, when Satie came to write film music a few years later for René Clair's *Entr'acte*, his idea found its perfect application.

Satie's fellow-conspirator Milhaud also wrote at this time a pair of compositions which struck people as being as much of a joke as 'musique d'ameublement', though his purpose was entirely genuine. From a visit with some friends to an agricultural exhibition he brought back a catalogue of farm machinery. 'I had been so impressed by the beauty of these great multicoloured iron insects, magnificent modern brothers to the plough and the scythe, that I thought of celebrating them in music,' he wrote. The *Machines agricoles*, which he composed for voice and seven instruments, consisted of extracts from the catalogue. Each one is dedicated to a member of the Six, with Jean Cocteau to make up the number. 'La moissonneuse Espigadora' (harvester) is hymned in rustic mood for its giant blade capable of operating on up to fifteen hectares in a day. A nostalgic phrase in the style of Milhaud's later ballet *Salade* illumines the remark that this harvester is particularly useful in regions where the straw is of poor quality. 'La fouilleuse-draineuse' (sub-soil and draining plough, which sounds even brisker in German as *Untergrunddrainpflug*) is a lively commentary on the machine's long round ploughshare. In 'La déchaumeuse-semeuse-enfouisseuse' (harrow-plough, seeder, stubble-burier) a notably sweet tune wreathes itself around the subject of stanchions and reinforced parts guaranteed to bear the weight of the sowing case. Binders and reapers are also featured, and the suite ends with 'La Faneuse' (tedder) which comes to rest in an unexpectedly conventional way.

The public, to Milhaud's annoyance, took *Machines agricoles* as yet another token of perverse humour. He argued in defence that they had been written in the same spirit that led past composers to glorify the harvest and the 'happy ploughman'. Machines now were so prominent that they formed a legitimate subject for the artist. Georges Antheil was to write his piano pieces *Airplane Sonata* and *Mechanisms* (true, he kept a pistol in his pocket at recitals if the need arose to shoot his way out of the riotous assemblies that gathered), which culminated in the *Ballet mécanique*. Honegger was to compose *Pacific 231* and Prokofiev his *Pas d'acier*. Milhaud felt hard done by.

A companion piece to the *Machines agricoles* was the *Catalogue de fleurs*. This was written for the same combination. The text was chosen from a seedsman's catalogue by the elegant Léon Daudet, son of Alphonse, man about town, and escort to Proust on the latter's excursions into the night-life of the Twenties. The straight and factual style of the catalogue is matched by music of a deliberately plain quality. Where an earlier composer and poet would have given the crocus a romantic aura, Milhaud invested it with sharp commonplace. The violet and the begonia were treated in similar brusque fashion. Even so, the mere enumeration of a flower's varieties had a certain poetry about it. The different types of hyacinth, for instance, were catalogued as: 'Albertine blanc pur. Lapeyrouse mauve clair. Roi des Belges carmin pur, Roi des bleus, bleu foncé. Mademoiselle de Malakoff jaune vif à bouquet.'

The *Catalogue de fleurs* was first heard in a recital at the Conservatoire, a setting guaranteed to ensure maximum disapproval of the work. Milhaud complained:

I have never been able to understand why thinking people should imagine that any artist would spend his time working, with all the agonizing involvement that accompanies the process of creation, for the sole purpose of making fools of some of them . . .

In his role of propagandist for the new music, however, Milhaud invited enmity. An article he wrote entitled 'Down with Wagner' brought him insults and anonymous letters of abuse. Though he was fond of classical music, he protested strongly at the permanent diet of Beethoven and Wagner that the Paris concert organizations went on serving up. Each day, in fact, he detested Wagner a little more. The art, the philosophy, the aesthetic of Bayreuth stood for everything he hated. His opponents counter-attacked with vigour. He had

D

composed some music for Claudel's *Protée*. A suite he drew
from it was programmed for a concert in October 1920, and
his proud parents were invited for the occasion. Before the
overture ended there were dissident shouts from the audience.
The fugue that succeeded it, scored for three trumpets and
three trombones, aroused a violent uproar that drowned the
orchestra. The police intervened, and Milhaud had the satisfaction of seeing a distinguished critic bustled out by two burly
representatives of the law. There came a brief respite when the
conductor rebuked his unruly patrons, but the performance
foundered again in tumult. Milhaud's father and mother
watched in fearful astonishment. Their son, on the contrary,
was delighted. 'The indifference of the public is what's
depressing,' he said. 'Enthusiasm, or vehement protest, shows
that your work really *lives*.' Saint-Saëns was one for whom
Protée 'lived'. He wrote to the conductor of the concert : 'I
am sorry indeed to see that you are opening the door to mad-
house ravings and trying to force them on the public when it
protests. Several instruments playing in different keys have
never produced music, only a vile din.' Milhaud had Saint-
Saëns' protest framed and joyfully hung it on the wall of his
studio in Aix.

II

Much of Blaise Cendrars' formidable energy during the early
twenties was channelled into managing les Éditions de la
Sirène, the publishing firm he ran with Cocteau. It would be
truer, perhaps, to say that Cocteau lent the firm his name, his
blessing and his gift for publicity, as well as bringing out his
early poetry under the imprint, while Cendrars did the actual
work of producing books. Financial support came from Paul
Laffitte, an entrepreneur who combined an unusual ability in
money matters with a fine appreciation of literature. He was,
reported Cendrars, 'as clever as a shrew-mouse and remarkably
enterprising, but changeable as a chameleon, a Parisian to his
fingertips though born in Philadelphia . . .'.

The Éditions de la Sirène published anything that appealed
to its founders. It brought out quite a lot of music, including
Durey's *Carillons*, Auric's *Adieu, New-York!* and other works

by Honegger, Milhaud and Tailleferre. When the enterprise closed down after a short but vivid butterfly existence, the music publisher Max Eschig took over the back-list that included these names. Cendrars' literary plans were bold and ambitious. He had on the stocks more than two hundred books in various stages of preparation. Particularly dear to his heart was a Balzac anthology he had wanted to compile ever since, as a boy, he came under the spell of the *Comédie humaine.* 'Paris par Balzac' would be a monument to the huge fresco of the capital which lay scattered in isolated pieces throughout the novelist's works. But Cendrars, with all his multitudinous activities, could never find the time to put it together. He wanted an assistant to shoulder the main burden.

One day there tiptoed into his office a tall, chubby-cheeked boy. The caller, who might have been seventeen years old but looked more like fifteen, wore an overcoat far too big for him. Although he had rolled up the sleeves, they still flopped raggedly over his hands. His shoes were down-at-heel and the leather was cracked. He timidly handed over a letter of introduction from a mutual friend. Cendrars learned that he wrote poetry and that his name was Raymond Radiguet.

'So you sleep under bridges at night?' inquired Cendrars, always eager to extract the last drop of Bohemian romance from any given situation.

No, the boy replied, he shared a room with another poet. During the day, he explained, he wandered the streets meditating a novel he planned. When it rained he went into a post office and wrote his narrative on the telegraph forms which a thoughtful administration had left at the disposal of the public. The novel, which he provisionally entitled *Julie*, was nearly finished. At that moment the Éditions de la Sirène were short of money and Cendrars could do little about publishing the book until new funds came in. On another visit Radiguet brought the finished manuscript. Cendrars glanced at it, was struck more by the author's precociousness than by his writing, put it in a drawer until more money was available, and half-forgot that he had done so.

In the meantime he set about indoctrinating Radiguet with his enthusiasm for Balzac. After long discussions in Cendrars' office they would end the evening at the 'Boeuf sur le toit'. The anthology began to take shape. The jazz finished, Doucet shut up his piano and dawn turned the windows blue, while Cendrars and Radiguet sat on at their table sketching a map of Balzac's Paris with cigarette stubs on the cloth. Cendrars, alas, never built his monument. Long before even the extracts were decided on, Radiguet had been taken up by Cocteau who nicknamed him 'Bébé', made him turn *Julie* into *le Diable au corps,* and launched him as a child wonder.

Radiguet was the son of a cartoonist whose work for the Paris newspapers earned barely enough to keep his family. The boy grew up at Saint-Maur on the banks of the Marne. His part of the river was not the one Poulenc knew, that of Nogent and its flashy amusement places. Radiguet's Marne was a quiet region where he went for family strolls on Sunday and dreamed beside the placid flow of the river. His manner was silent and withdrawn. At school he proved to be a mediocre worker, choosing to lose himself instead in Baudelaire, Rimbaud and Stendhal. His relations with his parents were veiled by a coldness that hid affection. On his deathbed – for he was to die at the age of twenty – he told his father : 'If only you knew how much I love you!'

An early poem he wrote offended Apollinaire, who detected in it traces of his own *Alcools.* Apollinaire's character was already affected by his war-wound, and his reaction was irritable : 'Don't despair, Monsieur,' he snapped sardonically at the sixteen-year-old poet, 'Arthur Rimbaud only wrote his masterpiece at the age of seventeen.' Other poets were not encouraging, and Radiguet, supporting himself with journalism, began to publish in the little reviews. Soon he was an intimate of everyone in Cocteau's circle. His first volume of poems, *les Joues en feu,* attracted Georges Auric, who found very much to his taste their evocations of surburban fortune-tellers and their mingled imagery of flowers and birds. He set a handful of them to music, as he also did with 'Alphabet', a poem containing some of Radiguet's favourite themes, including Mallarmé and the ever-present roses. On holiday near le Lavandou Auric cheerfully acted as his secretary, taking down *le Bal du comte Orgel* at his dictation and typing out the manuscript afterwards. Their fellow-feeling came in part from their both having been child prodigies. Auric, in fact, with his plump features and mischievous eye, looked scarcely much older than Radiguet.

Les Joues en feu intrigued Poulenc as well. Radiguet's poetry haunted him. He chose a quotation from *les Joues en feu* to head a piano piece called 'Badinage', and in 1920 he set one of the poems, 'Paul et Virginie'. It did not satisfy him. The melodic line he found for the opening words dwindled unhappily away for the rest of the poem. One rainy, melancholy day in 1946 he thought of Radiguet again and of the recently announced plans to film *le Diable au corps* 'for which I'd so much like to have written the music. I thought the commission had gone, as was only right, to Auric, Radiguet's best friend. Alas no.' Once more he returned to 'Paul et Virginie'. This time he found the music he wanted. He warned: 'If the tempo isn't always kept strictly the same, this little song, made up of a bit of music, much tenderness and silence, will be mucked up.'

Paul et Virginie figured also in Radiguet's acquaintance with Satie. The pince-nez'd Socrates was delighted to welcome an addition to the youthful circle that crowded round café tables to relish the sly humour of his conversation. From their discussions with Cocteau in the Coupole arose a project to turn Bernardin de Saint-Pierre's tearful romance into an opéra-comique. The idea was not such a surprising one for these two collaborators as might be thought. Satie had a child-like strain in his character, a naïf element of innocence which responded to the tale of a brother and sister who are raised from infancy on a tropical island (Mauritius) far distant from the corruption of society. The setting gave Radiguet, himself still a child, an opportunity to indulge in exotic symbolism. A libretto was read to Satie towards the end of 1920 and a note appeared in the fourth number of *le Coq et l'Arlequin* that *Paul et Virginie* would be 'Satie's next work and his farewell to composing'. Things did not turn out that way, and all that remains of this curious work is the manuscript of the libretto, where the dialogue is written in Cocteau's hand and the arias in Radiguet's.

In Radiguet it was possible for Cocteau to see a reflection of himself: the child prodigy doted on by admiring ladies in salons, the writer of dazzling precocity, the youth who had experienced everything but who could still remark: 'I'd like to know how old you have to be before you have the right to say: "I've lived." ' Under Cocteau's guidance he made the acquaintance of everyone in that circle both social and artistic for whom the name 'Jean' was a magic word. Radiguet's untidy hair was groomed into neatness. He started wearing a bow-tie and a monocle. He affected a smart walking stick that was always a little too big for him. He drank whisky and cocktails alike with vertiginous speed. His evenings were usually spent at the 'Boeuf sur le toit', and they ended at dawn when he returned home with some girl or other. These periods of idleness alternated with others of intense activity. Cocteau would shut him up under lock and key and force him to write. Like a schoolboy being punished, Radiguet would sometimes escape through the window or kill time scribbling nonsense on his writing-pad. His taskmaster would send him back to try again.

An early result of this tutelage was the 'comédie-bouffe en un acte mêlée de chants' which Cocteau and Radiguet worked on together and which they called *le Gendarme incompris*. The plot tells of a country policeman who, while on his beat through lands owned by the marquise de Montonson, observes a priest behaving in an equivocal manner. A charge is brought, the case is heard, and it turns out that the 'priest' was none other than the marquise. Dressed in a black robe and wearing a hat, the ancient noblewoman had been contorting her body into peculiar stances in order to get at some inaccessible flowers she wanted to pick. The marquise invites the judge to dinner, and the policeman, whose zeal for promotion had inspired the charge, is laughed out of court. The big joke of the proceedings is that the report which the policeman reads in broad, comic tones is none other than Mallarmé's prose-poem 'l'Ecclésiastique', where a priest, his blood stirred by the approach of spring, gambols among the shrubs of the bois de Boulogne in a highly unecclesiastical manner. Poulenc wrote the music for violin, 'cello, double bass, clarinet, trumpet and trombone. The part of the marquise was played by the versatile Pierre Bertin. Apart from two designs by Cocteau, Bertin has no other document relating to the play. The score also is not available since Poulenc, to Milhaud's regret, suppressed it. We do know, however, that no one in the audience, critics or public, recognized the Mallarmé text, and the reviews were particularly scathing in their attacks on its 'stupidity'.

Le Gendarme incompris first bewildered its audience at the Théâtre Michel on 23 May 1921. It was accompanied by another piece, this time wholly by Radiguet, called *les Pélican*. The characters were M. and Mme Pélican, their children Anselme and Hortense, the governess Mlle Charmant, and the valet Parfait. Anselme wishes to become a poet, and his father warns him that he will need to take a pseudonym. Echoing what many English readers have doubtless felt, Anselme replies: 'Pelican is no sillier a name than Corneille [crow] or Racine [root].' This exchange alone survives Radiguet's only play, for which Auric provided the incidental music. Cocteau remembered that after the performance the haughty playwright stalked through the corridors deliberately to embarrass the spectators who did not know what to say to him. 'I have never seen a soap-bubble blown up for such a time until it burst,' said Cocteau.

There were still more shocks to come for the audience in the Théâtre Michel. Satie now blossomed forth as a dramatist with *le Piège de Méduse*. This was a short play in which Pierre Bertin, made up with beard and pince-nez, bore an eerie resemblance to the composer of *Parade*. The action, which had all the meaninglessness of Dada, was interrupted from time to time by a stuffed monkey on a perch. This creature, known as 'Jonas', performed little dances between the scenes to music for a small ensemble conducted at the last minute by Milhaud, Satie having, typically, quarrelled with the original conductor. The musical part of the programme was completed by Milhaud's own *Caramel mou*, a 'shimmy' for jazz-band representing one of his earliest essays in the medium. At that time he was still investigating the sounds he had earlier encountered in the Hammersmith Palais. At home his gramophone tirelessly ground out the records he bought in Harlem on a trip to America. Negro jazz, like the Brazilian folk tunes he exploited for the piano suite *Saudades do Brazil*, was a source that fully absorbed his tireless curiosity. *Caramel mou*, suitably dedicated to Auric, was little more than an experiment in mimicry, an attempt to familiarize himself with new textures. It was performed by a Negro who danced after the manner of Harlem and sang words by Cocteau. The dancer was one of those whom Cocteau and his friends, dealers in genius of the 'instant' variety, had proclaimed as a great performer. Everyone believed this until the unfortunate man stepped on to the floor. His indecisive shuffling quickly destroyed all illusion. It did not really matter, Jean was sure to produce another genius to-morrow.

III

The years 1920 and 1921 were those when the Six flourished most as a group. In 1920 all their names were linked together in a joint production for the first and last time. The *Album des Six* presented six piano pieces in alphabetical order by composer. Auric began with a 'Prélude'. Its mocking tone was immediately revealed in the dedication to 'General Clapier'. A military fanfare, lavishly sown with 'wrong' notes, provided the theme of a jeu d'esprit which neither Auric nor anyone else has ever taken seriously. It was followed by Durey's 'Romance sans Paroles', a more thoughtfully worked out piece which developed a tune of folk-song quality. Honegger's 'Sarabande' was richer in texture and showed traces of his studies with Vincent d'Indy. He wrote little for the piano – unlike many musicians he did not use the instrument to try out ideas while composing – and apart from occasional pieces like these he preferred to work in orchestral terms. The 'Mazurka' which Milhaud contributed had been written some years earlier. More in the style of a slow waltz, it offered a character of melancholy charm. Poulenc was careless enough to allow his 'Valse' to be printed. This mechanical little piece must have been the sort of thing he indulged in at the keyboard while looking for an idea, and it added nothing to his reputation. Germaine Tailleferre rounded off the album with a 'Pastorale' of great busyness which hurtled playfully into a soft rallentando.

In the following year the Six were again to have worked together, this time on a stage production. The occasion was a new mime-play by Cocteau which had as its first title *la Noce massacrée*. This was later changed to *les Mariés de la Tour Eiffel*, the author believing that the new title had a more authentically Parisian ring. The impresario who commissioned it was Rolf de Maré, whose Ballets Suédois for a short period in the Twenties rivalled the Ballets Russes. Diaghilev was, in fact, partly responsible despite himself for their creation, since his associate Michel Fokine, after a disagreement with him, left Paris and was appointed ballet master at the Stockholm

Opera. There he found dancers of talent who responded warmly to his training.

One of Fokine's wealthy supporters in Stockholm was de Maré, a Swede of French extraction. He owned large estates and always gave his occupation as 'farmer'. This was true, for he had conscientiously studied in agricultural colleges and worked on probation at model farms. He was eloquent on the subject of clod-beetles and could strip down a tedder as efficiently as any of the labourers he employed. Cattle breeding and crop rotation held no mysteries for him. When his cows won prizes he asked for no greater happiness. At the same time, he was interested in music. On his travels through the Swedish provinces he collected folk songs and dances. When he grew tired of the spacious house at Hildeborg that looked out over the sea, he journeyed off to Asia, Africa (where he owned another home) and Europe, staying in each country long enough to savour its art and acquaint himself with its dance lore. Gradually he evolved the idea of founding a national ballet troupe.

Fokine had by then modernized and improved the techniques of the Stockholm dancers. He praised especially the talent of a young man called Jean Börlin who 'flew over the stage in great leaps, fell with all his weight and slid along the floor among the bacchantes. What a temperament! What ecstasy!' Börlin emerged as the star of the troupe which de Maré brought into being and which he named the Ballets Suédois. Though Börlin was said not to dance so well as Massine and to lack the star quality of Lifar, he had a simplicity, a youthfulness and a freshness which justified Fokine's high opinion. During his short life – he committed suicide in 1931 at the age of thirty-seven, penniless and alone in New York – he camouflaged his technical imperfections with an athletic grace which he owed to the perfect flexibility of his body. When he died the Ballets Suédois died too. Its existence was as short but as intense as Börlin's own life. In four brief years de Maré commissioned designs by Bonnard, Chirico, Léger and Picabia; a short film by René Clair; and music by Ravel, Auric, Honegger, Milhaud and Poulenc. He also commissioned a Negro ballet from Cole Porter, whose music was orchestrated by that deferent maid-of-all-work Charles Koechlin.

When de Maré approached Cocteau for a new ballet his

intention was that Auric should write the score. Auric, however, did not have the time, and Cocteau immediately saw an
opportunity to bring in all the Six. Each composer was allotted
a task. Durey, in the end, decided not to take part and
Germaine Tailleferre provided the music he was to have
written. For some time now he had been drifting away from
the Six. One reason for the estrangement was his friendship
with Ravel. Impressed by Durey's *Carillons*, Ravel had asked to
meet him and had expressed his 'warm artistic fellow-feeling'.
This appeared to the other members of the Six, encouraged
by Satie who was just then waging a malicious campaign
against Ravel, as a betrayal. Worse still, Durey protested at
their attacks on Ravel and loyally stood by his new friend. In
the year of *les Mariés de la Tour Eiffel* Durey moreover put a
distance between himself and the Six that was a matter of
geography as well as temperament. While touring Provence for
the first time he was attracted by the charm of Saint-Tropez.
It was not then a gaudy tourist centre but still preserved its
beauty as a place where artists could work in tranquillity. He
moved his family into a house on the slopes of Valfère above
the road that leads to the beach of les Salins. From his terrace
he commanded an expansive view of the gulf of Saint-Raphaël.
In the quietude of a home furnished with rustic simplicity he
found both a change from the nervous artificiality of Paris and
a background for his increasingly serious absorption in social
and political matters. Cocteau was annoyed by this show of
independence. It was as if a canvas on which he was painting
a picture had suddenly got up and walked away. His authority
had been contested. In a poem addressed to the Six he testily
omitted Durey's name. With the years his bitterness passed,
and he was reconciled in the late fifties to the extent of designing
a motif for the populist musical organization Durey supported.

Others remained faithful. One of them was the lovely
Valentine Gross. Cocteau had undertaken with her an unlikely
flirtation, and introduced her as his fiancée to his disbelieving
mother. The logical consequence of this rash venture never, of
course, took place, but his calculating charm had secured her
friendship. Later she married Victor Hugo's grandson, the
artist Jean. Their guests at the ceremony included her quondam
wooer, Radiguet, Auric, Poulenc and Satie. A souvenir of the
occasion was a notebook to which they all contributed. Cocteau

spangled it with a drawing of Auric captioned 'Get your Muse's hair cut' and with poems. Auric returned the compliment with the name of Picasso attached. Radiguet added an unpublished quatrain – something about initials lovingly enlaced – and Poulenc wrote out the music of 'la Carpe' from *Bestiaire*. Milhaud happily plagiarized Auric with a copy of *Adieu, New-York!* Fortified by this rare nuptial tribute, Jean Hugo worked on the designs for the costumes and masks required by *les Mariés de la Tour Eiffel*.

'Is it a ballet?' wrote Cocteau. 'No. A play? No. A revue? No. A tragedy? No. It is, rather, a secret marriage between ancient tragedy and an end-of-year revue, between chorus and music hall number.' The plot was mimed to commentaries issuing from cardboard loudspeakers each placed on either side of the stage. A newly-married couple arrive on the first-floor terrace of the Eiffel Tower accompanied by their family and an old friend, the General. A banquet and a speech are given. Then a photographer sets up his camera to photograph the wedding group. Each time he tells them 'Watch the birdie!' something incongruous happens: a Trouville bathing beauty leaps from the camera, telegrams shower down, a lion jumps out and devours the General, an overgrown child appears and knocks down the family as in a coconut-shy (whence the original title, *la Noce massacrée*). In between times the unpunctual habits of a stray ostrich cause alarm. Finally the General is restored to life and the photographer gets his wedding picture.

The device of restricting the players to mime and of explaining the action by means of commentary enabled the author to keep a tighter control than if he had written an ordinary play. The idea, which Sacha Guitry used in his film *le Roman d'un tricheur*, was elaborated by Cocteau:

A play ought to be written, designed, costumed, accompanied with music, acted and danced by one man alone. This all-round athlete does not exist. So it becomes necessary to replace the individual by what most resembles him: a friendly group. There are many cliques but few such groups. I have the luck, with several musicians, poets and artists, to belong to one.

Having assured for himself the maximum of unity in presentation, Cocteau goes on in his preface to develop some of the ideas already expressed in *le Coq et l'Arlequin*. Young composers of today, he warns the listener, have created for themselves

a new clarity, frankness and good humour. The simple-minded listener is misled. He thinks he is hearing a café-concert band. His ear makes the same mistake as his eye does when it fails to distinguish between a flashy piece of fabric and that same fabric copied by Ingres.

Again, Cocteau argues that instead of seeking after exoticism the artist must take his inspiration from everday things.

The poet must bring objects and feelings out from the veils and mists that surround them, must show them suddenly, so glaring and so quick, that a man can scarcely recognize them. Whereupon they impress with their youth, as if they had never become venerated in old age. This is the case with the old, powerful commonplaces which are universally accepted as we accept masterpieces whose beauty and originality no longer surprise us because we know them too well.

Another theme from *le Coq et l'Arlequin* which finds expression in the buffoonery of *les Mariés de la Tour Eiffel* is the conservatism of a public fettered by tradition in its appreciation of art. When the manager of the Eiffel Tower – a splendid creature with straw hat, walrus moustache and imposing girth – receives a telegram, he observes that it is dead. 'It's precisely because the telegram is dead that everyone understands it,' he is told. Bourgeois stupidity is embodied in the character of the General. After he has disappeared into the lion's jaws the chorus remarks: 'He was so gay, so young in heart. Nothing would have amused him more than such a death. He'd have been the first to laugh at it.' As the orator at his funeral remarks: 'Goodbye, goodbye, old friend. From your earliest campaigns you showed intelligence far above your rank. You never surrendered, even to the facts. Your end is worthy of your career. We saw you braving the wild animal, careless of danger, not understanding it, and only taking to flight when you did. Once again goodbye, or rather, au revoir, for your type will go on perpetuating itself as long as there are men on earth.'

The nonsense element has a strong affiliation with Lewis Carroll, that idol of the Surrealists. 'Have you seen the ostrich?' someone inquires. 'No. We haven't seen anything.'

'It's odd. I could have sworn it was skipping about on the terrace.' 'Perhaps it was a wave you mistook for an ostrich.' 'No. The sea is calm.' We are here in the country of *Sylvie and Bruno:*

> He thought he saw a Banker's Clerk
> Descending from a bus :
> He looked again and found it was
> A Hippopotamus . . .

The presence on the Eiffel Tower of a lion and of a lady bicyclist riding to le Chatou are explained away : 'There can't be a lion on the Eiffel Tower. So it is a mirage, a simple mirage. Mirages are in a way lies told by the desert. The lion is in Africa, just as the cyclist was on the road to le Chatou. The lion can see me and I can see the lion, but we're nothing more than reflections for each other.' The fantasy is varied with choice banalities such as : 'You'd never think he was seventy-four years old,' or : 'That child is the very image of his mother/father/grandmother/grandfather.'

It is the photographer who holds the key to the play. After he has enticed the bathing beauty from Trouville back into his camera by pretending that it is a bathing hut, he sighs : 'If only I knew in advance what surprises my broken-down equipment has in store for me, I could put on a show. Alas ! I tremble each time I say those wretched words. Does one ever know what's going to come out ? Since these mysteries are beyond me, let's pretend to have organized them.'

Since the action of the piece occurred on 14 July, Auric's *Ouverture* set the scene with brassy street-corner music, snatches of military marches and popular dances where sailors on leave waltz with typists over the pavement. Milhaud wrote a spruce little *Marche nuptiale* to which the party made its entry with the ironical chorus : 'The bride, gentle as a lamb. The father-in-law, rich as Croesus. The bridegroom, handsome as a dream. The mother-in-law, false as her teeth. The General, dim as a brush.' For the *Discours du général* Poulenc wrote a polka in which two cornets played a sprightly tune interspersed with lush 'raspberries'. His *Baigneuse de Trouville* started as a galop and veered into a slow waltz of the type Satie favoured in his days as a Montmartre café pianist. Poulenc worried that his music would not 'come off' with the broad effect required for the theatre. It was a larger orchestra than he was used to and he felt he could have done better. In the event it was perfectly danced by the Swedish ballerina Carina Ari (later to marry the composer Inghelbrecht who conducted for the Ballets Suédois), and Radiguet praised it as: 'A coloured picture postcard which took on the force of an allegory.'* Germaine Tailleferre deputized for Durey with a fairground *Valse des dépêches* in steam-organ style. Her *Quadrille*, which contained the hallowed movements of 'Pantalon', 'Été', 'Poule', 'Pastourelle' and 'Finale', unwound with all the exuberance of a Garde Républicaine brass band. The General's demise was celebrated by Honegger's *Marche funèbre*. Its lugubrious mockery of formal pomp was all the more effective in that he incorporated, *adagio* and in a minor key, the theme from Milhaud's *Marche nuptiale*. At the double forte he also introduced in counterpoint the waltz song from Gounod's *Faust,* a joke that Saint-Saëns had played with Berlioz' *Danse des sylphes* in the *Carnaval des animaux*. An unwary critic praised Honegger for having written 'real music at last'. As well as his *Marche nuptiale*, Milhaud wrote the crisp *Fugue du massacre de la noce.*

Rolf de Maré presented this 'choreographic farce' at the Théâtre les Champs-Élysées on 18 June 1921. Pierre Bertin and an actor called Marcel Herrand delivered the commentary as 'loudspeakers', and the different characters were mimed by members of the Ballets Suédois. The first-night audience was divided between cheers and catcalls. Later performances were more enthusiastically received. At the dissolution of the Ballets Suédois the costumes and music were bundled into packing cases and sent off to Sweden. No more was heard of the 'choreographic farce'. De Maré died in 1964 and bequeathed his archives to the Stockholm dance museum. On a visit there Cocteau discovered the existence of music which both he and its five composers had thought to have vanished for ever. Nearly forty years after that distant June season when the lion swallowed the General and the ostrich pirouetted on the Eiffel Tower for the first time, the orchestration was reassembled. In a Paris recording studio Milhaud brought to life once more the sounds of *les Mariés de la Tour Eiffel.*†

* The idea for the Trouville bathing beauty came from Poulenc, who, with Paul Morand, once appeared in such a fancy dress at a party.
† Text and music recorded on Disques Adès, 15 501.

6

THE DARK FOREST –
POULENC AND 'POOR MAX'

I

JUST over a week before the Eiffel Tower wedding party
assembled for their photograph in the Théâtre des Champs-
Élysées, the Ballets Suédois presented another and very
different work by Milhaud. *L'Homme et son désir* was composed in 1917 when Milhaud and Claudel were in the habit
of spending every Sunday out on the hills overlooking Rio de
Janeiro. They were joined for what Claudel described as
'picnics of ideas, music and drawings', by Audrey Parr, the
wife of the Secretary to the British Legation. She drew, with a
quick and fluent pencil, instant sketches to illustrate the ideas
that boiled up from Claudel's teeming imagination.

A visit from the Ballets Russes, who gave an impromptu
performance of *Parade* in the Legation ballroom, turned
Claudel's thoughts to the dance. The presence of Nijinsky
suggested to him a theme for a ballet, and the two men walked
off into the forest where Claudel, surrounded by the riotous
tangle of the *floresta*, explained his idea. Soon after this
Nijinsky's health gave way. Claudel was by now too involved
with his plan to relinquish it, and he continued work on the
ballet with Milhaud and Audrey Parr. His 'petit drame
plastique' was inspired by a night in the mysterious Brazilian
forest and portrayed that moment when the stillness began to
be peopled with movements, indeterminate cries and distant
glimmers. Claudel visualized a four-tier stage draped with blue,
green and purple around a central pattern of black. The scene
was conceived vertically, like a page of music where every action
was noted on a different stave. Across the top moved the Hours
dressed in black and wearing gold headdresses. Below was the
Moon, escorted over the sky by a cloud. At the bottom the

waters of the primeval swamp reflected the image of the Moon
and her escort. On the intermediary platform, between sky and
swamp, Man fell a victim to primitive forces and became the
sport of veiled shapes representing Image, Desire, Memory and
Illusion. He slept in the blaze of the tropical moon, watched
by the animals of the forest. He stirred in his dreams, moved
uneasily, and launched into the eternal dance of Desire, Longing and Exile. His obsession grew ever more frantic and violent.
A woman spun ceaselessly round him. He seized her veil, un-
winding it until he himself was wrapped up in it like a
chrysalis. Still joined to him by one last shred of cloth, tenuous
as the fabric of dreams, she covered his face with her hand
and they both moved off. The Hours of Darkness passed on.
The Hours of Daylight began to appear.

The first edition of Claudel's scenario was a curious one and
probably unique. He copied it out fifty times by hand. The
manuscript was mounted on cardboard and illustrated with
cut-out figurines by Audrey Parr. On the back Milhaud added
themes from his score. Dated 'Petropolis, Brazil, 1917', this
original item was inserted between blue boards and presumably
distributed to friends.

Milhaud wrote for a large orchestra. He divided it up into
several groups following Claudel's arrangement of the stage.
At one side of a tier he placed a quartet of soprano, contralto,
tenor and bass, and at the other an oboe, trumpet, harp and
double-bass. The percussion were allotted the next tier. Above
them were the woodwind, a little way off from the strings. His
aim was to give complete independence, melodic, tonal and
rhythmic, to each of the groups. Some of the instruments he
wrote for in common time, for others he wrote in triple time,
and for others still in six-eight. After every four beats he put
in an arbitrary bar line and added accents to keep the rhythm.
Muted strings trace a long sprawling figure pianissimo to introduce the scene. Their hazy meandering is joined by a wordless
chorus and by gentle throbs from the percussion, which has
been augmented with hammer beats on a plank and a wind
machine. The rhythm sharpens at the appearance of the Moon
and the harp plays silvery arpeggios. In the third section, where
the Man is hustled by veiled shapes, the beat of the percussion
grows insistent against pizzicato strings. He sleeps standing up,
wavering like a reed in the current of a stream, while a tenor

voice, and then the oboe, intone a simple, nursery-like tune. Thirty-one bars of fifteen solo percussion instruments with ad lib repeats portray the animals and things of the forest who come to gaze on him as he sleeps. Then the clarinet breaks in with a pastoral melody, the one Milhaud also used in the last movement, 'Et vif!', of his 'little symphony' *le Printemps* which he wrote in the same year. The 'Danse de la passion' builds up to a frenzy, tapers away into murmurous drum beats, and erupts into a violent climax. The seventh section lapses gradually into the misty sonorities of the earlier bars while the Man follows his partner off the stage.

L'Homme et son désir is one of the most striking works Milhaud has ever written. In it he captures the strangeness and immensity of the forests that dominated his stay in Brazil. An ever changing pattern of tone and rhythm conveys the restless crepitation of the foliage and the susurrus of unseen things that scurry continually behind it. The music is never still. Percussion is the element that supplies the vital pulse of activity, and Milhaud handles it with virtuoso skill. In addition to the usual instruments, he calls for metal castanets rather than the customary wooden ones, a whip, sleigh bells, a whistle, and the long narrow drum used in Provençal folk music. Over it all soar the wordless voices with their suggestion of great space and towering perspective.

Diaghilev was told about the new ballet. The ideas put forward in *le Coq et l'Arlequin* had interested him and he began to pay attention to the Six. Though he liked the music of Poulenc and Auric, he was always a little cool towards Milhaud's work. Still, he agreed to hear the composer play *l'Homme et son désir* at the home of a mutual friend. (The complexity of the score, said Milhaud, almost ruled out a piano arrangement. A version was prepared which, though blurring individual notes, at least allowed the main thread to be followed.) After Milhaud had finished playing, Massine and Diaghilev chattered together in Russian. The atmosphere was cold and sceptical. There was no chance of the ballet entering Diaghilev's repertoire. Rolf de Maré then agreed to produce it, despite the large forces required, and rehearsals began immediately.

Audrey Parr designed the costumes, snipping them out of cardboard and colouring them on the spot. Claudel had just been appointed Ambassador to Japan and at that time was in constant attendance on the heir to the Japanese throne who was visiting Paris. He would suddenly materialize on the stage of the darkened theatre, and, in morning coat and top hat, demonstrate to Jean Börlin, the choreographer, some new steps he wanted to see incorporated. Though his friend Gide inclined to the unadventurous in his musical tastes, Claudel showed a surprising side of his character by fervently supporting the new. His long collaboration with another member of the Six, Arthur Honegger, was further evidence of his enthusiasm for modernity. Honegger, with his Swiss Calvinistic background, might have seemed a more likely collaborator for Claudel, an Old Testament figure, than the Provençal Jew Milhaud. Yet while they were preparing *l'Homme et son désir,* Claudel wrote to Milhaud after a reading of Saint Paul:

It's very strange to see how all the Jews I meet are quickly on good terms with me and have confidence in me. Probably it's because I am deeply religious, and I do not think there is any Jew, however unpleasant he may seem, who is without religious feeling. But how they've forgotten the Bible! Here are people who limit their ambitions now to forming a little Eastern state on the lines of Bulgaria or Montenegro!

Some time before the production of the ballet Claudel had second thoughts about the title. Given the mood of the Parisian public, he inquired, might not *l'Homme et son désir* seem ridiculous? Would not *l'Homme et la forêt* give a better idea of the subject? Whatever arguments there were, the ballet opened under its original title on 6 June. The performance evoked no hostility from the audience, and even the passage for solo percussion went smoothly. Later performances were given to a steadily dwindling house. At one of them the picture dealer Ambroise Vollard lowered his giant bulk into a seat. He had come because he could find no one to accompany him to the cinema, which was his favourite art form since he slept better there than in bed. Because of the small number of spectators the management had cut down on heating. Always terrified of draughts, Vollard draped over his head an immense lily-white handkerchief that came down over his shoulders. Soon regular undulations showed that the owner beneath was comfortably asleep. The Théâtre des Champs-Élysées having been designed to seat close on two thousand spectators, and there being then little more than twenty in the auditorium, the acoustics were much improved by the vacuum and helped the 'Danse de la passion' to drown Vollard's healthy snores.

II

L'Homme et son désir showed just how fragile were the links with which Cocteau had tried to bind the Six into a group with a common aesthetic doctrine. By its subject and its treatment the ballet completely, though involuntarily, ignored his exhortation to seek poetry in the commonplace. Another of Cocteau's injunctions, that the Six should avoid foreign influences and stay French, was soon to be ignored. The music of Schoenberg, who had already intrigued Durey, began now to attract both Milhaud and Poulenc. Milhaud conducted the first French performance of *Pierrot Lunaire* at one of Jean Wiéner's contemporary music concerts. Great care was taken over this. To make sure the words could be understood, the singer Marya Freund made a French version of the German text. Although the poems were originally written by a Belgian, Schoenberg had used a German translation on which to base his prosody. The result was therefore a translation of a translation. There were twenty-five rehearsals in all, and the labours of Milhaud and his friends were rewarded with invitations to repeat the performance in Brussels and London. After conducting the difficult score so many times, Milhaud confessed, 'all my nerves were on edge. I was exasperated by the recitative running over the whole range of the vocal register and jumping unexpected intervals. So after conducting it in London I decided that would be the last time.'

Milhaud's disenchantment with Schoenberg did not last. At another of Jean Wiéner's concerts he directed the vocal piece *Herzgewächse* which was sung by an unbearably shrill soprano with Poulenc at the celesta and Wiéner himself, as a change from playing jazz in the 'Boeuf sur le toit', at the harmonium. In May 1920, the first issue of *le Coq et L'Arlequin* carried a message from Paul Morand: 'Arnold Schoenberg, the Six composers greet you.' (The seeds of decay were already planted.) In 1922 Milhaud and Poulenc delivered the greeting in person.

They found Vienna still suffering from poverty and inflation. Despite the hunger and wretchedness most people endured, there were excellent productions of Strauss and Mozart operas to be heard. At the home of Mahler's widow the French composers met Berg and Webern. When, a few days later, Poulenc fell ill and had to be operated on for an abscess in the throat, that learned musician Egon Wellesz brought him a pot of jam – a gesture of great friendship in a city where even essentials were scarce. By way of experiment, Schoenberg and Milhaud took turns to conduct *Pierrot Lunaire*. To Poulenc's ears Schoenberg's reading was distinguished for its accuracy, Milhaud's for its sensuality. An invitation to Schoenberg's home took Milhaud and Poulenc to Mödling, a suburb of Vienna. They talked of *die Glückliche Hand* and *Erwartung*. Milhaud was given the score of the *Five Orchestral Pieces* Schoenberg had used to conduct the first performance and which bore his pencilled notes.

Schoenberg, said Poulenc, looked like a teacher from some provincial German music school. At Mödling he lived in a pleasant house with its own garden. The walls of the rooms were hung with his own paintings, facial studies in which only the eyes were visible. They bore signs of Kokoschka's influence. It was a hot day and the party sat down for lunch beside an open window. While Milhaud and Schoenberg debated gravely the problems of twelve-note music, a small boy playing in the garden outside sent his ball flying through the window. By accident or design the missile landed precisely in the middle of the soup tureen. A geyser of thick brown liquid shot up to flood table and guests. The diversion was not unwelcome to Poulenc. His interest in Schoenberg, genuine though it was, can be explained by the attraction of opposites.

A journey to Italy the following year brought more new friendships – the composers Malipiero and Casella, and the contessa Pecci-Blunt. Known to Poulenc as 'ma chère Mimi', the contessa was one of those hospitable muses, like the princesse de Polignac, who took a maternal interest in him and appreciated his overgrown schoolboy's charm. With Milhaud he had hoped to arrange a concert engagement which might justify their Italian trip, but the Santa Cecilia, Rome's oldest chamber music society, took fright at the bad reputation of the Six which preceded them. They had to be content with a recital in a

private house and such tourist delights as those offered on a
visit to Neapolitan puppet theatres in a carriage driven by a
one-eyed, one-armed, one-legged coachman whose reckless vivacity in traffic was enhanced rather than diminished by his
physical peculiarities. A little later Milhaud played his *Ballade*
for piano and orchestra at a Rome concert. Rehearsals were
cordial. The performance was not. At the very first bars there
were shouts. Tumult continued to the end. The conductor
fled off-stage so quickly, Milhaud remembered, that 'he looked
as if he were swimming out through the violins.'

Poulenc came home inspired to write the piano suite *Napoli*.
The three pieces it contains, though mainly lyrical, are not
exempt from crackling discords which, one feels, he may have
inserted through a naughty desire to make the flesh creep. The
Paris flat to which he returned was the one that had belonged
to his maternal uncle 'Papoum'. Now that 'Papoum' had gone
to join the Goncourts whose artistic tastes he so admired, his
musical nephew lived in the bright rooms overlooking the
trees of the Jardins du Luxembourg. When Poulenc was not in
the capital he spent as much time as he could in Touraine,
a region he cherished with special affection. At an early age
he had been introduced by an aunt to the country of the Loire,
and the neat, unassuming countryside suited his mood. The
surroundings were perfect for work. His aunt used to spend
four months at her house near Amboise and the rest of the year
in Cannes. Her father-in-law was a friend of Balzac who had
put him into his novel *la Cousine Bette*. Aunt Liénard was
herself a lively personality. She had heard Wagner conduct
Lohengrin and attended one of the last concerts Liszt ever gave.
At the age of seventy-eight she went to the first performance
of *les Noces,* eager to hear what 'cher Stravinsky' had to offer.

When the time came Poulenc too settled near Amboise. 'Le
Grand Coteau', an eighteenth-century house by the hamlet of
Noizay, was built up against a rocky mound. Its tall windows
faced a terrace from which steps led down to a sunken garden
laid out with strict symmetry. The house was sheltered on one
side by a group of centenarian lime trees and on the other by an
orangery. Farther down, in a spacious garden, there flourished
vegetables, a vine noted for the light golden wine it produced,
and masses of flowers. Flowers were Poulenc's joy. He would
often arm himself with a vast Panama hat, secateurs and a sun

shade before descending to the garden and snipping the gladioli. The sunshade was a necessary item for the hypochondriac who feared sunstroke and summer colds, and who stocked an armoury of medicaments which symbolized his fervent belief in cures ranging from homeopathy to acupuncture. Back in the house, wearing tweed jacket and flannels, he filled every vase with flowers and arranged them in a way a professional would have envied.

The furniture, the pictures, the ornaments, were all matched and laid out with care. In Poulenc's big study a grand piano, heavily loaded with photographs of friends, stood next to an upright. On winter evenings he sat in an ample armchair by the fireplace and listened to gramophone records. His taste was eclectic. He followed with the score operas by Verdi and Puccini or symphonies by Mahler and Hindemith. He played Mozart and Schoenberg with impartiality. He put on music by his friends Stravinsky, Falla and Prokofiev. Chabrier, of course, was the great favourite whom he loved as 'a doting father, always gay, his pockets full of tempting tit-bits'. Like many people who have a reputation for humour, Poulenc was subject to moods of dark melancholy, and on such occasions only Chabrier could console him. There was one composer whom Poulenc failed to appreciate. If he was ready to admit the greatness of Fauré, he had to confess that works like the *Requiem* 'make me curl up'.

Away from the distractions of Paris he could give all his attention to composing. He liked to be up at six in the morning. After a breakfast of buttered rusks, jam and tea, he firmly shut himself in his study. With his back to the window he sat at his desk or piano. He always felt a little ashamed of working at the piano when people like Milhaud were able to compose anywhere, in railway carriages or in waiting rooms. Stravinsky reassured him by quoting Rimsky-Korsakov's remark : 'Some people write with a piano, others without. You belong to the second category, and that's all there is to it.' Poulenc worked very slowly. His fingers explored the keys, striking a chord and beginning a phrase. Then he would alter it and start again. A sudden silence indicated that he was writing down the notes on his music paper. Erasures were meticulously carried out with a knife whose blade over the years had gradually been worn down in the process.

At lunch-time he emerged, the day's work done. Perhaps there were pictures to be re-hung, for his preferences in art were as wide as in music. The canvases he owned of Matisse, Dufy and Picasso stood for one side of his nature, the outgoing jollity of Nogent. Mantegna and Zurbaran corresponded to his religious feelings. Chattering in his rich nasal tones, he would plan the rest of the day's activity with the guests who were staying. (Despite the way people teased him for being careful over his money, he was a hospitable man.) In the afternoon he might go on an excursion to Tours in search of the *rillettes* for which the town is famous. An epicure of high standards, he marketed with a shrewd eye. Or he might need to go on an errand into the village. Wearing a cap with the peak back to front, 'Like Blériot!' he would joke, he settled his large bulk on a scooter and roared off in a whirlwind of dust, his nose snuffling at the breeze, his complexion whipped to an even ruddier shade by the air. When he was on his own he played cards with the local innkeeper and carpenter. At tea time on the terrace, in the pearly light that softened the outlines of the Touraine countryside and picked out the slate roofs dotted around, he questioned his guests about the latest scandal from Paris, back-stage gossip, and society chat.

Friendship was everything for Poulenc. He never married, and the place of a family was taken for him by a large circle of friends. The hints he occasionally let drop suggest that beneath his gaiety there lay depths of sadness. But like Ravel, he kept his inner life strictly to himself. There were people who were very close to him, such as Brigitte Manceaux, his niece. Another was Raymonde Linossier, a girl he had known since childhood. They grew up together and liked reading the same authors – Ronsard, La Fontaine, Baudelaire, Apollinaire and Éluard. Raymonde was the author of *Bibi-la-Bibiste* (literally 'Myself-the-Myselfist'), a fey little work that Ezra Pound declared had 'all the virtues required by the academicians: absolute clarity, absolute form, beginning, middle, and end'. Printed on fourteen large pages, including the title, it was practically innocent of text, so that its form was chiefly a matter of visual appreciation. Raymonde had a sense of humour. This, and an inborn modesty, prevented her from becoming the writer she might have been. She then took up oriental studies and worked in a museum. After her sister's marriage she settled in a flat on the quai Saint-Michel and died not much later. Poulenc's tribute to her was the posthumous dedication of his wartime ballet after La Fontaine, *les Animaux modèles.*

Poulenc was often to be seen in the company of a small, bald-headed little man with a darting eye and a smile of ineffable malice. His name was Max Jacob, and their friendship dated back to 1917 when Raymond Radiguet had introduced them. Wearing a felt hat several sizes too large for him, and carrying a stick equally out of proportion, Radiguet took Poulenc to Montmartre and the shabby ground-floor room near the Sacré Coeur where Max lived. The room was dark and bare. A backless cupboard stood in the middle, so that to cross the room you had to step through it, as through a doorway. 'Here is my drawing room,' Max said, pointing to one side, and, pointing to the other, 'there is my bedroom.' He saluted the eighteen-year-old Poulenc as a great composer, and Radiguet, who was fifteen, as a novelist of genius. While Poulenc blushed to the roots of his hair, Max passed on from the extravagant compliments with which he was apt to drench unsuspecting friends, and launched into a worried monologue. Nobody loved him! Picasso was spreading tales about him behind his back! Cocteau was up to no good! Apollinaire was running him down! And Max, in the alpaca jacket that made him look like a sacristan, bemoaned the treachery of his friends, then gradually cheered himself up by relating outrageous slanders about them.

Whenever anyone who knew Max Jacob talks about him, the conversation soon becomes interlarded with exclamations of: 'Ce pauvre Max!' Poor Max, indeed. He had the appearance of Mr Punch, the instincts of a Sultan and the urgings of a saint. He was a Jew who worshipped the Virgin Mary and a sinner who terrified himself after each peccadillo with visions of damnation. They did not prevent him from embarking on his next sin with renewed relish. Max was born in Quimper, and on the house in the rue du Parc a commemorative plaque by Cocteau shows him with laurels wreathing his bare cranium, a coy and rather youthful Roman emperor. His father was a tailor and antique dealer. Madame Jacob he always claimed to be a terrifying woman. Did Max say this because Apollinaire's mother was a dragon and he did not want to be outdone? When Poulenc went on a tour of Brittany Max asked him to call on his mother. 'You'll find her sitting in the shop window. Be sure to tell her that I'm somebody VERRRY famous and VERRRY respected in Paris. There's no point in mentioning names, she doesn't know who Claudel is, nor Monsieur Paul Valéry.' Poulenc found her as indicated, enthroned in the window and surrounded by a jumble of bric-à-brac where she spent the day watching passers-by in the street. Though Max feared her, Poulenc decided that she was not so terrible after all.

A favourite game played by Max and his brothers was to recount the dreams they had had. When he had finished his contribution they shouted : 'Max, you're lying.' At that moment, he said, he knew he was a poet. He had a gift for art, too, which he showed by drawing female nudes in his geometry book to the surprise of his mathematics teacher. One fine day he took some money from his mother's drawer and came up to Paris. For a time he subsisted by giving piano lessons. He made the acquaintance of a Spaniard who 'painted two or three pictures a day, wore a top-hat as I did, and spent his evenings back-stage in music halls doing portraits of the performers. He spoke little French and I had no Spanish at all, but we shook hands warmly.' Later on Picasso and Max shared a squalid room in the boulevard Voltaire. Picasso drew all night, and when Max got up in the morning to go to the shop where he worked as an assistant, Picasso would be ready for bed. A meeting with Apollinaire followed and Max's circle was complete.

He worked as an apprentice carpenter, as a notary's clerk, as a tutor, and, according to him, as a children's maid. In the end none of these varied occupations suited him so well as the one he eventually hit on and which kept him just above the poverty line : that of painting gouaches of the sort favoured by tourists and, later, by collectors. He painted views of Brittany and famous scenes in Paris, often working from postcards as Utrillo had done. To convey the soft light of the Paris sky, he mixed powder diluted in water with cigarette ash and coffee, a blend to which he added a judicious quantity of spit. Since many of his friends were painters and lived together in a ramshackle Montmartre tenement at 7 rue Ravignan, he moved in to join them. The glass-fronted studios made the building look like one of those wash-house boats on the Seine, and he dubbed it the 'Bateau Lavoir'. In that crumbling, draughty place lived Picasso, who painted the 'demoiselles d'Avignon' there, Juan Gris, Modigliani, the Douanier Rousseau and Van Dongen. Many years later, when their art had attained respectability, when in other words the telegram of the *Mariés de la Tour Eiffel* was dead, well-meaning, right-thinking persons wished to preserve the Bateau Lavoir as a national monument. Picasso, quite rightly, turned a deaf ear to pleas for endowment. In 1970 the problem was solved when the wooden structure, which had begun life in 1860 as a piano factory, went up in flames. None of the surviving artists, for whom it was a symbol of poverty and struggle, lamented its passing. Regret was limited to sentimentalists who were sixty years behind the times.

Max lived in a tiny slum room at the end of the courtyard. The light from its only window had to be augmented all day long by a brass oil lamp. Here he painted his pictures and wrote his poems. Annoyed by the tumult of children playing outside, he did what few other people would have thought of doing : he wrote a little poem and sang it to them—

> Les enfants qui jouent sur les marches,
> On ne les aime pas du tout . . .

He was a child-like creature himself and they loved him. So did the concierges, whose fortunes he told. He helped them with their family troubles and advised on their problems. The only feature they disapproved of in him was the faint smell of ether that always hung about his clothes, for he was as much an addict of it as Cocteau was of opium. 'It's not ether,' he would protest indignantly. 'It's the apricot plums I had for dinner!' His reputation for astrology spread afield, and the smart carriages that began to line up at the shabby entrance of 7 rue Ravignan earned him money for the horoscopes he made up with many a cabbalistic flourish.

One evening in 1909 he came home from working in the Bibliothèque Nationale and sat down, like any worthy bourgeois, to put on his slippers. Suddenly a vision appeared on the wall. In a flash of unearthly well-being he perceived a man wearing a long silk robe. It was the Host. Max was kneeling by his bed in a trance of happiness long after the sublime vision had vanished. When he talked about it, of course, everyone thought he was playing another of his practical jokes. A second vision came to him on the screen of a local cinema in the middle of a gangster film. The priests he approached were disbelieving. 'So you go the pictures?' said one, reprovingly. 'Well, Father,' replied Max, 'didn't the Lord come there too?' A final vision materialized in the Sacré Coeur. This time it was the Virgin Mary. 'What a twerp you are, poor Max,' she said. 'Not such a twerp as all that, good Holy Virgin!' snapped Max, stumping out in annoyance and upsetting the congregation.*

Within a week or so he was baptized into the Catholic faith. His godfather was Picasso, who, though ready to lend him money still, could never get used to his new Christian name of 'Cyprian', despite Max's request to call him so. Neither could anyone else. Many people did not take him seriously, and they looked on his apologia, *la Défense de Tartufe*, as mere play acting. But Valéry has pointed out that unbelievers always find it difficult to agree that sincerity of faith can coexist with shameful conduct. When they see a believer indulge in vice, they think his faith is a sham. The paradox is that the deeper a convert sinks into sin, the more he needs forgiveness. Faith is therefore inseparable from sin. (Or, as Dr Johnson once roundly observed to a clerical gentleman: 'Sir, are you so grossly ignorant of human nature as not to know that a man may be very sincere in good principles, without having good practice?') There was only one woman in Max's life – the improbable Madame Pfeipfer, or so Max said her name was – whom his father tried to persuade him to marry. His true sins lay elsewhere, with nameless boys, muscular policemen and the ether bottle. He lived in a state of eternal remorse and accused himself of the vilest crimes. In 'Nuit infernale' he wrote vividly of his condition: 'Something horribly cold falls on my shoulders. Something sticky attaches itself to my neck. A voice cries down from the heavens: "Monster!" and I do not know whether it refers to me and my vices, or whether it is pointing out the slimy creature attached to me.'

At the beginning of the twenties Max went on a retreat in

---

* A little later Max asked the notorious Kiki of Montparnasse to go to a film with him. 'What a twerp you are, poor Max,' said she without malice, unaware that she was echoing the very words of her holier sister. In the end she relented, and they went off arm-in-arm like two young lovers, Max twirling his ebony cane and reciting a poem he had written in her honour.

the priest's house at Saint-Benoît-sur-Loire, a score or so miles
from Orléans. The church and the ancient Benedictine
monastery there gave him the peace he had been seeking ever
since his conversion. The monks were curious about the little
man who, wearing clogs and workman's corduroy trousers, knelt
in the basilica, violently striking his breast and exclaiming aloud.
'He's a converted Jew,' they were told. He was given a tiny
cell at the end of a dark corridor. It contained a narrow
bed, an old chest of drawers, a table, two chairs, a few wooden
shelves to take his books and manuscripts, a crucifix and a
holy-water stoup. Through the little window he could see a bit
of the garden and the open sky. An occasional rustle of the
trees outside, the cluck of hens and the bark of a dog were
all that distracted the silence. He spent a month writing a
book and the remaining eleven months of the year in revising
it. 'You're very lucky to have so much talent,' he told Poulenc.
'By having talent I mean not being obliged to tear one's guts
out to write the most trifling little sketch.'

Having once nearly set fire to the place by throwing a lighted
match into a wastepaper basket, Max was asked not to smoke.
It was torture for him. Each time he wanted a cigarette he had
to go outside. Except for this deprivation, life at Saint-Benoît-
sur-Loire was the nearest he approached to happiness. Every
day he was up early to write a meditation before Mass. Sometimes he prepared the altar himself and served with an ardour
that astonished the congregation. Daily he followed the Stations
of the Cross, lumbering painfully up and down on rheumaticky
knees and prostrating himself so that his forehead touched the
carpet. At Mass his voice rang out with insistent clamour. He
sang with a careless vigour that disturbed musicians of precise
habits. 'Monsieur l'Abbé,' he would demand anxiously, 'do you
bear a grudge against me? Are you sure I have no enemies in
Saint-Benoît?' For apart from death, his greatest obsession
was fear of betrayal, and anti-Semitism had encouraged his
natural feelings of diffidence.

From the Twenties onwards he divided his time between
Saint-Benoît and Paris. After the dissipations of the capital his
bleak little cell offered the chance of meditation and repentance.
When his yearnings for Montmartre became irresistible, he was
off again. The salons of Paris welcomed him as an amusing
entertainer. Hostesses were captivated by his eyes, languorous

and oriental, which, says André Billy, were full of mischief, ingenuousness, melancholy, irony, covetousness, gentleness, kindness, cruelty and salacity. They lacked true gaiety. He resembled sometimes a dubious priest, sometimes an actor. On evenings out he wore a top-hat, a tie which he varied according to the days of the week or the signs of the Zodiac, dancing pumps, a monocle, and a coat buttoned up high to conceal the absence of linen. Often he carried under his arm a rolled-up mat to place on stony church floors that he might protect his suffering knees. Wearing this dandy's outfit one cold January night, he was knocked over by a car in the place Pigalle. His collarbone was shattered. At the hospital he sat for hours on an iron chair in an open yard. They gave him a cold bath and trundled him through icy passages into a foul public ward. There he caught pneumonia which affected his lungs. Twenty years later, in a concentration camp, German brutality helped his longstanding respiratory troubles to cast him into the arms of death. 'Dead!' he once wrote. 'We shall all be dead: the woman passing by, and myself, the big man who's lost his hat will be dead, and the delivery-man from Dufayel will be dead, and the hawker and his dusty wife, and me! I shall be dead.' Just before the Gestapo came for him, he was resigned. 'I shall die a martyr,' he said. His last words were: 'I am with God.'

Max was often cruel to his friends. He mimicked them with a feline wit. His victims were left speechless and embarrassed. The next moment he would be truly repentant, giving them presents, writing little poems in their honour and painting pictures of them. His mercurial behaviour was the result of insecurity. 'It was fear,' said Poulenc, 'a fear of displeasing Picasso, fear of quarrelling with Breton and Éluard, fear of Reverdy, fear of Cocteau; fear was one of Max's basic characteristics.' Afraid that his religion would be mocked, afraid that his talent would be questioned, afraid that he would be persecuted by Gentiles, Max concealed his personality with a show of clowning. Though religion may not have given him the full peace of mind he wanted, his conduct at the end of his life shows that it at least was sincere. He bore with dignity the yellow star the Nazis made Jews wear on their clothes, and he died glorying in the thought of a better world to come.

Max's reputation as a clown has obscured the value of his work. More than half remains unpublished. His novels are satirical anecdotes told by a keen observer who adores the quaintness of human nature and excels at parody. The religious writings are mystic and benevolent. Perhaps his concentrated excellence is in the poetry, and more especially in *le Cornet à dés,* with its half-deliberate echo of Mallarmé. Believing that long works are to be avoided since the spirit of beauty can only be captured for short periods of time, he preferred to write little prose poems. Within these limits he creates a world of fantasy and strange images which, in their unusual juxta-position of objects, make one think of Surrealist paintings. Like Satie, he uses brevity to make an unforgettable impression. An art auction reminds him of a public execution, and he sees the condemned pictures strewn in a yard while butchers watch the proceedings through binoculars as if they were a Revolu-tionary mob. He contemplates a book and reflects that its binding is like a gilded railing that encloses the wonders within – multi-coloured cockatoos, boats with sails made of postage stamps, sultans wearing paradise on their heads. He looks down the rue Ravignan and the milkman becomes Ulysses, the ladies on fifth-floor are Castor and Pollux, and the old rag picker is Dostoevsky. Childhood memories commingle with parodies of Baudelaire. Free association gives rise to puns and allusions and metaphors which he sprinkles from his magic dice-box in a lavish but artfully controlled flow.

This digression on Max Jacob, who was one of Poulenc's closest and best-loved friends, helps to explain much in the composer's own character. Both men had a disconcerting mix-ture of buffoonery and seriousness in their make-up. Their urgent gaiety sprang from a deep awareness of the tragic in life. Where Milhaud's Jewish faith is as much a part of him as the sunshine is of Provence, Max and Poulenc lived their Catholicism with the intensity of a Goya painting.

Poulenc held *le Cornet à dés* to be on a level with Baudelaire's *le Spleen de Paris* and Rimbaud's *Une Saison en enfer.* In 1921 Max wrote some poems for him which he set to music. The poet jubilated in the thought that 'your music will earn me an income until the end of our days and the days of our heirs (I've a nephew). I think that each time it's played I shall be entitled to twenty-five centimes.' Unfortunately Poulenc was dissatisfied with his music and tore it up. Max had to wait for the golden shower of centimes until 1931, when Poulenc used some other poems for his 'secular cantata' *le Bal masqué*. This carnival in sound was scored for chamber orchestra with the piano as master of ceremonies. 'It's a hundred per cent Poulenc,' said the composer. 'If a lady in Kamchatka wrote to ask me what I was like, I'd send her the sketch Cocteau did of me at the piano, my portrait by Bérard, *le Bal Masqué* and the *Motets pour un temps de pénitence*. I think she'd have a very clear idea of Janus-Poulenc.' In the same year the *Cinq poémes de Max Jacob* drew on the poet's memories of his Breton background. Much later, in 1954, Poulenc set two other poems and gave them the title of *Parisiana* to show, by contrast, their essentially boulevard atmosphere. All these works fall outside the scope of this book, but it is enough to mention them to show Poulenc's response to Max Jacob.

There is no doubt about Max's attitude towards Poulenc. 'You're my favourite composer,' he exclaimed, adding with typical Jacobean caution: 'Don't say so to the others, though.' He was thrilled that Poulenc should choose his poems. 'You know I'm really very flattered at the thought of inspiring you. This is quite sincere and outside the usual conventions of politeness. Oh yes ... I authorize whatever your precious fantasy pleases, O Master. My only claim to glory will be to figure beside your name.' His letters to Poulenc, some of them written in poetry, were of the sort that lightened many a dull morning for his friends. He chattered about the guests at Saint-Benoît ('St Garden Party, pray for us!'), retailed the gossip he loved ('the grocer's wife and the commercial traveller here ...'), and bemoaned his inability to be serious. His correspondence was as entertaining and fantastical as his conversation.

Towards the end of his life, when he was hunted by the Gestapo and forced to display the yellow star denoting his race, Max wrote a last prose poem. It was called 'Neighbourly love', and, in Poulenc's opinion, wonderfully expressed Max's humanity:

Who saw the toad cross the street? He's a very little fellow: a doll couldn't be tinier. He crawls along on his knees: would you say he was ashamed? ... No! He's rheumatic, one leg drags behind, he brings it forward! Where is he going to like this? He comes out of the drain, poor clown. No one has noticed the toad in the street. Once upon a time people didn't notice me in the street, either. Now children laugh at my yellow star. Happy toad! You haven't got a yellow star.

7

KING DAVID – THE WIDOW ON THE ROOF – THE CREATION OF THE WORLD

I

The Six were closely linked with poets and writers. The names of Auric and Radiguet were inseparable, as were those of Milhaud and Claudel. Poulenc will always be associated with Apollinaire, Jacob and Éluard. Honegger was no exception. He worked with Claudel in the 1930s on *Jeanne d'Arc au bûcher* and the *Danse des morts,* and with Valéry on *Amphion* and *Sémiramis.* He set, like most of his comrades, poems by Cocteau. His studio in the boulevard de Clichy was stacked with books. Besides all his published scores there were studies of his music and articles about him. Thousands of volumes on psychology, philosophy and literature in general bore witness to his eclecticism. Each was meticulously numbered and arranged. As though to prove that he, too, had his share of frivolity, there were also shelves full of the detective novels he liked to read in bed.

He lived with his wife Andrée Vaurabourg and his daughter on the third floor of a tall, anonymous block at Number 71. From the window of his studio he could pick out the shape of Sacré Coeur, and, to the right, the Moulin Rouge with its eternally revolving sails among the neon lights. Photographs of composers whom his fellow members of the Six would never have allowed into their homes – d'Indy, Fauré, Ravel – decorated the walls. Under a bust of Debussy, another of his renegade preferences, hung an enormous collection of pipes. Honegger was an inveterate smoker. He composed in a permanent blue haze. His repertory of pipes must have run into hundreds : they were scattered everywhere throughout the room, in distant corners behind books, under manuscript papers, forgotten in ashtrays. They ranged from great dropsical Meerschaums to

Jean Cocteau in 1960 at the age of seventy-one. Doctor honoris causa of Oxford, he is seen with some of the 'props' from his last film, *le Testament d'Orphée*

Le groupe ~~dit groupe~~ des six n'a été qu'un groupe de six amis dont le seul plaisir était de se rejoindre et de travailler ensemble. Il n'a jamais été une <u>école</u> mais un <u>mouvement</u>. C'est pourquoi je suis fier d'avoir toujours été son porte parole.

Jean Cocteau

1951

Cocteau's own definition of his role with the Six. 'The group known as the Six was nothing more than a group of six friends whose pleasure it was to meet and work together. It was never a *school* but a *movement*. That is why I am proud of always having been its spokesman' (*Courtesy of Rollo Myers*)

The Six in 1922. Standing, left to right: Milhaud, Honegger, Tailleferre, Poulenc, Durey. Auric, absent, was represented by Cocteau's sketch. Cocteau is seated at the piano

The Six in 1952. Standing, left to right: Poulenc, Tailleferre, Auric, Durey; seated: Honegger, Cocteau, Milhaud (*Courtesy of Rollo Myers*)

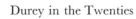
Durey in the Twenties

Milhaud in the Twenties   Milhaud today

Poulenc at the beginning of his career

Poulenc at the keyboard with Wanda Landowska (*Courtesy of Rollo Myers*)

Honegger as a young man

Honegger – the last photograph

Erik Satie in 1910,
aged forty-four

Auric (left) with the
comtesse Etienne de
Beaumont and
Salvador Dali

Rolf de Maré, impresario of the Ballets suédois, in his office at the Théâtre des Champs-Elysées

LE BŒUF SUR LE TOIT

The Ox on the Roof – designed by Raoul Dufy

Max Jacob, poet and
painter, at his easel

unassuming nose-warmers. A small table held two pots of tobacco which were ever mysteriously full.

Two large writing desks stood in the middle of the room. Behind them was a music stand where he put manuscripts when he was orchestrating. On the piano lay a song by Mistinguett whom he admired. He never moved it, even when working there. Persons from Porlock were warned off by a notice on his door: 'Work in progress. Please do not disturb.' It was written in a number of languages to make quite sure that the message would be received. He did not answer the bell when it rang and he made a habit of ignoring the telephone, often leaving the receiver off. This iron refusal to be interrupted in his work at first distressed the sociable Poulenc, who was accustomed to long daily telephone chats with Auric and Milhaud. Honegger's friends had to limit their social meetings with him to Saturday evenings at Milhaud's flat and the 'Boeuf sur le toit'. Yet though Honegger maintained a Swiss reserve among acquaintances, he was in reality a man of humour and warm feeling.

In common with others of the Six, Honegger wrote a lot of music for the stage. He began with a Debussyst prelude to Maeterlinck's play *Aglavaine et Sélysette*. As a most unlikely contrast he was also involved with Max Jacob's *la Mort de Sainte Alméenne*, of which neither the text nor the music has been published. The image of Honegger as a dour man is belied by his friendship with Max. His ballets in the twenties included *Vérité-Mensonge*, which he wrote for a puppet show by André Hellé, the designer of Debussy's *la Boîte à joujoux*, and *Skating Rink*, a piece commissioned by Rolf de Maré for the Ballets Suédois programme that included Milhaud's *l'Homme et son désir*. Honegger's ballet was designed by Fernand Léger and was the result of a dangerous challenge: the circular motion of the skaters was supposed to represent the monotony of everyday life, with only occasional diversions to vary it. *Fantasio* was written for the once-famous mime Georges Wague, and *Sous-marine* for the dancer Carina Ari. *Roses de métal* provided a curiosity in that it experimented with Bertrand 'dynaphones' which foreshadowed the later 'ondes Martenot'.

Honegger also composed a deal of incidental music. By the end of the twenties he had worked on plays by André Gide, Romain Rolland and Shakespeare. The suite he wrote for

Cocteau's *Antigone* – a modest affair for harp and oboe – was later turned into a full-scale opera. He had been fascinated by the character of the heroine. She was, he enthused to his friends, 'a saint', and he saw her as representing the victory of nobility over cowardice. Antigone haunted him for several years until 1927, when his opera was finally produced. Using a libretto by Cocteau that was concise and compact, Honegger aimed at replacing recitative with 'a melodic line created by the word itself, by its own plasticity, and intended to emphasize the word's contours and to throw it into greater relief'. Each syllable was scrupulously given its full value, consonants were treated with deference, and the melodic phrase was dictated by Honegger's insistent care to make each word clearly stand out. Instead of providing a commentary on the action, the orchestra followed behind, as it were, and discreetly paralleled the text. The austerity of the work and the concentration it demanded from its listeners worked against success. The first performance, with scenery by Picasso, and a later revival, failed to attract admirers.

The disappointment of Honegger's hopes for *Antigone* was a little softened by his bizarre encounter with Gabriele d'Annunzio. The lively Italian poet had written a play called *Phaedra* to which Honegger contributed music. At the performance in Rome little could be heard save the jeers of young Fascists who were annoyed at the absence of their hero d'Annunzio. (He was in prison at the time.) Later he invited Honegger to visit his estate. In the middle of the garden stood a land-locked battle-cruiser watched over by a fully armed marine. D'Annunzio took his guest up on to the bridge and pointed out the beauties of Lake Garda. 'And now,' shouted d'Annunzio, 'to greet the musician who is visiting the poet, we shall launch into the innumerable and limitless infinite the seven notes of the scale ... *Fuoco*!' A cannon roared sonorously and nearly swept the astonished composer off his feet. By the seventh shot he had recovered enough to appreciate d'Annunzio's novel gesture. His conversation, Honegger found, was brilliant, and he understood why this man, so unattractive physically, had such success with women. The poet was justly proud of his linguistic gifts. 'Most French writers are content with fifteen hundred words,' he declared. '*I* know fifteen thousand!'

Since Honegger claimed to be a slow, even painful worker,

his facility for turning out incidental music seems a contradiction. He explained that when he had a visual or literary stimulus he could write fast. It was the purely symphonic works that gave him most trouble. Film music was particularly congenial. 'The subject is supplied by the picture,' he said, 'which instantly suggests an orchestral transposition.' In his time he wrote music for over thirty films, sometimes in collaboration and always accepting with good humour the often outrageous attitudes of cinema people. He had the consolation that film music was a good source of income. His first score was for the classic silent film *la Roue* of Abel Gance, that dauntless pioneer who was the first to use the wide screen and stereophony, and who for nearly fifty years devoted himself to proving that a man's reach should exceed his grasp. *La Roue,* with its railway setting, was a foretaste of Honegger's tone poem *Pacific 231.* Later he collaborated with Gance on the epic *Napoléon,* and few years were to pass without a film score by him for adaptations ranging from Bernard Shaw to Dostoevsky.

The speed with which Honegger could write when he had an external inspiration is shown in the case of *le Roi David,* the oratorio that gave him immediate fame. He started it on 25 February 1921, and finished on 28 April. The initiative came from the Swiss poet René Morax. At Mézières, in 1910, he had founded with his brother, an artist, the Théâtre du Jorat. Its design was based on Greek and Roman models, and the theatre was 'popular' in its aims. There, in a spacious setting with Alpine glaciers distantly shimmering over beech and fir tree, Morax put on a play every two years and drew his cast from among the local populace. The war brought this project to a standstill. In 1921 he planned to re-open the theatre with a Biblical spectacle about the life of King David. The text was written, the scenery and costumes were designed by Morax' brother, and rehearsals began. Only at this point did Morax start to look for a composer to provide the music. 'I can see only one solution,' said Ernest Ansermet, to whom Morax had rushed for advice at the last minute : 'Honegger.'

Up to now, so far as Switzerland was concerned, Honegger had been a prophet without honour in his own country. The accident of French birth had not diluted his affection for the country of his ancestors, and no doubt that is one of the reasons why he accepted the commission. There were many problems to be faced. He had to work at very great speed. The cast for which he wrote was an amateur one of varying abilities. He was also restricted to an orchestra of fifteen players. These he divided up into six woodwind, four brass, a harmonium, a piano, two kettle-drums and a double bass, to which he was allowed to add a gong. His experience in writing for the small groups used in theatrical music served him here, and he utilized the strange combination of instruments so as to give his score much of its piquancy. No sooner had the ink dried on the various sections of the manuscript than they were posted off to Mézières, where housewives, shopkeepers and farmers transformed themselves into Israelite crowds and rehearsed anxiously. So intense was Honegger's preoccupation that, called to Zurich where his mother lay gravely ill, he took his music paper with him and scribbled all the way there and back.

The first performance on 13 June brought a large and curious audience. Among them was the music critic Émile Vuillermoz, already a sharp-tongued enemy of Poulenc. He wrote an enthusiastic review in which he sought to divide the Six by praising Honegger and comparing his friends unfavourably with him. Cocteau rose to the bait and counter-attacked. The argument between him and Vuillermoz continued for many years, off and on, until the liberation of France in 1944, when harmless squabbles over a work featuring a Jewish hero could be seen in a light that neither adversary had foreseen. In the meantime the publicity which *le Roi David* was receiving made it known far beyond the confines of Mézières in a way that tended to overshadow the guiding spirit of the place, though the gentle, bearded Morax did not grudge his young musical colleague a dominant share of the glory.

A rich banker who happened to be the friend and patron of Gabriel Fauré was at the performance. He had the idea of presenting *le Roi David* and Fauré's *Requiem* in the same programme – a combination which both pleased and flattered Honegger, who by no means shared Poulenc's opinion of Fauré and found him, rather, a welcome antidote to the influence of Reger and Schoenberg. The concert was given soon afterwards in the little church of Annecy-le-Viex, where Fauré was spending summer with his banker friend. It took place in 1923, the year before the composer of the *Requiem* died. Frail, thin, his hair and moustache snowy-white, he sat beside Honegger on a bench under the trees and looked with dim benevolence into the camera lens. His bony fingers emerged from a gaping shirt-cuff to hold delicately a cigarette. Honegger, grasping the bowl of a pipe in his fist, gazed confidently out with all the youthful exuberance of his thirty years. Not long after, thanks again to the wealthy banker, *le Roi David,* re-cast as an oratorio, was given in Paris. It confirmed Honegger's reputation – although, as he afterwards pointed out, he never earned from this immensely successful work any more than the wretched 420 francs which a Lausanne publisher gave him for the outright purchase of the score.

The triumph of *le Roi David* was immediate and unanimous. The rare phenomenon of a major work by a serious composer being taken up by the general public has only occurred again in recent years with Benjamin Britten's *War Requiem.* In both cases it seems as if the imagination of listeners who were not particularly musical had been caught by the broad appeal and generous emotion of a work that transcended normal cate-gories. *Le Roi David* was heard at a time when people were still exhausted and confused by the experience of war. They were, many of them, repelled by much of the new music and not in a mood for experiment. Those who had traditional tastes were delighted that Honegger should have taken an old form and rejuvenated it with a quality of invention which, though modern in technique, was humane and accessible. A pattern had already evolved in which, if you disliked Milhaud, you were bound to welcome Honegger. It was a situation that amused both composers without causing ill feeling, and when they gave joint concerts of their music they chuckled at the sight of rival factions among the audience.

Morax based his text on the first Book of Kings and the first and second Books of Samuel. The work is in the form of a triptych. Part I shows David the shepherd battling with Goliath. Saul pursues David jealously and is killed. Part II is chiefly occupied with the dance before the Ark and leads to the angel's prophecy and a triumphant Alleluia. In Part III the King David, 'old and stricken in years', cherishes a criminal love for Bathsheba. His son Absolom rebels and dies. The king feels death approaching and hands over the crown to his son Solomon. An adagio evokes the king's passing with a firm, clear-cut chorale tune.

With *le Roi David* Honegger was able at last to express the ideas he had conceived in his studies of Bach and Handel. Solo pieces alternated with orchestral interludes and mixed choruses. Instead of recitatives he used a speaker to provide continuity. Traditional harmony was subtly mingled with atonal techniques, notably in the orchestral introduction to Part I, where brass and woodwind dialogue together before ending in a conventional chord of D major. After hearing the oratorio given so many times throughout the world Honegger began to grow a little weary of it. At the end of the day he could only speak with approval of three items. One was the number 'L'Éternel est ma lumière' sung by tenors and basses with a syncopated horn accompaniment. Another was the dance before the Ark, which is built up into a clashing frenzy by the deft use of what are really very small forces. The other item to retain Honegger's affection was the psalm of penitence in Part III. This is a sombre appeal by David for pity after the death of the child Bathsheba has given him.

Honegger was perhaps a little too harsh with himself. The faults of *le Roi David* are the too-obvious echoes of Bach which, occasionally, hover on the edge of pastiche. Otherwise the boldness of the writing and the unaffected simplicity of the texture have kept the vigour which conquered earlier audiences. An important feature of the work is the interpolation of psalms at various points. There is a deep and impressive melancholy in the setting of 'Ne crains rien et mets ta foi en l'Éternel.' Another psalm, 'Pitié de moi, mon Dieu, pitié de moi', has a heart-catching leap of a fifth in the opening 'Mon Dieu'. The care for words that Honegger showed in *Antigone* was evident also in *le Roi David*. He explained at great length to Morax how he intended to set the line : 'Saül tua ses mille et David ses dix mille.' The emphasis was to be put on 'dix', Honegger said, because it was more important for David to have slaughtered *ten* thousand than ten *thousand*. Another instance was the precision with which he accented the name of Saul. Throughout the whole of the work, indeed, Honegger was ceaselessly experimenting with accents and rhythmic possibilities.

Le Roi David comes over when heard today with its lyrical energy untouched by the passage of close on fifty years. The brutal rhythms of the dance before the ark and the screeching incantations of the witch of Endor are beautifully contrasted with the serene lucidity and the dark melodies of the psalm settings. The oratorio marks the end of Honegger's allegiance to Schoenberg. 'By taking his ideas to their logical conclusion,' Honegger said of him, 'he came to a dead end, an art of abstraction. He lost touch with the public.' Unmoved by musical fashion, Honegger believed himself to be justified by the audiences who crowded to hear *le Roi David*. To those who accused him of working in a dying medium he replied :

It seems to me essential that in order to move forward we need to be firmly attached to what has gone before us. We must not break the link of musical tradition. A branch cut off from the trunk quickly dies. We need to be new players of the same game, because if you change the rules you destroy the game and take it back to where it started. A self-imposed limitation of means appears to me more difficult but also more useful than obstinate audacity. There is no point in breaking down a door that you can open just as easily.

II

Honegger's deliberate choice of popular appeal rather than the heady but hermetic delights of Parisian novelty struck Jean Cocteau as being in the line of Durey's 'betrayal'. He had, though, little time to lament this apparent defection, for in the December preceding the arrival of *le Roi David* in Paris Raymond Radiguet had died.

In March 1923, the publisher Bernard Grasset brought out Radiguet's novel *le Diable au corps* with all the brassy panache of a tycoon launching a new detergent. It was Grasset who bought for two thousand francs an unsuccessful novel by Louis Hémon, *Maria Chapdedelaine,* and made it into one of the greatest best-sellers of the inter-war period. He introduced Giraudoux, Mauriac and Maurois to the public. He was apt to reveal in confidence that, by dint of bullying Proust into constant rewriting, he deserved credit as part-author of *Du côté de chez Swann.* At other times he would airily claim that he had published it without reading it. Deeply involved with the fortunes of his authors, Grasset was reported to have fought a duel because the Académie had chosen not to award one of them a prize. The nervous strain of his compulsive buccaneering showed in his drawn features, his pallor, and the anxious rabbit twitch of the nostrils.

When the manuscript of *le Diable au corps* had been rescued from Cendrars' office Grasset immediately saw possibilities for exploitation. The twenty-year-old author was described to the press as being only fifteen. The walls of Paris were covered with sensational posters. Large advertisements in the papers reported the discovery of a genius. Photographs showed Radiguet signing a contract for huge sums. An inexhaustible stream of puff and testimonial lauded the book as a masterpiece. Critics were horrified by the indignity of such methods. The public, especially men who had fought in the war, was scandalized by the brief tale of a boy and his seduction of a woman while her husband was away at the front. In the book she gives birth to a son and dies soon afterwards. Radiguet denied that the novel was in any way autobiographical and claimed that it was pure fiction. But in 1953, long, long after public indignation subsided, an elderly man disclosed that he had been the deceived husband. Until 1952 he had lived in cold suspicion with his wife and unwanted son. Her death in that year released him from silence. He claimed that Radiguet had stolen the diary in which his wife noted their assignations. In his copy of the novel the margins were black with annotations: 'False!' ... 'This is what happened to my wife and *me*! ... That's what she said to *me*! ...' Cocteau denied the man's story. So did the son. True or false, the obsession caused by *le Diable au corps* had ruined the father's life.

The campaign directed from Grasset's little office in the rue des Saints-Pères brought Radiguet money and notoriety. If, though, the techniques used by Grasset were those of a huckster, the 'product' he launched was of a rare and precious quality. *Le Diable au corps* has become a minor classic in French literature. In the last months of his life Radiguet was able to enjoy the material rewards of genius. He entertained his friends to champagne dinners in expensive restaurants where his pallid features, short-sighted look and badly cut hair tumbling over his collar were respectfully greeted by maîtres d'hôtel. He now wore elegant white gloves when he rolled his thin little cigarettes. There was enough money for him, the eldest and dutiful son, to send remittances to his family. Yet his new life of luxury was pervaded with unease. He began to set his affairs in order.

He started going to bed early. There was, he felt, not much time left. A new novel, *le Bal du comte d'Orgel,* occupied his mind, and Georges Auric took it down to his speedy dictation. The comte d'Orgel was inspired by the cool, aristocratic Étienne de Beaumont, and the acute analytical manner owed something to *la Princesse de Clèves.* He had always admired the classic purity of Madame de Lafayette, and succeeded in passing on his enthusiasm to Cocteau, whose education up to then had been somewhat haphazard.

Radiguet took up quarters in the hôtel Foyot and shared his life with a girl who, though history records her as the daughter of an Amsterdam rabbi, was known as 'la Polonaise'. One evening he was taken with a fit of shivering. An expensive doctor diagnosed influenza and gave him injections of sea water. It was discovered too late that he was suffering from typhoid fever. In his delirium he murmured that God's soldiers were coming to shoot him. Cocteau tried to reassure him. Radiguet whispered : 'Your information's not as good as mine. The order's given. I heard it.' When his father arrived at the nursing home he was met by an attendant with the words : 'Do you want to see your son? He's in the mortuary.'

'Poor child!' Radiguet's father told Poulenc, 'so much youth and talent, so much kindness.' He had not forgotten his family in the days of success. The money he sent, the gifts he made were not enough for his generosity. He used the influence of his new friends to help them, and through Poulenc was able to find his brother a good post in the composer's family firm.

The funeral arrangements had a chic attributable to the hand of the dressmaker Coco Chanel, who was in charge of them. The flowers in the church were white and so was the coffin. It arrived in a white hearse drawn by two white horses that reminded one of the mourners of a Uccello picture. Picasso and Brancusi were among the congregation, and so was the Negro band from the 'Boeuf sur le Toit'. After the service the hearse moved off through the rain and the fog, a bunch of red roses lying on the white pall of the coffin.

Cocteau went mad with anguish. Dressed in black, he shut himself up in his room, inconsolable. He could not forget his cherished 'Radigo's' tragic swollen face, the half-open mouth, the lolling head. Max Jacob sought to comfort him with visions

of Radiguet 'au ciel comme les enfants!' Other friends, less
charitably, nicknamed Cocteau 'le Veuf sur le Toit'.

III

A few weeks before Cocteau went into mourning a new ballet
by Milhaud, *la Création du monde*, had its first performance.
Blaise Cendrars, hot from compiling his Negro anthology, had
proposed the subject to Rolf de Maré and the Ballets Suédois.
His idea was to portray the creation of the world as it is told
in African legend. The artist whom de Maré chose as designer
was Fernand Léger, who had already worked for him on the
ballet *Skating Rink* with Honegger. Léger was the son of a
Norman cattle dealer, and, had it not been for his father's
early death, would have probably followed that trade himself.
He studied architecture, was providentially turned down for
art school, and made the acquaintance of Chagall and Apollinaire who helped him find his path as an artist. Cendrars the
indefatigable became his friend and made vigorous propaganda
on his behalf. The war of 1914 crystallized his artistic ideas:
at the front, the angular scenes of destruction, the lines of the
big guns, the glitter of light on white metal, the view of men
at grips with the machines of war, gave him the inspiration for
his Cubist experiments. 'For me,' he said, 'the human face and
body have no more importance than nails and bicycles. They
are nothing more than nails and bicycles. They are nothing
more than objects of plastic value that I must use as I wish.'

Léger was disconcertingly ugly. His nose was big, and a
pair of oddly small eyes nestled in the sun-baked features of
a Norman peasant. One evening in 1919, as he was taking
an apéritif outside a café, he perceived a lady feverishly pedalling down the road on a smart new bicycle. She wore bridal
dress and her veil flew in the wind. Dismounting breathlessly,
she explained that she had just been married in her Norman
village. After the wedding, unable to resist the temptation of
a bicycle among her presents, she sprang on the machine and,
in her exhilaration, had pedalled all the way to Paris. Charmed
by her beauty and by the quite Surrealist spontaneity of her
action, which recalls, indeed, *les Mariés de la Tour Eiffel*,
Léger made the necessary arrangements for her to become his

wife – after, presumably, negotiating with the dazed husband she left at home.

While they were working on *la Création du monde,* the three collaborators explored districts of Paris which Milhaud had never visited before. In the evening after dinner they put on caps and raincoats to go down the colourful rue de Lappe. The mingled strains of bals-musette hovered in the air, sustained by the accordion with help from cornets, trombones and an occasional violin. Men danced with their girls in crowded cafés where the proprietress circled among them tirelessly repeating 'Money, please!' and pocketed the dues in a large bag slung over her shoulder. Around the Bastille quarter exiles from Auvergne danced their native *bourrées* to the sound of a hurdy-gurdy, while a few streets away there were women from the Antilles wearing Madras handkerchiefs on their head who sketched out the languorous steps of the beguine. As Milhaud and his friends walked through Paris, Léger talked of the décor he wanted to create. He visualized a transposition of primitive Negro art, with African divinities painted on the drop-curtain and scenery to represent power and darkness. However hard he tried, though, he was disappointed at the result, which he never thought terrifying enough. Then he struck on the idea of skins which would represent flowers, trees, animals, and which, blown-up, would be released at the moment of creation and fly away like balloons. But the equipment needed would be too cumbersome, and in the end he contented himself with animal costumes of the sort worn by the dancers in African ritual. They were painted in dazzling colours and represented grass-skirted hierophants, strange beaked animals and totem figures. From a back-drop cubed and squared, there glowered horned creatures and undulating clouds.

The score of *la Création du monde* was written in a new flat Milhaud had just taken. It was in the boulevard de Clichy, not far from Honegger, and there he has lived ever since. The place is large and comfortable, and from the first floor overlooks the noisy boulevard and the café underneath. He has always composed with facility. The din of Montmartre troubles him not at all, and the everyday noises of the home are a positive inspiration. He shared the house-warming with Paul Morand, who was also moving at the same time, and on a hot summer night troops of their friends poured into the flat, crowded on the stairs, and overflowed into the café below. Montmartre fair was in full swing, and through the open windows came snatches of barrel organ music, the crack of pistols in shooting galleries, and the roar of caged animals. A bird-catcher arrived to entertain the guests. Canaries and tame sparrows preened themselves coquettishly on his hands and shoulders, and then fluttered round the room. A dramatic little sketch ended the show. A canary fired a tiny cannon at another bird which fell and lay motionless. It was placed on a hearse and drawn round the table by a pair of birds. But a canary magician brushed the corpse with its wing, the bird came to life, and it flew swiftly away to the applause of the spectators.

La Création du monde gave Milhaud the chance he had been seeking of using jazz techniques for an extended work. He modelled his orchestra on those he had seen in Harlem, and wrote his score for seventeen soloists including piano. The percussion arrangements, not so elaborate this time as in *l'Homme et son désir,* called for tambourine, metal and wood blocks, cymbals, two side drums, and a big drum. The overture consists of a dulcet melody sedately played by the saxophone with the accompaniment of a regularly repeated pattern of thirds from the piano. Abrupt trombone glissandi bite into the atmosphere of serenity from time to time and add a dash of spice. The curtain rises to quick, nervous piano glissandi, while the double basses play a brusque syncopated figure which is later taken over by the saxophone. The three gods of creation appear on the mountain tops. They perform their incantations and depart, leaving fetishes to call into existence apes and insects. Rain birds flitter over the stage. The animals swirl about and form a circle to dance around their creators, each of whom emerges in turn and leads their steps. Witches, vampires, fetishists, oath-makers and soothsayers incite them to frenzy. All this time the music has been growing wilder, and now it blazes into excitement with a staccato jazz figure incessantly hammered out on the piano. At the height of the delirium a crash on the drum signals the birth of man and woman. They face each other and embrace. The tender saxophone tune of the overture comes back, and the springtime of the world begins.

Milhaud's achievement lies in his genuine synthesis of jazz

elements with classic western procedures. He is the most succesful in a venture which several of the Six attempted, and his contribution is perhaps more valid than Ravel's experiment on the same lines. The jazz fugato is a brilliant exercise where Milhaud convincingly shows that he has fulfilled his original ambition. The blend is perfect and the idiom absolutely right. Moving swiftly from incantation to frenzy and back to peace again, the music beautifully expresses the mystery and sweetness of its theme. Having done what he set out to do, Milhaud went on to other things. The critics, of course, said that the music was better suited to the dance hall. Ten years later they were philosophizing on the nature of jazz and learnedly arguing that *la Création du monde* was his best work.

On the same programme with *la Création du monde* Rolfe de Maré chose to feature a novelty which Milhaud again had put his way. Returned from a tour of the United States, de Maré wanted to mount an authentic American ballet but did not know where to find a composer for it. Milhaud introduced him to a friend he had made in the drawing room of the princesse de Polignac, 'an elegant young American who always wore a white carnation in the buttonhole of his impeccable dinner jacket, who sang in a soft and serious voice his own songs which had exactly the qualities de Maré was looking for', and whose name was Cole Porter. For de Maré, Cole Porter wrote *Within the Quota*, a ballet which told the story of a young Swede and his adventures on arriving in New York. The score, says Milhaud, captured the essence of Manhattan with its nostalgic blues and throbbing ragtime tempo. To close this pleasant interlude, it is only necessary to add that the everobliging Charles Koechlin orchestrated the work in a tone of complete sympathy with Broadway rhythms of a more boisterous nature than the fugue and counterpoint of which he was a master.

Only a few weeks later the protean Milhaud, having exorcized his jazz demon, appeared on the bills of the Opéra-Comique. His entry into that venerable establishment was occasioned by the first performance of *la Brebis égarée,* an opera he had written before the war to a libretto by Francis Jammes. This work, it will be remembered, was the cause of his meeting with the poet, whose verse he had admired from youth. The plot, one of those commonplace tales that Jammes, as if accepting a challenge, delighted to transform with his rare poetic gift, awakened Milhaud's lyrical urge. His setting had warmth and expansiveness. The audience at the Opéra-Comique, more used to the less demanding pleasures of Massenet and Gounod, were little pleased with this story of a Biblical 'lost sheep'. There was uproar during the first act and police had to be called in. The management was terrified, though the conductor riposted with an angry rebuke to the audience. *La Brebis égarée* achieved no more than five performances. Milhaud was still not respectable.

8

THE BLUE TRAIN – *SALADE – LES BICHES* – BORES AND BIRDSELLERS – SATIE IS DISPLEASED

I

ONE evening early in the twenties a lady prepared for a visit to the Opéra. She was known to her parents as 'Gabrielle', to her three thousand employees as 'Mademoiselle', and to the rest of the world as 'Coco' Chanel. As she was running her bath the geyser exploded and covered her with debris. When she had wiped off the dirt she found that half her hair was missing. There was no time to lose. Calmly, she snipped off the ragged ends and washed what remained. Her entry at the Opéra was sensational. Next day there was hardly a chignon to be seen in Paris. The mode for short hair had begun.

From 1920 onwards Chanel had been a queen of Paris. Her origins – she came from the bleak and distant Auvergne – were suitably mysterious, and no one has yet been able to establish her precise age. She was reputed to be the daughter of a wine merchant who died when she was six years old. Of her mother there was no mention. She liked to foster the legend that she was brought up by two spinster aunts. At the age of fifteen, it is said – and she did not deny the romantic tale – she was abducted from Vichy by a dashing army officer. Many other men fell in love with her dark complexion. She was launched on the Parisian scene by a wealthy admirer who, as a means of keeping her occupied and free from temptation, set her up with a clothes shop in Deauville. There she had her first inspiration: pullovers for women. Within twenty-four hours the season's fashion leaders were sporting the novel garment on the promenade.

When Chanel arrived on the scene the star of Paul Poiret was already declining. For years he had dictated the fashions of Paris. He dressed his clients in swathes of expensive material bearing multi-hued designs of oriental inspiration. The colours he used were rich and exotic. The friend and patron of Derain and Vlaminck, he also commissioned Raoul Dufy to experiment with new textiles. He was a master of the lavish gesture. The receptions he gave were famous for their extravagance. One such was 'The Thousand and First Night', when his guests wore sumptuous Persian costumes and were ushered into their host's presence by a Negro wearing a gold tunic. In the park attached to his eighteenth-century country house pink ibis wandered over the turf with a melancholy eye. On a blue and gold dais the 'Sultan' received his friends. In the next room his 'Sultana', barred inside a golden cage, toyed with a parrot. The garden was turned into an Eastern souk where domestics sprayed scent over the delighted crowd, and a girl, naked save for a pearl in her nostril, danced to an invisible orchestra. But time was running out for Poiret. The revolutionary simplicity of Chanel's ideas triumphed over his preference for the elaborate. 'Until recently women were beautiful and statuesque, like the prow of a ship,' he lamented. 'Now they look like underfed little telegraph boys.'

Poiret had failed to take account of the change in social life : fashionable women, like everyone else, now travelled in buses, crossed Paris in the Métro, and climbed into taxis where there was no room for imposing hats or spectacular robes designed with languid houris in mind. Chanel catered for the new freedom with short dresses, practical trousers, comfortable jackets and neat little cloche hats. The line was youthful. The heavy velvets and rustling silk Poiret loved she replaced with georgette and shantung. Under her guidance complexions which had been noted for their whiteness now showed the effect of the vogue for sun tan. Just as her discovery of short hair had been a happy accident, so her introduction of costume jewellery resulted from chance. Afraid one evening of risking pearls worth many millions, she wore copies instead. So, inevitably, did countless others when the idea became known. They rushed to buy her scent, her cardigans, her jerseys and her unfitted dresses at the boutique she was the first to open. The river of Chanel Number Five has never ceased to flow since.

She set up headquarters in the rue Cambon and took a home in the rue du Faubourg Saint Honoré, near the British Embassy. The house once belonged to the duc de Lauzun, a protégé of the marquise de Pompadour. Since it was classed as a historic monument Chanel was unable to change the green and gold decorations which irritated her, so she concealed the walls behind Coromandel screens. Three colours were predominant: beige, white, and chocolate. Whatever the season, the great bouquets of flowers disposed around her rooms were white. The big Louis XIV chairs were draped in white velvet. From the high windows you could see the terrace, the stone steps and the fountain in the middle of the lawn. The formal garden, stretching across to the avenue Gabriel not far from the Champs-Élysées, ended at a line of century-old trees.

She was small and very slim. Her hair was dark and her eyes shone with a hard brilliance. Her dress was simple and usually black. She spoke quickly, following the line of her thought to a logical conclusion without pausing for chit-chat. Her judgements were swift and firm. At her office in the rue Cambon she was alert and authoritarian, giving her orders with the military incisiveness of a Napoleonic general. Yet with her audacity there went an unexpected shyness. She was happiest in the rue Cambon, despatching her mannequins to the cat-walk as a commander sends off his troops to the attack. Men were fascinated by her combination of stark elegance, haughtiness and timidity. The Duke of Westminster asked her to marry him. 'There have been many Duchesses of Westminster,' she replied. 'There is only one Coco Chanel.'*

Chanel gathered round her figures like Picasso, Stravinsky, Diaghilev and Cocteau. On several occasions she rescued Diaghilev from bankruptcy. She paid Radiguet's medical expenses, and her generosity subsidized many artists including Cocteau. It was her money that financed revivals of *Parade* and *le Sacre du printemps*. This link between high fashion and art, which is, of course, highly suspect to Anglo-Saxons, who are traditionally unable to distinguish between frivolity and lightness of touch, brought about several important productions of the twenties. One of them was the ballet *le Train bleu*. Diaghilev had just discovered a new star who was known to the public as Anton Dolin, and he asked Cocteau to devise a ballet for him. Impressed by Dolin's agile acrobatics, Cocteau produced a scenario having as its subject beach sports in the south of France. The title came from the Blue Train, the

* She later denied the remark. It is, none the less, *ben trovato*.

luxurious equipage that used to whisk the beau monde to the Riviera.

Diaghilev had many problems at this time. Chief among them was Massine's defection to Étienne de Beaumont, whose 'Soirées de Paris', a season of new ballets, threatened to outshine the Ballets Russes. Diaghilev, in vain, warned Poulenc and Auric not to work for his new rival. But he wanted the music for *le Train bleu* in a hurry, so he turned to Milhaud. He knew that the urgency of the task and the light-hearted nature of the ballet would prevent Milhaud from writing a complicated score like that of *l'Homme et son désir* which he had disliked and rejected. So, swallowing the unpalatable fact that Milhaud was already under contract to de Beaumont, he gave him the commission.

'Cette vieillerie,' as Milhaud now dismisses *le Train bleu,* is a delectable period piece. Chanel designed the costumes free of charge. They included a white dress and Suzanne Lenglen bandeau for Nijinska, who danced the part of a tennis champion. For Lydia Sokolova, Chanel invented a pink knitted bathing suit then considered rather daring, a wrap of the inevitable georgette, and a cap of dark suède that quickly became a fashion. As an accessory, she provided one of those heavy pearl stud earrings made of china and coated with wax that she had popularized. Leon Woizikovsky, dressed as a British golfer in pullover and plus-fours, attempted with conspicuous gallantry to smoke a pipe. And Dolin, superbly bronzed to Chanel's great approval, cavorted in a series of breath-taking high leaps that left him with bleeding knees and feet after each performance.

Cocteau described the entertainment as an 'opérette dansée'. He organized his band of gigolos and 'poules – a word whose nearest equivalent would be the dusty phrase 'fast women' – after the style of a fatuous operetta chorus. They struck attitudes taken from coloured picture postcards, and at the end of every scene froze as in a snap-shot. There were numbers imitated from Moulin Rouge quadrilles, set pieces based on Charlie Chaplin slapstick fights, and a grand finale that aped the traditional ending of popular adventure films. It was all very energetic and very camp.

Diaghilev used the ballet to open his Paris season of 1924. He was not very pleased with the scenery, but as there was no time to change it he made the best of a bad job and enlarged a Picasso painting for the curtain. During the overture the audience found themselves staring at two giant and muscular ladies who frolicked beside a Picassoesque sea. As 'Beau Gosse', Anton Dolin made his entry to a bounding piece in three-four time with brusque syncopation effects. Lydia Sokolova as 'Perlouse' fluttered on to a quick little number rather like a children's round. The 'poules' and the gigolos drifted in time with a nonchalant melody that unrolled like waves lapping lazily on the shore, their peaceful evolutions disturbed only by the shadow of an aeroplane chattering overhead. The tennis champion (Nijinska) danced a duet with Beau Gosse, miming the gestures of operetta singers to a pert but not unfeeling tune in the bass. The famous waltz of Perlouse and the golf player (Woizikovsky), where she was thrown up to be caught as she descended by her partner, was an anxious experience for Sokolova : each time she came down she feared that her woollen costume would slip from his grasp . . . but each time he caught her firmly, and the café-concert air ran smoothly to its end. The finale came with a spectacular squabble between the tennis champion and the golfer, for whom Milhaud wrote a 'Fugue de l'engueulade' (or, in the colourful terms of American slang, a 'Bawling-out fugue'), which developed with no less rigour the device he had already incorporated in *la Création du monde*.

The score of *le Train bleu* was written in three weeks between 5 and 20 February. At the same time Milhaud was working on *Salade,* the ballet commissioned from him by Étienne de Beaumont. This he wrote between 15 February and 5 March, and so he always referred to the two works as 'my twins'. *Salade* took its subject from an episode in the Commedia dell'Arte called *Insalata*. The titles, both in French and Italian, have a secondary meaning which may be politely rendered as hash-up, mess, or disorder. They are entirely suited to a plot of daunting complications, an imbroglio involving the intrigues of rival lovers, the outwitting of stupid guardians, and a scene where the leading characters, dressed for some arcane reason as Peruvians, dance a tango. Like Stravinsky's *Pulcinella*, *Salade* is described as a 'ballet chanté', and, again following Stravinsky's example, Milhaud utilized some old Italian music, adding to it a few serenade themes he had noted down while in Sardinia. The choreography was devised by Massine, who himself danced Punchinello.

The 'marche-ouverture' sets the tone with its comic pompous rhythms and vivid colouring. By contrast, the heroine Rosetta is personified in a charming little berceuse. The boastful swagger of Captain Cartuccia, with whom Rosetta is being forced into marriage by her ambitious father, is amusingly portrayed in a thumping march tune with interjections by the chorus who relate Cartuccia's current adventure :

> Le Capitain' fait la cour à la mère
> Mais couche avec la fille au blanc museau !
> De la mère il reçoit plus d'un cadeau
> Mais à la fille il en fait un plus beau !

['The Captain courts the Mother but sleeps with the white-faced Girl ! From the Mother he gets many a present, but to the Girl he gives a much finer one !'] Coviello, servant to Rosetta's father, engineers with Figaro-like ingenuity the counterplots which enable both Rosetta and her friend Isabella to marry the men of their choice. The dance numbers, to which the various characters in bewildering disguise play out their intrigues, include a polka, a burlesque tango ('Souvenir de Rio'), and a maxixe, where the composer draws amusedly on his Brazilian memories. The finale is impatient and gaily percussive.

With scenery and costumes by Braque to match its bubbling gaiety, *Salade* brought the sparkle of southern sunshine to de Beaumont's 'Soirées de Paris'. A few years later, when Milhaud was invited to compose a new work he could play on an American tour, he went back to the ballet and took from it twelve items which he arranged for piano and orchestra. He called his suite *le Carnaval d'Aix*. It has deservedly become one of his most popular works. The overture served as an evocation of the busy cours Mirabeau in his native town, and, with a little readjustment, the movements stood for portraits of the characters from the Commedia dell'Arte. The piano is used as leading instrument rather than as the star of the proceedings, since Milhaud as soloist had no pretensions to virtuosity. The sprightly humour of the piece and its Italian verve make it very pleasant listening. Such was its appeal that in 1935 even the Opéra could no longer resist it, and the ballet version was given there with choreography by Lifar, to be revived after the war in 1948.

11

It was Satie who had brought Milhaud into favour with Diaghilev. In the unexpected role of a subtle and tactful diplomatist, the first and only time doubtless that he had ever played the part, Satie persuaded the impresario to commission recitatives from Milhaud for a production of Chabrier's *Une Éducation manquée*. He cunningly pointed out that the need to adapt Chabrier's style would keep Milhaud in check and stop him writing the sort of music Diaghilev found little to his taste. At last Satie triumphed, Milhaud overcame his earlier hesitation, and at rehearsals Diaghilev was unable to tell the difference between genuine Chabrier and the article manufactured by Milhaud.

Satie, Auric and Poulenc were all engaged on similar tasks for Diaghilev at the time. The idea of producing three delightful little Gounod operas, those in which the composer's talent is most exquisitely displayed – *le Médecin malgré lui, Philémon et Baucis,* and *la Colombe* – called for music to be written for the spoken passages. Satie took on the first of the operas ('doing a Gounod', he called it), Auric worked on the second, and Poulenc tackled the third. More important was the original work that occupied Poulenc for the moment. This was a ballet he had suggested to Diaghilev, who took up the notion with enthusiasm and also kept nagging him impatiently to finish it. It was to be called *les Demoiselles,* and Diaghilev, always aware of the latest trend in art, wanted Marie Laurencin to design it.

Marie Laurencin, in her person, was the incarnation of femininity. Her creole ancestry showed in her sallow complexion and the fizzy hair that Apollinaire described as 'black as a forest by night'. Her eyes twinkled darkly from a slim oval face. The lips were full and mischievous. When the Douanier Rousseau painted her with Apollinaire, he measured the size of her nose, mouth, ears, forehead and body, and transferred the proportions scrupulously to his canvas. Finding her a little thin, he plumped her out in the folds of a capacious dress. The matronly figure he drew missed entirely the charm, the lightness, the vivacious look of Marie, whom he gave the appearance of a barmaid or of some gorgon behind a post-office counter.*

Marie knew little about her father. It is said that he came from Picardy. Her mother, who was Norman with a dash of creole, brought her up as a child in the most respectable fashion. The little girl – and a little girl she remained in many ways for the rest of her life – wore neatly hand-embroidered collars and white gloves. With her mother, who gave her the name of Laurencin, she had a deep and affectionate relationship untouched by jealousy. Marie loved feminine things : silken threads, pearls, cotton reels, which she took away and hid, adding them to a little store she would meditate over in solitude. At school she discovered the queens of France and mused for hours over their pictures in the history books. From Clotilde by way of Sainte Radégonde, Bertrade de Léon, Adelaïde d'Anjou, Marguerite de Provence, Charlotte de Savoie and on to Louise de Lorraine-Vaudémont, the music of their names filled her with a mysterious excitement. She read a lot, devouring in her quiet little room all the books that came her way. Her favourite was *Bleak House,* which she read and re-read at least five or six times. After Dickens she acquired a passion for Jane Austen and Virginia Woolf. In later years she carefully bound her books to harmonize with the colour schemes of her home. As a child she was made to read aloud, usually from Racine, and to this she owed perhaps her clear bright speaking voice.

On 14 July each year she would slip out and wander along the banks of the Seine, 'my river' as she called it, listening to popular songs and watching people dance in the streets. She was riding on top of a horse-drawn omnibus, peering at the upper windows of the houses she passed, when the succession of dark interiors, with their glimpses of the shadowed life that went on within, gave her the idea of painting. For a time she went to art school. The teachers repelled her with their cold pedantry. On her own, she discovered the drawings of Kate Greenaway and was enchanted by their quaint costumes, tremulous lines and gentle colouring. She evolved her own style and created a dream world of fluffy ladies vanishing into the mist on the

* Apollinaire disliked the picture, refused to work with it in the house, and eventually sold it to a dealer.

backs of elegant horses. It was a universe where pensive girls caught the attention with their big eyes and melancholy mouths. Doves fluttered indistinctly and fawns glided playfully through a haze of soft colour.

Marie was elusive. 'Loves luxury,' she said of herself. 'Very proud of having been born in Paris. Knows all the tunes in *Sylvia*. Likes neither speeches, rebukes, nor advice, not even compliments. Eats quickly, walks quickly. Paints very slowly.' When she wanted to, though, she could be decisive. Lady Cunard, dissatisfied with the portrait she had done of her, sent it back with the complaint that the horse on which she was shown posing was not a good likeness. Marie tartly changed the horse into a camel and proposed to exhibit the picture. (The visual pun was particularly offensive, as 'chameau' is a very rude thing to call a lady.) Lady Cunard quickly repented and commissioned her to decorate a ballroom.

Was it the thought of her obscure father that caused Marie to emphasize her feminine qualities? She disliked painting portraits of men and always charged extra when asked to do so. Their roughness displeased her. They were out of place in her little home, where fragile knick-knacks decorated the shelves and the mild tones of a clavichord were often heard. Yet her piquant beauty, her tantalizing 'little girl' mannerisms made her very popular with men and correspondingly detested by women. The latter doubtless saw, with their clearer eyes, the shrewdness that lay beneath Marie's studied naïveté. If she was capable of declaring that she would only accept the Légion d'honneur if the ribbon were pink, a favourite colour, she was hard-headed enough to make a good living from her reputation in fashionable society for portraits that were meticulously detailed, bland, pretty, and unlifelike.

In 1907 Picasso told Apollinaire that he had discovered a 'fiancée' for him and introduced him to Marie. Apollinaire inaugurated their acquaintance by lending her books by Thomas Hardy and Sacher Masoch. The choice of authors was appropriate to a poet of catholic taste who wrote erotic novels on the side. After this original beginning they lived together for some time. He adored her. 'She is gay,' he exulted, 'she is kind, she is witty, she is like a little sun, she's a feminine version of myself.' She made him sick with jealousy. He introduced her to his painter friends and Braque praised her talent. There were evenings when Max Jacob, Picasso and Apollinaire would chatter and argue long into the night while Marie, bored by their craze for Negro art, sat in a corner reading Marivaux. After his friends had gone the burly poet would make love to his delicate mistress in an armchair. His bed, which he compulsively kept unwrinkled and immaculate, he chastely reserved for sleep.

In the autumn of 1912 Marie brutally shattered the idyll. She fell in love with a German artist and married him. On the outbreak of war the couple fled to Spain, where Marie introduced her new acquisition as 'My husband, a Hun!' The French government smartly impounded as enemy property all the paintings she had left behind and auctioned them. They fetched, with difficulty, the insulting total of thirty francs. After the war she tired of her husband and came back to Paris. They were divorced, and ever afterwards she was fluent in abuse of him. Apollinaire borrowed some of her traits for the character of 'Tristouse Ballerinette' in *le Poète assassiné*, that symbolic fantasy of the poet as a solitary figure abandoned by friends and mistressess, and stoned by an uncomprehending mob. He saw himself as the victim not only of woman's malignity but also of the Baudelairian malediction that hangs over every poet. Marie/Tristouse, he wrote sombrely, had 'the dark and child-like face of women who are destined to make men suffer'. He was not, it should be admitted, the most tactful of suppliants, and she, one cannot deny, was a creature of whim. They doubtless had an equally maddening effect on each other.

Marie's experiences with him did not cure her of a taste for poets, as she soon afterwards began a liaison with the elliptical Saint-John Perse. It would be fascinating to know the story of this episode. Unfortunately that majestic bard does not seem to have spoken about the affair, and it is difficult to see Marie as the inspiration behind the ceremonial obscurity of his verse. In later years she rarely spoke of Apollinaire except to complain about his off-hand manner. Poulenc was one of the few to be privileged with her reminiscences of 'le Mal-aimé'. One Monday afternoon, she told Poulenc, Apollinaire asked her to go out with him. She did not feel like leaving the house and gave as her excuse a trip to the Louvre. At that time the Louvre, in common with other museums, always closed on Mondays. Apollinaire said nothing. A little while later, when friends were talking about the Louvre, he remarked with irony:

'Ah yes, I go there every Monday!' and pointedly avoided Marie's gaze.

Poulenc was also the victim of Marie's playfulness, as Apollinaire must often have been. He was much taken with Apollinaire's *Trois poèmes de Louise Lalanne* and made of them three songs which are among his best. He sent the score to Marie, for whom the words of the first and third poems awakened memories of a distant joke. In 1909, under the name 'Louise Lalanne', Apollinaire contributed articles about women writers to a magazine edited by a friend. Delighted with the success of the trick, Apollinaire promised to write some poetry that could be attributed to 'Louise'. The day came, as it always does for journalists labouring under the tyranny of a deadline, when the 'copy' had to be ready. Apollinaire was short of ideas. Marie searched through her old school exercise books and produced some poems she had written as a girl. Apollinaire chose two of them, added one of his own, and 'Louise' duly contributed on time. Twenty years later Marie was able to tell Poulenc that he had expended a moving simplicity and tenderness on her own schoolgirl verse. Fortunately Poulenc had a sense of humour. She made up for the deception by saying that his music for *le Bestiaire* seemed uncannily to have caught the very tones Apollinaire used in reciting his lines, tones that were deep and melodious. Perhaps she really had loved Apollinaire. When she died the letters he had written her were placed, according to the directions of her will, in her coffin beside the portrait of her mother.

When Diaghilev thought of commissioning Marie to design Poulenc's new ballet, her art was still spontaneous and fresh. The stylized figures had not yet ossified into mannerism, and the hazy colouring was not become a simple mechanical device. After 1930, impelled by commercial success and an astute dealer, she turned out dozens of pictures of dreamy girls floating in pastel tints. (She increased her fees when the subject was a brunette, as she loathed painting black hair.) Diaghilev's flair picked on her when she was at her best. He saw the ballet as a modern *les Sylphides*, a spectacle of atmosphere, and Poulenc supplied what little scenario there was. The original title of *les Demoiselles* was changed, for the better, to *les Biches*. The word means hind or doe, but its zoological flavour has acquired undertones which are nicely shown in the phrase associated with Louis XIV, whose 'parc aux biches' catered for the monarch when he wished to frolic in pastoral surroundings with damsels honoured to be chosen for his pleasure. 'Ma biche' is a term of endearment. 'The Darlings?' Such a phrase is certainly closer than 'House Party', which was the tweedy name for the ballet when given in London.

The atmosphere, said Poulenc, was to be like those 'fêtes galantes' as painted by Watteau. He thought of lords and ladies in trim parks escorted by lute players under shady trees, of couples dallying on mossgrown benches, of flowing dresses that a mischievous breeze occasionally lifted to reveal the gleam of a stocking. Masks and bergomasks danced in an airy vision beneath the moonlit branches, and the scent of roses mingled with the cunning perfumes of a shepherdess in disguise. Eyes glittered perversely behind jewelled fans. Alone in his white-faced melancholy, the clown Gilles sat apart and remembered kisses long ago . . . but the park was chill and frozen now. Everything was suggested, nothing was explicit. A shroud of hints and whispers and murmurs cloaked the scene.

Les Biches, a modern transposition, was set in a spacious country drawing room. The glittering white wall at the back was cut into by a large window suggesting a terrace and formal gardens beyond. The only furniture was a long blue sofa. Marie Laurencin's drop curtain, on which the playful outlines of *biches* gambolled around nymphs and ate out of their hands, played on the twin meanings of the title. She worked at her designs with Poulenc in a house she had taken at Draveil, an old village on the bank of the Seine where the forest of Sénart clusters oak and birch around. Sudden perspectives opened out on to the river, and in May the lily of the valley covered its flanks with a profusion of white.

There was little plot to the ballet. Twelve girls, white plumed and white robed, were joined by three athletic oarsmen. A quartet of women dancers completed the cast. They made advances, withdrew, and re-formed in a series of duos, trios and concerted numbers that followed an ambiguous pattern of flirtation that was not quite innocent. But, as in Watteau, suggestion was all. Nijinsky's sister devised the choreography. Poulenc greatly admired her allusive art: you could, he said, enjoy it equally well, whether you ignored the dancers' gestures or whether you chose to imagine the worst.

The music, which has become well-known as an orchestral suite, was a succession of independent pieces. The overture introduces us to that blend of gaiety and melancholy that flavours the whole work. In the Rondeau that follows – or, at least, in the version Poulenc revised fifteen years later – the orchestration is wittily varied. He is generous of good things to each department of the orchestra. The trumpets are given their chance with attractive solos, while horns, trombones, clarinets and oboes each have a share of the fun. The strings come into their own in the second section with a broad melody that sweeps irresistibly on helped by a solo from the 'cellos. The trumpet briskly returns to lead them all to the final pizzicato.

Next comes a 'Chanson dansée' based on old popular songs in which the tenors, with much rolling of r's and mincing articulation, inquire: 'O, what is Love?' The basses, apart from a few helpful tra-las, are unable to answer this profound question and content themselves with blandly repeating it. To the accompaniment of a bassoon solo, they join with the tenors to hit on a possible solution: Love, they cheerfully trill, is a pussy that's on the watch and will catch you soon. ('Chat' can have the same ribald meaning as in English.) This little bit of nonsense ends with their assuring us that Love and cats like to play together, and that when you flatter them they draw in their claws.

After the brassy fanfares of the 'Chanson dansée', the tones of the famous Adagietto come as a gentle diversion. The oboe first introduces the lovely theme, a tune that looks wistfully back to old, unhappy far-off things. It is preserved from sentimentality by the trumpet, which, cool and silvery, repeats it in accents of precision. After some boisterous passages the bass clarinet, aided later by the horn, emerges and brings the theme back to serenity. Here is the most perfect expression of that 'fêtes galantes' mood Poulenc was aiming at. Regret and tenderness are mingled in exquisite proportion, and the courtly style unites them with fluent grace.

The atmosphere turns swiftly to buffoonery again with 'Jeu'. The gentlemen of the chorus lament the plight of the father who has four daughters to marry off and who doesn't know how he'll manage it. Daughters riposte that they will marry for love. Father enjoins them to obedience. They dream, stubbornly, of the lover who will admire their pretty eyes and

rounded charms in the merry month of May. The debate ends
on a folk tune air with the father still worrying about a house-
full of unmarried girls. They are all brushed aside in the scurry
of a Rag Mazurka that gallops itself at one point into a cake-
walk, takes breath among the lugubrious drone of horn and
bassoon, and subsides uneasily into the woodwind phrases
that link it with the Andantino. This opens on a ravishing
pirouette from the violins. It turns into the melody of the
Adagietto before dissolving in a shimmer of harps leavened by
acid peeps from the woodwind. The vocal chorus have the last
word in their 'Petite chanson dansée' – a last word offering
laurel wreaths to the beloved, and gilly-flowers and capucines
for the marriage – before a whirlwind galop dashes into the
Finale.

From his hotel in Monte Carlo, where the ballet had its
performance, Poulenc wrote jubilantly to a friend :

The first night of *les Biches* was, if I may say so, a triumph. They
had to give eight curtain calls, something which is extremely rare
for Monte Carlo. I must tell you that Nijinska's choreography is
so beautiful that even the old English lady roulette fiend couldn't
resist it. It's the absolute essence of the dance. And the rehearsals
were meticulously done. We had no less than seventy-two of them,
about two hundred and seventy hours' work. That's the way to
produce something worthwhile. The scenery, the curtain, the
costumes are completely successful. I can't wait for you to see it
all. As for the music, although it's immodest to talk to you about
it, I won't hide from you the fact that I'm very pleased with my
orchestration. It's very striking and I think the colouring very
personal. Auric, who is difficult on this point, has given me his
entire approval. . . . Satie was here a few days for his recitatives in
[Gounod's] *le Medécin malgré lui*. I think he was very pleased
if I can judge from his excellent mood during his short stay.

A little more practical than her musician friend, Marie
Laurencin wrote to the composer from Paris :

It seems that *Biches*
move
the *riches*
of Monte Carlo.
It would be so kind of you to ask the Boss where my
sketches are

especially the finished one for the curtain – and a framed
water-colour and the dresses.
It was agreed they should be returned to me.
I'd be glad to be paid, too. And that's it.
I'm delighted with the success. It was none of my doing.
Your music was responsible.
The choreography haunts me
    and the sofa!

This was Marie at her most typical, combining pleasantry with
an ever so slight scratch of the claw.

On holiday in Villefranche, Cocteau, still suffering from the
loss of Radiguet, found a partial remedy in the score of *les
Biches* that Auric played over to him. He wrote of Marie
Laurencin's contribution:

Her scenery and costumes were just right. They firmly under-
lined the action. In front of this artist's pictures we have always
felt the sadness of realizing that plants and animals do not love
us and do not care about us. Perhaps a kiss would break the spell?
Who would dare offer it?

Poulenc was barely twenty-five at the time of this first great
success. He revelled in it with boyish pleasure and talked of his
music with such ingenuousness that no one could have accused
him of boasting. Behind the scenes at the Théâtre de Monte
Carlo, among the dusty potted palms and stacks of scenery, he
spoke about the work to Rollo Myers.* At an old upright
piano he played through the *Adagietto,* pointing out felicities
with unaffected delight and indicating such details of orchestration as the divided violins in the undulating figure it contains.

Les Biches, of course, owes something, as do all works of
art, to others. A passing glance at Mozart, a touch of
Stravinsky here, a whiff of Tchaikovsky and Scarlatti there,
by no means spoil enjoyment of the delicious work. Beneath
the wit and playfulness lies sorrow. The music flows gaily on,
mocking, airy, nervous. It pleases. But it saddens also.

The steps the dancers followed are lost in time. Though
the music remains, we have to imagine the pinks and pale

---

* Rollo Myers was then in Monte Carlo to report *les Biches* for the
Daily Telegraph and did, in fact, write one of the first notices of the
work to appear in the English press.

blues of Marie Laurencin, and the blue velvet costume Vera Nemtchinova wore as she danced the Adagietto.

How rightly Stendhal uses the word sublime! [wrote Cocteau] Nemtchinova's entry is truly sublime (no Wagnerian would understand me). When that little lady emerges on points from the wings, with her long legs, a too-short jerkin, and her right hand, white-gloved, held up near her cheek as if for some sort of military salute, my heart beats more quickly . . .

In Paris the conductor of *les Biches* was André Messager. The choice was a clever move by Diaghilev who counted on Messager's prestige to help the new ballet. A composer of brilliant operetta and a conductor whose name will always be linked with the first performance of *Pelléas et Mélisande,* Messager brought high qualities of professionalism to the score and helped considerably towards its success in the capital. His long years of experience in the theatre were heavily tested at one point: the lights on his desk suddenly failed, and he had to direct the music from memory. The composer of *Monsieur Beaucaire* was unruffled and he guided the orchestra safely to the end of the ballet without losing a single oboe on the way.

Another ballet Diaghilev introduced during his 1924 Monte Carlo season – though it did not enjoy the same enthusiastic reception that greeted *les Biches* – was Georges Auric's *les Fâcheux*. It was taken from the incidental music the composer wrote for a production of the 'comédie-ballet' Molière had quickly thrown together at the order of his patron, Nicolas Fouquet, the unscrupulous and enormously rich minister under Louis XIV. *Les Fâcheux* was given at a lavish entertainment held by Fouquet in the grounds of his magnificent home at Vaux-le-Vicomte. (The king attended, laughed heartily at the play . . . and, a short while after, imprisoned the luckless Fouquet who had shown himself too clever, and tactless, by half.) Molière was given no more than a fortnight to write and produce *les Fâcheux*. It is, under the circumstances, just the sort of thing one would expect from a superb actor-manager. Éraste is anxious to marry Orphise, the ward of Damis. His courtship is persistently interrupted by a series of bores – a stupid marquis, a dancer, a duellist, a card player, two 'précieuses', a huntsman, a pedant, and a mad visionary who tirelessly propounds a scheme for turning the whole of the French coast into seaports.

(It would not be difficult to think of contemporary bores appropriate to a modern version of the play.) Despite all these hindrances, Éraste finally wins approval from Damis for his marriage with Orphise.

The scenario gave Molière and his talented company a chance to display their gift for improvisation and the portrayal of different 'types'. It also implied that there are two sorts of bore: the genuine sort, who will drive you to desperation whenever you have the ill-luck to meet him, and the circumstantial bore, who, though welcome at all other times, happens to catch you at the moment when you are busy with something important. The action of *les Fâcheux*, which is really a procession of grotesques, lends itself well to ballet since it enables the dancers to show off their different styles. In Boris Kochno's arrangement the number of bores was slightly altered to include a pair of gossips, and the corps de ballet was made up of battledore and shuttlecock players and bowlers. The choreography, as for *les Biches*, was the work of Nijinska. Cocteau fancifully suggested that the dance was dictated by the interplay of beige, yellow, maroon and grey which arose from Braque's costumes and scenery. 'Houses grow, windows take on life, trees breathe,' he commented.

An overture of metallic brilliance leads to the opening scene, where, in the play, Éraste complains to his servant in tones that will find a sympathetic response today:

> Sous quel astre, bon Dieu, faut-il que je sois né,
> Pour être de fâcheux toujours assassiné!

The music here chatters out the staccato figure which has dominated the overture and which deftly imitates the remorseless drone of all the bores who ever lived. Having despatched his servant to bring Orphise to him, Éraste is confronted with the first of his tormentors, the dancer Lysandre. He makes his bow to a charming pastiche in eighteenth-century style and then launches into a dance with music far too graceful, one feels, for such a tiresome creature. Next, the devotees of battledore and shuttlecock rush on and engulf Éraste in their turbulence. While they are milling about Orphise makes a discreet entry. She dances a slow, elaborate and much ornamented number, but is frightened off by the arrival of the two loquacious gossips. The stage becomes more crowded still with the bowlers. They are accompanied by what sounds to the wondering ear like a parody, mischievous or otherwise, of the allegretto grazioso theme played by flute and oboe in the third movement of Dvorak's G major symphony. Éraste's tribulations are still not ended, for now the card player trips on to add to the bustle going on all round him.

At last the bores withdraw. Orphise returns and is left alone for a few minutes to dance a slow Satiesque number with Éraste. Her guardian Damis appears. Éraste's servant, helped by his mates, falls on Damis and threatens him. Éraste, with ostentatious bravery, rescues Damis from the mob. This piece of cunning stage-management misleads Damis, who, impressed by Éraste's gallantry, consents to his marrying Orphise. Thudding brass chords in the orchestra announce the return of each and every bore. At first terrified by the noise of the skirmish, they soon are able to strut in all their old glory, vying among themselves as to who shall be the most *fâcheux*. The lovers are united while the music slips into a rondo, complete with Alberti bass, repeating the theme of Lysandre's dance. As Damis gives them his blessing trumpets shriek the clattering tune of the overture and the curtain falls.*

Les Fâcheux was composed with the ready craftsmanship of those adaptable eighteenth-century musicians who were prepared to turn out a masque, an opera, a pageant or a little light music whenever their royal masters commanded. That, indeed, is the sort of role Auric would have filled had he lived in those days. It is not a dishonourable one. One can see him, amiable in his peruke, doling out the hastily-written parts to the members of his orchestra and urging them on in their last-minute tasks with humour and a wit that was cat-like. Tragedy, comedy, history, pastoral, pastoral-comical, historical-pastoral, tragical-historical . . . there would surely, in Hamlet's words, be nothing he could not have put his hand to with cheerful expertness. If his courtly audience did not like what he put before them, he would have shrugged his shoulders and studied their tastes – and his – more carefully in the future. Where Poulenc, however clumsily on occasion, expressed himself in what he wrote, Auric was quite happy to produce well-tailored music, neatly honed and pleasantly witty, that did not seek to rise above

* The concert transcription for piano, made later by Auric, included three of the items from the ballet.

the nature of a *divertissement*. If in some respects this was a failing, it became a strength in the field where he was tending more and more to specialize : that of incidental music, which demands qualities of unobtrusive suggestion, fast-moving variation and fleet allusiveness.

Something of the misfortune that besieged its sponsor after the first production of Molière's play seems to have clung to the emergence of *les Fâcheux* as a ballet. Diaghilev liked the way Braque's scenery had been executed deliberately to give the impression of a sketch, though not everyone approved it. There was sharp disagreement between Nijinska and Boris Kochno, whose suggestions were often angrily ignored by the choreographer. Diaghilev, too, had his criticisms, and the three of them would argue long after rehearsals had been interrupted and the dancers sent away. The steamy atmosphere of the Ballets Russes, hot with intrigue and simmering with jealousy, was luxuriant of venomous duels between warring camps. Nijinska gradually lost interest and even gave way to requests that Dolin, as Éraste, should make his entry on 'points', like a ballerina. When, a few years later, Massine revised the ballet, he had little more success in evolving a satisfactory plan of the dance.

Auric, Poulenc and Milhaud were the only members of the Six to be commissioned by Diaghilev. He could not be expected to find what he wanted in the music of Honegger, who was more at ease with Rolf de Maré and the Ballets Suèdois for whom he wrote *Skating Rink*. Durey was by this time immured in Saint-Tropez. Germaine Tailleferre, though equally ignored by the Ballets Russes, did, however, work for Rolf de Maré. Her ballet was called *Marchand d'oiseaux* and showed, as had *les Fâcheux,* a modish partiality for the eighteenth-century harpsichordists. The overture, with its figurations coming straight from Domenico Scarlatti, might have been taken for a modern orchestration of some unpublished sonata tricked out with the 'wrong notes' that had, in the twenties, become obligatory. The curtain rose on the house of two sisters, the elder proud, the younger modest. Someone has left at their front door two bouquets of flowers. The elder sister chooses the smarter and more expensive one. True to character, her junior prefers the humble bunch of wild flowers. The charm of the scene is somewhat diluted, for Anglo-Saxon ears at least, by the tune of the slow waltz. Its opening bars have a disconcerting kinship with Eric Coates's 'A Sleepy Lagoon'. A snatch of chorale brings on a crocodile of convent-children walking to church. Their orderly ranks are scattered by a mob of school-boys, who, stepping out the rhythms of the overture, drag them into a round. The bird-seller of the title, young and handsome, enters to a pavane. The elder sister snubs him. The young one smiles at him. A richly dressed stranger appears. The haughty sister makes up to him. One of the schoolboys mischievously rips off the stranger's mask to reveal an aged, ugly merchant of the neighbourhood. While the elder sister flees away in shame, her younger sister and the bird-seller dance a triumphant finale, 'très vite', over which the shade of old Domenico tenaciously hovers.

A more substantial work than the *Marchand d'oiseaux* was the piano concerto that Germaine Tailleferre wrote at about the same time. Again, the Scarlatti figuration recurs, in this instance as the propelling force of the opening movement. Piano and orchestra dialogue in the best of good humour until they suddenly tire of their play and finish abruptly. The finest moments in the concerto are provided by the adagio, which moves gently forward with a long-breathed Ravellian melody. The finale returns to the earlier mood of glancing haste, verges hesitantly on fugue, changes its mind, and plumps straight into the concluding D major chord. Though no less accomplished an exercise, Tailleferre's *Ballade* for piano and orchestra, which was published in the same year as the Marchand *d'oiseaux,* is subtler than the concerto. The ideas are worked out in greater depth, the invention is longer sustained, and themes are treated with a degree of ingenuity that shows a thoughtful acquaintance with the resources both of the piano and the orchestra.

Tailleferre was never as close to Satie as Auric, Milhaud and Poulenc were. Her master was Ravel. She was luckier in her choice of mentor than were her colleagues of the Six. Milhaud was the only one with whom the umbrageous Satie did not quarrel. The happy days of Monte Carlo in 1924, when he applauded *les Biches* and *les Fâcheux*, were succeeded by a number of incidents which permanently estranged him from Poulenc and Auric. The first of these concerned his umbrella, an article of furniture to which, it will be remembered, Satie was devotedly attached. It had a sacred character for him. One day Auric, quite accidentally, thrust his own umbrella into Satie's where it reposed on a stand. He was immediately showered with a spray of invective. 'Guttersnipe! Boor! Hooli-gan!' screamed Satie beside himself.

Worse still, *les Biches* and *les Fâcheaux* had been warmly praised by the critic Louis Laloy, who became a close friend of Poulenc and Auric. Now Laloy was regarded by Satie as an enemy. What right did he have to come between Satie and his friends? The old man jealously warned Poulenc about his choice of companions. Soon afterwards Auric was unwary enough to express some reserves in an article he wrote on Satie's music. The published reaction was furious. Satie observed:

Very good, my little friend. Let him carry on; let him 're-Laloy' himself from top to bottom. Oh yes. What was my crime? I didn't like his faked-up, re-jigged *Fâcheux*. Those who say my late friend is nothing but a twerp exaggerate; he is, very simply, just an Auric (Georges) – which is already more than enough for one man (?) alone.

Auric knew his Erik and refused to lose his temper at this pettish onslaught. At about this time Poulenc went into a shop to buy some counters for the poker games he was in the habit of playing with Auric, Honegger and the singer Claire Croiza. He was transfixed at the sight of a child's rattle on the counter. There was something about the head which decorated it that reminded him irrevocably of a friend he knew well. The lurking malice, the quizzical eye, were Satie to the life. Auric hurried in and purchased the bauble. With Poulenc's approval he wrapped it up and posted it to Arcueil. They could not resist the joke. But Satie could. He promptly transferred his patronage to another group of young composers who were hailed for a time as 'l'école d'Arcueil'. The better-known members were Roger Désormière – the genial 'Déso' who won fame as a conductor – and Henri Sauguet. Another was Maxime Jacob, who is not to be confused with the poet of *le Cornet à dés*. A further misleading resemblance is that he, too, was a Jewish convert to Catholicism. He did something Max would dearly have loved to do by entering the Benedictine Order. After writing incidental music for an unholy piece by Alfred Jarry, and for a light comedy by Marcel Achard, he became 'Dom Clément', found an austerer muse in Paul Claudel, and was noted for the purity of his organ playing in the monastery church of En-Calcat.

Milhaud alone of the Six retained Satie's friendship. Auric and Poulenc were never forgiven. When Satie was ailing and near the end a mutual acquaintance, Raymonde Linossier, tried to reconcile him with them. The musician remained proud and incorrigible. Had he not carried on his feud with Debussy right up to the latter's deathbed? Had not Debussy's quavering hand fumbled at Satie's letter of reproach as, with tears in his eyes, he murmured: 'Forgive me'? Why should two saucy young rogues be treated differently? 'What's the point of my seeing them again?' he inquired irritably. 'Debussy died without my seeing *him* again, didn't he?'

9

MERCURY – DADA, A FILM, AND *RELÂCHE* – SATIE GOES

I

In the few months of life that remained to him Satie was responsible for two more ballets. The first of these was *Mercure*. The second, *Relâche,* confirmed his reputation among detractors as a jesting nincompoop.

Mercure, like Milhaud's *Salade,* was written for Étienne de Beaumont's 'Soirées de Paris', which were still unsettling audiences with a string of incongruous spectacles. One evening there was a Cocteau adaptation of *Romeo and Juliet* which was startling in concept and strange in its all-black setting. Another evening saw the Dadaist grotesqueries of Tristan Tzara's *Mouchoir de nuage* hurled across the footlights. By comparison with Dadaism, a movement that sought the violent destruction of all values and conventions, *Mercure* seemed positively harmless. Indeed, much of its primly academic character helped to strengthen this impression of innocence.

The rehearsals were held, as was normal for the 'Soirées de Paris', in the comte de Beaumont's own home. In the eighteenth century it had been the Spanish Embassy. Ballet troupes invaded the salon and tried out their fouettés, avoiding by a hair's breadth the fragile Empire chairs that cowered beneath outflung legs. Sketches for scenery were poised precariously beside Monet landscapes on the wall, and Spanish antique chests were negligently strewn with rehearsal clothes. At the end of it all the 'artistes de la danse', more accustomed to the dehydrated sandwiches and bitter coffee of stage-doorkeepers' fare, were rewarded with collations of cold pheasant and the best champagne.

Picasso designed the scenery and costumes for *Mercure.* They

were elaborate affairs, ranging from pin-headed trellis-work con-
structions to airy charioteers and horses traced in fascinating
curlicues. Elaborate and sophisticated, they clashed sharply with
the music. As if to emphasize his stubborn independence, Satie
had written a score that was belligerently simple. It was dedicated to de Beaumont's wife and opened with a 'marche-
ouverture' of modest, almost self-effacing proportions which
seem appropriate to its noble dedicatee. The 'Danse de
tendresse' of Apollo and Venus is a café-concert waltz purified
of its gross associations and bearing directions such as 'Caressant', 'Très chanté' and 'très expressif' which are more the
trademark of Massenet than of Satie. The Signs of the Zodiac
come out and surround the two dancers. Mercury arrives. In
his jealousy he cuts the thread of Apollo's life and then, with
his magical powers, restores him. The scene ends with a return
to the 'marche-ouverture'. The second tableau shows the
Graces bathing. The eight bars, once repeated, of the 'Bain
des grâces', have a dazzling 'whiteness', a slow and steady movement that suggest the perpetual opening up of new vistas. It
is music that could be played endlessly. Although, of course,
there is progression, the total effect is of a hardly perceptible
stirring.

While the Graces are disporting themselves in the water –
which we know, from the music, must be crystal-clear and
hardly rippled by any wave – Mercury steals their pearls and
is chased away by an angry Cerberus. In the third tableau
Bacchus throws a party. Mercury invents some new dances to
entertain the guests, including a 'Polka des lettres' in which an
impertinent little tune preens itself on the trumpet. It is succeeded by the graver measures of the 'Nouvelle danse'. The
'Chaos' which follows is created by a cold-blooded mingling
of elements from the 'Polka des lettres' and the 'Nouvelle Danse'.
Finally, Proserpine is abducted by Pluto with the aid of Chaos
and a fast march rhythm.

Mercure, sub-titled 'Poses plastiques en trois tableaux', was
given at the Théâtre de la Cigale on 15 June 1924. This time
it was not the respectable bourgeois who protested but a group
of Surrealists in the audience. 'Long live Picasso !' they bellowed.
'Down with Satie.' Their disturbance forced the management
to lower the curtain in the middle of the show, after which
the performance was allowed to reach its end. Satie, unmoved

by the sudden enmity of the Surrealists, who were doubtless as vague about their motive as was everyone else, sat quietly in his box with Milhaud. He left in time to catch the last train to Arcueil. 'When I came out of the theatre,' he wrote to Milhaud next day, 'I passed a group of would-be Dadaists. They didn't say anything to me.' Milhaud's own ballet *Salade,* which followed on an evening soon after, was troubled by annoyances more traditional than aesthetic. A musicians' strike ten minutes before curtain-rise made it necessary for him to accompany his ballet at the piano by candle-light.

The accusations of fairground jokery left Satie apparently indifferent. He was used to them by now. If anything, they encouraged him to further audacity, and *Relâche* deserves to be counted among those works of his that most outraged opinion. The original idea came from Blaise Cendrars, who gave it to his old friend Satie as the subject of a ballet for Rolf de Maré. Then Cendrars went off on one of his trips to Brazil, and while he was away Francis Picabia stepped in, added all sorts of notions of his own and generally transformed Cendrars' contribution into a Dadaist free-for-all. Picabia was an artist, poet, novelist and showman of flamboyant techniques. As a young man he studied with Pissarro and was influenced by Sisley. The early pictures he exhibited were heavily Impressionistic. His talent was so diffuse that within a bewilderingly short space of time he painted in styles that could be variously identified as belonging to Orphism, Cubism, Abstraction, Dada and Surrealism. With the painters Marcel Duchamp and Fernand Léger he established a small but influential group who founded the 'Section d'Or'. With the writers Tristan Tzara, André Breton and Philippe Soupault, he inaugurated the technique of 'mots dans le chapeau'. They argued that over the centuries words had become worn-out and rusty with the passage of time and ill-usage by mediocre writers. There was a need, they claimed, to put words in new settings for them to shine again with unexpected brilliance, as a jeweller gives diamonds fresh lustre by rearranging them. The method Picabia and his friends chose was to scribble words on bits of paper and throw them into a hat. After shaking them up the scraps were picked out and sentences were constructed which faithfully respected the chance order in which the words emerged. The idea had a logical beauty about it. The results had not.

Picabia read very little, and, like most good revolutionaries of the time, attacked with rich and foul invective writing by Gide, Proust and Valéry of which he had never perused a single word. His own poetry, which at its best attains a refreshing jauntiness, often is flavoured with the sharp tang of wisecracks. He will write sardonically :

> On peut tout demander
> à une femme
> quand elle est nue
> et qu'elle pense
> à sa lointaine destinée.

He was ready with salon wit to explain the title of his poem, 'Jesus Christ rastaquouère'. (A *rastaquouère* is a flashy adventurer who lives by his wits.) To those who reproached him with sacrilege, he answered : 'Look up *rastaquouère* in the dictionary. You'll find it means : a person who has no visible means of support. Isn't that precisely the case with God?'

Picabia was rich – a circumstance that endeared him not at all to his friends in rebel literary groups. It exasperated his enemies, who saw in this unjust dispensation of fate another good reason for detesting him. In his time he owned more than a hundred motor cars and drove them with the panache of a film star. When anything went wrong with his current model, he bought another, preferably a Rolls Royce. He also had three yachts which he named, with a pleasing simplicity, l'Horizon I, l'Horizon II, and l'Horizon III. On one of them he abducted a newly-married bride who had taken his fancy. The husband later joined them in response to a friendly telegram from Picabia. He then departed to catch his last train home, leaving his wife behind. She stayed on for months, during which time she had the engines taken out of the yacht. They wasted space, she said, and their removal enabled her to get on with keeping sheep aboard the vessel.

When he tired of the lady and her sheep, Picabia retreated to his country house near Antibes. It stood on a hill surrounded by cemeteries. People who saw in this yet another example of a Dada whim for the macabre were cheerfully corrected by Picabia. They were, he said, fake cemeteries. The fields where he had set them up belonged to him. The idea was to force down the price of neighbouring properties he wanted to buy.

His house, known as the château de Mai, was run on informal lines. Chickens wandered curiously from room to room. There was even a ghost which the owner had designed with mechanical expertise so that it stalked through the night clanking noisy chains. He had done this in order to instil fearlessness in his children. When they grew up he intended to replace the ghost with 'a creditor waving an unpaid bill'. His studio was a vast shed where he covered his canvases with ordinary house paint which he had chosen because of its durability. This he mixed with aviation fuel, afterwards varnishing the completed picture with car polish that never turned yellow and protected his work. Down in his garage stood a decade of Ford motor cars. He found them so reliable that he bought them in groups of ten at a time. It was a highly practical move, he argued, since you could buy ten Fords at the price of a single Hispano. 'Wouldn't you rather have ten Fords than just one Hispano?' he asked persuasively. 'Of course you would . . .' Thirty years later, in 1953, he had nothing left of an immense fortune which only the most tenacious effort could have squandered. He died at the age of seventy-four, paralysed, speechless and destitute.

With Picabia in charge of the revels it was inevitable that *Relâche* would lead to another of those enjoyable 'scandals' which André Breton and his friends of the Twenties were so adept at engineering. As Breton wrote in his *Second manifeste du Surréalisme:*

It must be recognized that the primary aim of all Dada spectacles has always been to cause the greatest possible confusion, and that in the minds of the organizers it was a matter of nothing so much as creating the highest pitch of misunderstanding between performer and audience.

One of the devices Picabia intended to utilize for this inspired purpose was the projection of a film during the interval 'to clear the auditorium'. He asked a journalist called René Clair to make it for him. Born René Chomette, the son of a provincial wholesaler established in Paris, Clair had celebrated his twentieth birthday on the day of the Armistice in 1918. His impression of the victory parade was coloured by sombre memories, still fresh, of service on the battlefield. One of the poems he wrote then contained the lines :

Mon ami mort était couché
tout au long des Champs-Élysées.

He also contributed a few songs to the repertory of Damia,
a popular singer nicknamed the 'Duse of the music hall'. As
film critic on a Paris newspaper he was already engaged in the
sphere that appealed to him most of all. In 1920 he made
several appearances in films produced by the dancer Loïe Fuller
and by Louis Feuillade, the sponsor of those interminable *Fantômas* serials that enthralled the Surrealists. Three years later he
was behind the camera for good and working on his own
production, *Paris qui dort*, the first of many films which, in
their unique and stylish manner, were to be admired and
widely imitated, not least by Charlie Chaplin.

Picabia's commission was a piece of luck. The young cinéaste
hastily engaged a cameraman, two assistants and a props
manager. One of the most delicate administrative tasks was
to find somewhere at night to garage the cumbersome hearse,
and the camel that drew it, which the scenario demanded. This
scenario, scribbled by Picabia on Maxim's writing paper, suggested an opening scene in which a cannon was fired. Later
events included a chess match, a hose that gets out of hand and
drenches the actors (a reminiscence of Lumière's early film
l'Arroseur arrosé), two marksmen aiming at an ostrich egg, a
bearded dancer slowly revolving on a transparent rostrum, and a
funeral procession led by the famous camel and hearse. 'I gave
René Clair a tiny scenario made out of a trifle,' exclaimed
Picabia, 'and he turned it into a masterpiece : *Entr'acte*. The
entr'acte in *Relâche* is a film that translates our dreams and the
events, as yet unmaterialized, that happen in our minds; why
relate what everyone sees – or can see every day?'

The opening scenes of *Entr'acte* reward the alert viewer with
the sight of Picabia and a bowlered, bearded Satie admiring
a cannon on a Paris roof top. The composer raises his umbrella and indicates a distant target. Stern and dignified, he
convinces Picabia that the deed must be done. Picabia opens
the breech and Satie hands him the shell. The cannon is fired
and the two conspirators hop about in joy. A ballerina, whose
pince-nez and false beard recall the amateur gunner of the
previous scene, turns remorselessly in her tutu. Man Ray and
Marcel Duchamp play chess. Jean Börlin, wearing hunter's

rig and a hat with a feather in it, shoots a pigeon. From time to time it is possible to catch glimpses of Rolf de Maré and a young Marcel Achard. The grand finale is the progress of the hearse, which carries a wreath bearing a monogram linking the initials of Erik Satie and Francis Picabia. The leader of the procession, an official personage in three-cornered hat, sets off in slow motion at the head of the mourners. Camel and hearse break into an accelerated rhythm and as they sway dizzily along a suburban road everyone runs to keep up. The conveyance lurches into a fairground and whizzes on to a scenic railway. From there it gains the open country and comes to rest in a field. The coffin opens and a man springs out. He is Jean Börlin, now transformed into a magician. A few waves of his wand and everyone vanishes. He gives a last flourish and disappears too.

While René Clair devoted himself to the search for the novel close-up and the startling trick effect, Picabia was spattering Paris with declarations and manifestos each as joyfully pointless as the other.

The air needs cleaning, the air is stagnant; you talk too much. Be quiet and do something, or go to see *Relâche.... Relâche* isn't art. *Relâche* isn't a false pearl. No more art, just life, the joy of instantaneous invention. MONTPARNASSE, you must create the *REVOLUTION* and throw all old conventions into the sewer. *There is no more painting, no more literature, no more music* with a big P a big L and a big M. This manifesto is dedicated to the people whose country is THE WORLD and whose ideal: THE SUN. FRANCIS PICABIA invites you to go and see *Relâche* on the 27 November, the seats are cheaper than in PARADISE.

As for the action of the ballet, Picabia described it in the form of a riddle: 'My first is a pretty woman wearing a dress and a coat by Jacques Doucet. My second is a handsome fellow brilliant as a diamond. My third is a fireman wearing the Légion d'honneur, and he's here in case of fire!* My fourth is a camel. My fifth are men in evening clothes. My sixth is the

---

* *Pompier* = fireman – and is also a slangy word of abuse of outdated artistic convention – doubtless a cheeky reference to the audience Picabia expected, many of whom would have the Légion d'honneur and be representative of official morality. At one point in the ballet a fireman does indeed wander across the stage.

dog's tail. My whole is a success. What is it?' The answer is *Relâche,* with its pretty woman who has a 'dance without music', its men wearing evening dress and its film entr'acte featuring a camel. The reference to the dog's tail is a private joke which no one ever grasped. Picabia described *Relâche* as an 'instantaneist ballet in two acts, a cinematographic entr'acte, and the dog's tail'. As René Clair points out :

For the sake of future historians of the theatre, I must add that people have never quite known why the ballet was 'instantaneist'. As for the dog's tail, no one saw hair nor hide of it. But Picabia, one of the great 'inventors' of those days, wasn't averse to making things up.

We must accept Picabia's sage remark : 'When will people get out of the habit of explaining everything . . .'

There is, in fact, little to explain about *Relâche.* A woman comes on to the stage, lights a cigarette, and smokes it while listening to the music. After her 'Danse sans musique', she is joined by a man with whom she performs a 'Dance of the revolving door'. Men wearing top hats and evening dress take off their outer clothes to reveal clowns' combinations underneath. Then comes a 'Wheelbarrow dance'. One of the dancers gravely places a wreath on the head of a woman in the audience. The ballet ends with a mimed song. Picabia gravely observed,

Like infinity, *Relâche* has no friends. To have friends you need to be very ill, so ill indeed that you can't keep them away any longer. If Satie ever liked *Relâche,* he probably did so in the way he liked Kirsch, a leg of mutton, or even his umbrella! *Relâche* has no meaning. It is the pollen of our age. A speck of dust on our fingertips and the drawing fades away. . . . We must think about it from a distance and try not to touch it . . .

Satie himself was unwell at the time he wrote the ballet, and, as we have seen, was, in Picabia's phrase, doing his best to keep his friends away. Among the few admitted to his intimacy was Rolf de Maré, with whom he was on the best of terms :

Cher Exquis Directeur [he told him], I am working for you : it's progressing a bit, but I still haven't found the true direction. It will, though, come out smartly and surely, have no doubt. [. . .] Every best wish to Börlin, please. Let him know that I am working hard *for him.*

And then, in the January of 1925, six months before his death, Satie was writing to de Maré that he was too tired and dogged with pain to accept some invitation or other:

I would very much like to have seen you that evening to give you in person my New Year greetings and my best wishes for a good journey. I would, too, have told you what a charming impresario you have been to me.

The music of *Relâche* does not show Satie in an accustomed light. There is, of course, the expected use of popular songs – 'Cadet Roussel' appears unmistakably, and there are references to such immortal airs as 'As-tu vu la cantinière?' and 'R'tire tes pieds, Tu n'vois pas que tu m'ennuies' – and the men dancers put on their coats to an accompaniment of strict fugal writing. The phrases in general, however, are not shaped with the usual hard compactness. The 'Dance of the revolving door', for example, has a wistful sentimentality implying that he was now too weary to hold up the jester's mask. As in *Mercure*, the directions to the players include the phrases 'caressant' and 'très chanté', for all the world as if the mellifluous shade of Gounod had touched Satie's austere manner. The extended melody of the 'Wheelbarrow dance' is suspiciously close to lyricism, and the bars signalling the Woman's first entry, which are to be played very slowly, have a strange sweetness about them. Seen as a technical whole, the ballet has an interesting mirror-like peculiarity in that both acts are interchangeable and could just as well be played backward or forward without loss of continuity.

Satie's most original work on *Relâche* is contained in the incidental music he composed for René Clair's film sequence. He was touchingly anxious to give of his best.

And the film? [he wrote to Clair.] When?... Time passes (and doesn't pass again). Have got cold feet at the thought of being forgotten by you. Yes.... Send me quickly the details of your wonderful work. Warmest thanks.

From the date of this letter, 23 October 1924, it is clear that Satie composed the music for *Entr'acte* in less than a month, since the first performance was intended for 20 November. When at last the film was edited he sat in the projection room and timed each scene with mathematical precision. The individual 'shots' are very brief, and he was able to evolve a theme eight bars long which, by altering when necessary the tempo and key signature, he fitted closely to the action. Thus he could switch abruptly, and without losing unity, from the cannon on the roof to the bucking motion of the scenic railway in Luna Park. The same little 'cell' is capable of delicately graded variations for other scenes. (Although, of course, the funeral march indulges in not unexpected mockery of Chopin.) When used strictly as film music, the score functions perfectly: it is wedded so firmly to the action that, on its own, it has no reason for existence. The *Entr'acte* suite is the most logical and convincing example of 'musique d'ameublement' among the attempts that had been made by Satie and others in that direction.* He, naturally, carried off the whole thing in jest and retained enough of his old waggishness to tell Clair that he had written music that was pornographic. Then, assuming an expression of dignity, he added that he did not 'wish to bring a blush to the cheek of a lobster, still less an egg'.

The first performance of *Relâche* was intended for the night of 17 November 1924. The date was changed and put back until the 20th. On that evening – it was a Thursday – a hopeful audience poured into the Théâtre des Champs-Élysées, the men in classic evening dress and white ties, the women bareshouldered, befurred and flashing with diamonds. It was to be an elegant first night. Had not Paul Poiret designed the costumes? Poiret was in decline but he remained an amusing figure, and there was sure to be something to provide a topic for chat. An air of puzzlement descended on the gentlemen and their ladies when they saw that the doors of the theatre were firmly shut. They jostled each other in irritation. Some of them smashed the glass. A lugubrious official stepped forward and announced that the theatre would not open, as the first night had had to be postponed. Now the word 'relâche' means 'closed'. It is the legend that appears on theatre posters when there will be no performance. The baffled audience thought they had been deliberately fooled. They climbed back into their cars, half angry, half chuckling at the prank of which they had been victims. The real joke, however, was that the 'relâche'

* Darius Milhaud has arranged the score for piano duet as 'Cinéma'. In 1967 Henri Sauguet conducted the orchestra for a sound version of the film.

took place for a genuine reason. At the final rehearsals Jean Börlin, who danced a leading role, had fallen ill. The management agreed to put off the first night and, in the confusion, forgot to tell the press. In such a way did Picabia become responsible for a notorious practical joke of which he was, for once, guiltless.

When, on 27 November, the theatre eventually opened, the audience was in a more than usually captious mood. They eyed, a trifle edgily, the curtain designed by Picabia, which, amid a swirl of zig-zags, arrows and squiggles, informed them that 'Erik Satie is the greatest musician in the world.' It rose to show a décor consisting of a triangular construction blazing with light. When their eyes grew accustomed to the dazzle they saw that it was made up of hundreds of small glittering discs piled up in symmetrical rows. Gramophone records, said some. Reflectors, said others. Another theory suggested cymbals. There was not much time for speculation on the interesting nature of the scenery, as the orchestra now broke into the opening chords of the overture. Gradually, through the dissonances, the audience recognized the tune of a ribald students' song. Determined to join in the spirit of the thing, they bellowed out the chorus with hearty relish. Their amusement turned to anger as the ballet went on. They were annoyed by a change of scenery that brought on a curtain scrawled with insulting remarks. They were furious when Jean Börlin made his entry in an invalid carriage of the type used by war-wounded soldiers.

The projection of René Clair's film began with a susurrous of muffled laughter and groans. The bearded ballerina and the camel received the precise length of shrift that might have been expected. When the funeral hearse lumbered on to the scenic railway the whole audience, to Picabia's great delight, roared disapproval. Many of them stood on their seats the better to scream annoyance. Disorder was complete. Through it all the conductor, Roger Désormière, a lock of hair pugnaciously flying, drove the orchestra on. The little film, only twenty-two minutes long, reached its end amid whistles and one or two cheers, for by that time the gaiety and wit of René Clair had won a few supporters. Many who objected to the ballet were amused by the film, and some of the most conventional critics wrote favourably of it next day. '*Entr'acte* doesn't believe in anything very much,' Picabia said, 'except perhaps in the pleasure of life; it believes in the pleasure of inventing, it respects nothing if not the wish to *burst out laughing,* for laughing, thinking, working, have the same value and are indispensable to each other.' This mellow observation, as René Clair says, could stand as a summary of Picabia's own work and personality.

The second half of *Relâche* wound its rowdy way to an uproarious curtain call. Satie and his colleagues drove on to the stage in a small Citroën car and acknowledged with bland courtesy a raging audience. The ballet was performed another dozen or so times. Paris quickly tired of the joke, there were few spectators left willing to expose themselves to ridicule, and early in the following month the word 'relâche' was inscribed on the posters with real meaning. Picabia shrugged his shoulders. 'I'd prefer them to protest rather than applaud,' he said.

Relâche, appropriately, was the last production of Rolf de Maré. Within a period of five years he had mounted twenty-four new ballets, nearly all of them original creations. In his own way he was as remarkable a figure as Diaghilev, and his troupe, the Ballets Suédois, comprised the only serious rival to the Ballets Russes. The range and variety of their contribution to the art were unique. The fusion of new elements with ballet was a constant aim. In *la Création du monde* it was painting that supplied the novelty: Léger's designs had the effect of 'mobiles' long before the term came into fashion. *Les Mariés de la Tour Eiffel* introduced drama into the ballet. And with *Relâche,* which brought the audience into the action, there was the added ingredient of film. After *Relâche,* de Maré said, he could not discover any more new paths to follow: 'Since I was unwilling to retrace my own steps and repeat myself I decided to disband les Ballets Suédois.' His final gesture was to import the revue that gave Paris its first sight of Joséphine Baker. He went back to his world travels, researching into the history of ballet and assembling a rich collection which has since become the Dance Museum of Stockholm. In 1964 he died. The eyes, kind and sincere, were closed for ever. The mouth, 'witty and slightly arrogant . . . the mouth of a fairy-tale prince' as Picabia described it, was shut. Yet Rolf de Maré survives because he was both creator and curator, and because he did so much to preserve the fugitive trace of an art that is, more than most, doomed to evanescence.

I I

Satie was ill, very ill. His doctors told him he had cirrhosis of the liver. He still travelled every day from his drab home in Arcueil to see his friends in Paris. Sometimes it was Braque or Derain who gave him lunch. Sometimes it was Milhaud. He ate little and sat with his back to the fireplace, coat still on, hat pulled down over his eyes, umbrella firmly clenched. There he remained for hours, dumb and motionless, until it was time to catch the train for Arcueil. His friends persuaded him to take a room at a hotel. Still esconced in an armchair and fully dressed in his street clothes, he spent the days fixedly contemplating himself in a full-length mirror that stood before him. An elaborate arrangement of strings and pulleys enabled him without stirring to open the door for callers. Since he regarded the telephone with abhorrence, his friends soon learned not to ring him.

Later he moved from these quiet surroundings to a hotel in Montparnasse where he felt happier among the noise and chatter of artists. He was now so unwell that he took to his bed. Never having known serious illness before, he inspired perpetual dramas in which thermometers and medicaments were the villains of the piece. When asked if he wanted any relatives to be told of his state, he grew evasive. It became necessary for him to go into hospital, and Étienne de Beaumont arranged for him to have a private room. The friend who packed his case asked Braque to stand between herself and Satie to shield her from the invalid's view, for he would fly into rages if each item were not placed in certain exact positions. His only toilet articles were a toothbrush made of couch-grass and a pumice stone.

In the hospital Satie kept his sense of humour despite much pain. He remarked of a priest who came to visit him: 'He looked like a black Modigliani on a blue background.' The publisher who called to discuss the printing of his score for *Relâche* was asked for immediate payment. 'You never need money so much as when you're in hospital,' remarked Satie in a tone of bourgeois shrewdness. As soon as he was paid he slipped the bank-notes inside the old newspapers stacked on his case, together with documents, forms, bits of string, and all the other junk he could not bear to throw away. This included handkerchiefs. Someone who went out to Arcueil to collect his laundry was astonished to find that the parcel contained eighty-nine of them.

As soon as Poulenc learned of Satie's illness he wanted to visit him. The composer of *Relâche* was touched but obdurate. Neither would he allow Auric to come near him, since the article 'Adieu, Satie' had deeply wounded him. 'No, no, I prefer not to see him; they've said "goodbye", and now I'm ill I choose to leave it at that and let things stay as they are. There must be no compromise to the end.' Their place was taken by the sculptor Brancusi, Jean Wiéner, Roger Désormière, and a young musician called Roger Caby who for many months nursed him with devotion and cheerfully put up with his fits of temper.

On 1 July 1925, he slept all day so deeply that flies crawled undisturbed over his face. During the past few days he had been kept alive on a diet of champagne and paregoric. He died in the evening without regaining consciousness. His brother Conrad learned the news in a press report. Years previously they had quarrelled over some minor family affair and had never met again. Now, moved by the death of a brother whom he was really very fond of, Conrad helped Milhaud rescue the manuscripts left behind, the notebooks and the drafts.

Satie was buried at the church of Arcueil. The cheap coffin was treated to look like mahogany so that people should realize that an important composer was being interred and not a penniless musician. There were few flowers – a wreath of roses and hortensias from Poulenc, others from the Ballets Suédois and Satie's publisher, and from his neighbours in Arcueil a simple bunch of violets labelled : 'To M. Satie, from the tenants'. Most of the congregation was made up of respectable persons in their Sunday best : the shopkeepers of Arcueil, café acquaintances, butchers and confectioners. Satie would never have guessed that the mourners at his funeral – several hundred of them – would consist chiefly of simple folk who knew nothing of his music but who had affection for him as a man.

When Milhaud and Conrad Satie penetrated into the obscure apartment where the composer had lived alone for so many years they found an interior of squalid disarray. Though Satie himself always dressed with impeccable neatness and kept himself scrupulously clean, his room was covered in filth and dust. They saw a broken-down bed, a table heaped with a jumble of disparate articles, and a half-empty cupboard on which there lay a dozen corduroy suits, all unworn and long out of fashion. In each corner straggled newspapers, walking-sticks and old hats. On top of the piano, a wretched instrument whose pedals were done up with string, there was music affectionately inscribed by Debussy. Behind it mouldered the scores of *Jack in the Box* and *Geneviève de Brabant* which Satie always thought he had lost on a bus. An old cigar box contained over four thousand scraps of paper on which he had drawn, in an exquisite hand, strange landscapes, imaginary architectural plans and Gothic fancies. They were ranged in meticulous order.

As French law demands, a public auction of his belongings was held. His friends decided to buy as much of his personal belongings as they could and to force up the bidding to increase the value of his estate. Étienne de Beaumont came away with a portrait that depicted Satie, stained-glass window style, playing the organ. Braque purchased another picture and, for sentimental reasons, the ruined piano. Milhaud went home the possessor of walking sticks, drawings and ballet designs done in red ink.

Some years later in Arcueil the dead end that leads from the sombre rue de la Citadelle under a massive aqueduct was given the name of Erik Satie. (Massenet, to the north of the suburb, has been dignified more spaciously with an avenue.) It was a deserved civic tribute to a local resident well-known for his charitable work in organizing holiday treats for poor children. In 1966, a hundred years after his birth, a park was named after him, and a statue put there. Would he, one wonders, have preferred his dead-end to the sculptor's funerary art?

When Satie died there was discussion about whether he had received the last rites of the church. Since the hospital where he spent his last days belonged to a religious foundation, a friend was able to discover that he had communicated. This meant, at least, that the nuns were authorized to administer the Sacrament. There was little doubt that they had done so. Nonetheless, on a gate opposite his hovel at Arcueil, an unknown hand scrawled in chalk : 'This house is haunted by the Devil.'

IO

ORPHEUS AND ESTHER - MINIATURE OPERAS - *PACIFIC 231* AND *JUDITH*

I

SATIE left this world at a moment when the spirit of the Twenties had reached full bloom. During 1925 France enjoyed the luxury of being governed by four different administrations in turn. January opened with Édouard Herriot still clinging to his shaky perch. He was a familiar face in the pre-1939 comedy of government, sometimes playing the lead as Prime Minister, at other occasions turning up in the supporting role of Foreign Secretary or Minister of Education. As a young man he had gained his doctorate with a thesis on Madame Récamier and her friends. When he was not forming governments he wrote biographies and histories of French literature, though it is for his fifty years' tenure as Mayor of Lyon that he will best be remembered, and not for his life of Beethoven. In April he was succeeded by Jean Painlevé, a mathematician whose two great joys in life were the differential equation and the manipulation of parliamentary majorities. Painlevé's government lasted for six months. But, if on 27 October he fell, on the 29th he rose again, and for just over three glorious weeks he acted as his own successor, this time combining the job of Prime Minister with that of Minister of Finance. Such virtuosity, especially when it involved a proposal for heavy taxes on capital, was unwelcome, and in November he stood aside to make way for that somewhat battered ornament Aristide Briand, who now became Prime Minister for the eighth time. Unlike his immediate predecessors Briand had no leisure to spare for literature or mathematics and chose instead to devote himself wholly to politics. He was a charmer with a gift for lyrical oratory. He also created a record for longevity in office which no Anglo-Saxon, let alone Frenchman, could equal.

175

When, in 1926, his own administration collapsed, he became Foreign Secretary, a post he held with an unshakeable grip for six years while government after government, including one of his own, rose and fell around him.

The year of 1925 also saw the fortunes of André Citroën at their height. He was the son of a Polish diamond merchant from the ghettoes of Warsaw. A few years earlier he had started mass production of the little five-horse-power car that made him famous. (It was the model in which Satie had taken his bow after the first performance of *Relâche*.) His name already featured in the satirical ditties sung by the chansonniers of Montmartre, whom he would delight to hear and whom he would encourage with suggestions for making their references to him wittier and more pointed. He was not the type of businessman to construct an empire by means of patient, ant-like activity. He preferred the bold gesture and played for high stakes that gave his accountant sleepless nights. The qualities of daring that built, within three years, a massive industry that helped make France second only to America as a car manu-facturer, were carried over into his private life. His passion for gambling made him lose seven million francs in a night. 'If I hadn't been a gambler,' he used to joke, 'what couldn't I have done!' After an evening's play at the baccarat tables he would go through the streets of Montmartre pressing thousand-franc notes into the hands of beggars. Propelled by audacious risk-taking and brilliant publicity schemes, his firm grew like a pro-digious mushroom. When a sponsor refused to give him the ten million francs he sought for expansion, he was always con-fident of finding another to guarantee him twenty. If Louis Renault was the inspired mechanic of the age, Citroën in 1925 was its visionary. The trick that made, literally, the whole of Paris talk about Citroën in 1925 was his decoration of the Eiffel Tower. One evening the Tower glittered into light. The whole of its upper length was emblazoned with the letters of his name, each one more than forty yards high. There was only one Eiffel Tower. There was only one Citroën.

Way below the flickering neon of the Eiffel Tower the ill-starred Exposition des Arts Décoratifs opened its doors. It was, in fact, lucky to have opened at all, for even at the inaugural ceremony few exhibits were ready. Top-hatted dignitaries splashed through puddles and stumbled in mud. Two months later some of the pavilions were still forlorn and incomplete. The general public was indifferent to this dying offspring of 'Modern Style'. The clovers, the lilacs, the thistles, the lilies of the valley which had featured so profusely in the designs of the Belle Époque were replaced by a handful of bouquets and roses. The voluptuous contours were straightened into angular lines. A splash of luxury was provided by furniture made of rare, almost theatrical materials: macassar ebony, shark-skin, mother-of-pearl, eggshell and ivory.

The ideas of Le Corbusier were influencing architecture and interior decoration. Houses were machines to be lived in. Terms such as 'le living-room' and 'le cosy' made their appearance, and drawing rooms lived in concubinage with dining rooms. There was a flourish of chrome metal, lacquered wood and wrought iron. Furniture designers borrowed from Cubism its geometrical forms and straight lines and neutral colours. Sofas assumed a look of clinical severity and chairs were built of steel tubes. Léger himself designed for Rolf de Maré an armchair of stark outlines and a desk that was chillingly square. In the sphere of applied arts Lalique created an attractive alliance between pressed glass and electricity, leaving behind him the fountains of the Rond Point des Champs-Élysées which still divert the eye with the play of light and water. Under the pressure of Jean Lurçat the craft of tapestry, dormant in France throughout the nineteenth century, took on a new life.

Another development which 'Art Déco' helped to focus was in the domain of poster art. The Japanese delicacies of Toulouse-Lautrec and the frilly creations of Chéret had given way to triangles, roundels and semi-circles that represented the saucer eyes and flashy teeth of Joséphine Baker as Paul Colin showed her in his posters. Colin was much in demand as artist and set-designer. For Rolf de Maré he drew advertisements announcing the *Revue Nègre*. At any given time he had fifteen posters on his easels in various stages of completion. Inspired by Joséphine Baker, he utilized the forms of Negro art so deftly that his drawings commanded high prices in Harlem. Other artists brought the shapes of Cubism into the street, and the French Railways, among many advertisers, took to presenting themselves to their customers in a whirl of line and tone that had a short time previously been confined within the experimental studios of Montmartre.

But the exhibition was not, on the whole, a success. It opened at a time when the Parisians most likely to appreciate it were going on holiday. 'The most you could say,' complained Paul Poiret, 'was that in the evening, between nine and eleven o'clock, you saw a horde of concierges and clerks pouring in because they liked crowds, noise and light.' Poiret was especially bitter. He had organized a display of curtains and drapes in his most elaborate manner, exotic and alarmingly expensive. He had, out of his own pocket, financed three luxury barges – *Amours, Délices* and *Orgues* – which were tied up on the Seine alongside the exhibition. These scintillating craft were decorated with pictures by Raoul Dufy, and aboard them, wearing an admiral's hat, Poiret welcomed his guests with champagne.

As the Exposition des Arts Décoratifs dragged on to its muffled conclusion Poiret fought inch by inch to retain some of the ground stolen from him by Chanel and Schiaparelli. Writs poured in on him, creditors lurked impatiently on the watch, and his floating palaces on the Seine were threatened hourly with distraint. He sold his country house and his art collection. The bankers moved in on his firm and brought mass-production methods with them. He sank by slow and dignified stages into poverty. He went on lecture tours of third-rate sea-side resorts. An exhibition of his paintings organized by friends revealed that although he had an unerring eye for talent in others he did not possess it himself. In the desperate struggle to survive he acted in a play with Colette. Unshaven, long-haired and wearing an old dressing-gown turned into an overcoat, he would recite La Fontaine for a derisory tip in shabby night-clubs. (His rendering of the fable about the grasshopper and the ant was noted for its grim humour.) He was often to be seen on park benches sharing his stale bread with the birds. When he died in 1944 a list of names was found written on the wall of his room. It included all those who had cheated him and stolen from him in a career that had known many splendours and frequent miseries.

The literary diversions of 1925 were of a pleasantly mixed nature. Cendrars blustered into print again, this time with *l'Or*, an epic about gold prospecting in California. Two film versions were quickly made of it. Maurice Dekobra published *la Madone des sleepings*, a novel which few people nowadays have read but one whose title has passed into the lore of the Twenties.

L'Europe galante was Paul Morand's elegant contribution to the festivities. In that year, too, Proust's *Albertine disparue* came out posthumously. The theme supplied a perverse titillation for those who had time to read the book : the narrator's love for the heroine is stimulated by her apparent Lesbianism, and his passion is increased by jealousy and suspicion. The social event of the year was, without a doubt, Paul Valéry's entry into the Académie Française as the successor to Anatole France, an author whom he loathed, but one whom, by tradition, he was obliged to praise in a 'discours de réception' of graceful phrases and sardonic implications.

For Darius Milhaud the most important occasion of 1925 was his marriage. The bride was his cousin Madeleine, whom he had known since childhood days in Aix. She was ten years his junior, fair-haired, lively, and a delightful mimic. The wedding brought to the synagogue of Aix those two ardent Catholics Paul Claudel and Francis Poulenc, and their presence at the ceremony demonstrated the wide range of Milhaud's friendships. The honeymooners set off on a long journey that took them to Naples and on to Pompeii where they travelled a dusty road crowded with herds of sheep and goats, donkey carts and decrepit vans. In Malta they stopped at tea rooms and refreshed themselves with warm tea and toast. The smell of incense and olive oil pervaded Athens, and they caught the distant gleam of icons through the open doors of shady churches. Rain and fog veiled the Dardanelles as they sailed on to Constantinople. Here some cousins of Milhaud's mother took them to restaurants to sample dishes he had known during boyhood in Aix : rose-leaf jam, loukoum, sugary pistachios and honey cake. They listened to Turkish music where all the instruments played nearly, but not quite, in unison, and Milhaud strained his ears to detect the tantalizingly imperceptible variation each of them introduced.

The Lebanon they viewed from the windows of an aged Ford motor car, its brakes tied with string and its motor leaking generously. When they arrived in Beirut Milhaud fell ill. Madeleine nursed him with a devotion that was to be called upon many times again in the years to come. They had to give up the notion of visiting Palestine and made their way slowly back home by way of Egypt and Italy. The malady that declared itself in the Lebanon was the precursor of an ailment which reduced Milhaud to a permanent state of invalidism. Not long afterwards a violent attack of rheumatism drove him to bed, where he lay motionless for weeks. During the long convalescence the use of his legs returned but gradually. If he walked for any length of time he risked being immobilized again with excruciating pain. A period of relative good health would be followed by another attack. There was no way of telling when it would come. Sometimes the agony would rise from the legs and feet to strike at the arms. Through the wakeful nights of suffering he would try to distract himself by making shadow pictures. Holding his hand against the night-light he succeeded in throwing a silhouette on the wall. Soon his fingers grew quite agile, and in turn the pointed profile of Jean Cocteau, the rounded beard of Erik Satie, the large nose of Poulenc, and the aquiline features of Étienne de Beaumont would flash over the wall. Afterwards, when he was better, he tried to recapture the shapes. He could not do it. His fingers were out of practice.

The waters of Vichy did nothing to cure his tortured legs. The gold needles of acupuncturists gave only a slight relief. Once, his doctors wrapped the swollen feet in monstrous layers of wool and sticking plaster. Two days later he was walking again. Another miraculous recovery was wrought by a village policeman who had a natural gift for massage and restored the composer to active life within days. There was, however, no permanent cure. He remained at the mercy of dolorous pains which were ever ready to pincer his nerves and nail him to his bed. An invalid chair, mounted on wheels sensitive to the slightest touch of his weakened legs, gave him back his mobility. The ailment seemed to redouble his appetite for life. His journeys across the world continued. Even when an Italian train stopped abruptly and shot him out of his chair to fall on the point of his agonized knees, he refused to give up the travel that was essential to a mind always curious of new sights and people. Very rarely did he complain. His sufferings he preferred to keep to himself. Once, though, when a friend called to see him during an attack he could not stay silent. 'J'en ai marre!' he whispered in a tired voice. His eyes filled with tears. The friend discreetly looked away and pretended not to hear. A few minutes later he was chatting jovially again.

The disabling rheumatism that had come into his life only

stopped him from composing when his hands could no longer hold a pen. At all other times he wrote music with his usual frenetic industry. By now he had become disenchanted with jazz. He had, with *la Création du monde*, done all that he wanted to in that direction. The charm was broken. The genuine article had been vulgarized by commercialism and snobbery. He returned to an older source for his next venture, an opera commissioned by the princesse de Polignac. His aim was to set the legend of Orpheus in a modern frame-work. The hero was to be a peasant from the Camargue and his Eurydice to be a mysterious stranger in that limitless plain, a gypsy girl like those Milhaud had seen in his youth dancing at Sainte-Maries-de-la-Mer in the pilgrimage season.

The libretto of *les Malheurs d'Orphée* was written by Armand Lunel, a close childhood friend of Milhaud and now a teacher of philosophy. As boys they had explored the country-side around Aix, striding over arid hills where an occasional cypress tree stood bleakly on guard in a shrivelled landscape. They had climbed up on rocks to hear the sharp cry of the grasshopper beneath torrid pines, and they had seen, from hill-top villages, the plains of the Durance stretched out before them in the heat. Composer and librettist sought to put into *les Malheurs d'Orphée* the memories of that luminous countryside which had marked them both for life. Orpheus is presented not as a charmer musician but as a healer of animals and men. He lives in a Camargue village and is planning to marry Eurydice, one of a number of gypsies recently arrived there. Her parents disapprove and wish to take her back, dead or alive. The lovers flee to the mountains. There she is stricken by illness and dies, in spite of Orpheus' medical skill. Her body is carried to the grave by a chorus of animals – an aged bear, a fox, a boar and wolf that has 'lost the taste for blood' – who sing a funeral chant. Orpheus returns to his village home and laments the despair that nothing can soften. Eurydice's three sisters believe him to have caused her death and fly at him like the Bacchantes of ancient legend. Torn to pieces by their furious attack, Orpheus dies, once more proclaiming his attachment to Eurydice. The sisters realize, too late, that they have been mistaken.

Les Malheurs d'Orphée, written in ten days of a golden autumn at Aix, was a new departure for Milhaud. It belonged to the class of chamber opera and was scored for an orchestra of thirteen players. The scenes were short and each of them was broken up into separate arias, duets and concerted numbers. Apart from Orpheus and Eurydice, the characters were treated as groups – villagers, animals, the heroine's sisters – and though they often sang as a chorus Milhaud succeeded in preserving their individuality. The piece had been scored in such a way that the music sounded just as effective in a large theatre as it did in a small one. The conductor of the first performance, which was given in Brussels, did not realize this. Fearing that the sound would be lost in the wide expanse of the Théâtre de la Monnaie, he doubled the strings. The unwieldy result convinced him that Milhaud had been right in the first place.

Honegger and his wife travelled with the Milhauds to Brussels for the première. The party crammed itself into a little Renault heaped with travelling rugs and cases while Honegger, wrapped in a voluminous hooded cape and fisherman's hat, slept peaceably in the dickey, oblivious of the rain that poured throughout the journey. *Les Malheurs d'Orphée* lasted forty minutes and had as its companion in the double bill Mozart's *Il Seraglio*. The Belgian audience heard both operas politely, or at least with none of the visible indignation that Parisians were apt to show at the modernity of Milhaud's earlier scores. The tribulations of Orpheus did not reach the French capital until the following year and eventually found their way to America, Germany and Italy. Milhaud's setting of them had a poignant simplicity which makes this little opera one of his most successful works.

Tragedy was also the theme of his next chamber opera, but tragedy with a contemporary background. The idea for *le Pauvre matelot* was Jean Cocteau's. He had read a newspaper item which caught his imagination and suggested a plot. A peasant couple, too poor to raise their baby son, gave him to relatives. He grew up and prospered. One day he decided to go back and visit the parents he had never seen. He arrived in his native village and spent the night in their house without revealing his identity. They, taking him for a wealthy foreigner, murdered him as he slept. It is a story which frequently recurs in folklore and literature. Camus is one of the writers who has been interested by it, as *le Malentendu* shows, and he also refers to it in *l'Étranger*. One can see how the tragedy lends itself to existentialist interpretations.

In Cocteau's version a wife has been waiting fifteen years for news of her sailor husband. She has refused to marry again and still clings to hope of his return. The husband comes back and speaks first to a neighbour who tells him of his wife's loyalty and her virtuous resignation. The husband decides to see for himself. The plot now echoes the medieval theme of patient Griselda, whose virtue was tested by her unbelieving husband in a series of temptations. Presenting himself unrecognized to the faithful woman, the man gives himself out as a friend of her husband. The latter, he says, is penniless, ill and in prison. He, the friend, is on the other hand very rich : he has pearls in his pocket and gold at his belt. May he spend the night under her roof? She agrees. When he has fallen asleep she kills him for the sake of his money, which she plans to use for the benefit of her unfortunate husband on his return. The curtain falls before she realizes her ghastly mistake.

Cocteau's libretto is written in the simple style of a 'complainte'. The dialogue, modelled on popular ballad, is set to music of the same nature. As the curtain rises on the squalid little bar kept by the wife the tune of a 'java' is heard as if ground out on a player-piano. The exchanges between the woman and her husband are accompanied by music which, in its smooth flow of melody, recalls the folk airs that used to be heard in the little streets round the harbour at Marseille, where Milhaud often strolled at the time he was working on his opera. The scenes are short and they lead up to the dénouement with a brutal logic. Cocteau's wordage is taut and the action is concentrated : each phrase and gesture are governed by the need for a steady development of relentless force. This is emphasized by Milhaud's restrained use of his orchestra. It does not enlarge on the action of the piece and remains in the background, ever alert and sympathetic to what is happening on the stage. When, for example, the woman prepares for murder in Act III, a throbbing ostinato increases the tension by its very understatement.

Le Pauvre matelot made its début at the Opéra-Comique, where it was last revived in 1945. It failed to please. One evening Milhaud, out of curiosity, witnessed a performance from the gallery. His neighbour, whose view was hindered by a pillar, asked if he would mind shifting a little. They watched the opera tightly squeezed against each other, the galleryite following the action with knitted brows and heavy breathing. At the end he stood up muttering 'Nasty! nasty!' and vanished abruptly. The verdict seems to have been shared by others, for in Paris *le Pauvre matelot* did not have a long run. Abroad it won great success, and not only for the practical reason that its small cast of four and modest stage requirements made it inexpensive to produce. It ran for three consecutive years in Berlin, where it was revived after the war. More than twenty provincial German opera houses mounted it, and since that time it has been played in many different countries. The opera, in fact, which has a duration of less than three quarters of an hour, has been performed more than any other of Milhaud's stage works.

For his next opera Milhaud chose a quite different story and setting. Armand Lunel, his collaborator on *les Malheurs d'Orphée,* had written a comedy based on old stories handed down in his family and on an eighteenth-century play. It was called *Esther de Carpentras,* and Milhaud saw it as an ideal subject for an *opéra-bouffe.* The Provençal town of Carpentras, which Milhaud knew well, is the ancient capital of the Comtat Venaissin, that realm which until the eighteenth century belonged with Avignon to the Popes. Long before Augustus planted a Roman colony there, the Carpentrassiens had occupied the site in the middle of a half-circle of barren mountains. Not far from the Gothic cathedral of Saint-Siffrein is a handsome synagogue founded in 1367. Rebuilt four hundred years later, it contains not only some rare and elaborate woodwork and church furniture, but also, among its Gothic foundations, a pool where girls on the eve of marriage took ritual baths.

The synagogue, with its adjoining terrace laid out for celebration of the Sabbath, represents many years of Jewish coexistence, always inescapable, sometimes unruly, with the Papal overlord. The plot of *Esther de Carpentras* tells of an incident which occurred in the town before the Revolution. The newly-appointed Cardinal Bishop is approached by three venerable Hebrews for permission to act the play of Esther on the day of Purim. His Holiness agrees. He is fresh from Rome and hot for evangelism. At the festival he plans to interrupt the play and call on the Jews to renounce their religion. Outside the synagogue preparations go ahead. The actors are recruited, by tradition, from among the audience, and the spectacle begins. The famous scene where Esther confronts Ahasuerus is about to start when the Bishop erupts and declaims an edict threatening the Jews with death or exile if they do not accept the Catholic faith. The girl who plays Esther comes on stage and takes him for the man who is acting the part of the tyrant Ahasuerus. Under this impression she speaks her words to the end. The Bishop, touched by her beauty and her faith, grants the Jews the right of staying in Carpentras and following their religion.

The plot is treated with great freedom. The thunders of the Old Testament are mingled with the lighter tones of the New, and scenes of drama follow moments of knockabout humour. The challenge of musicking such an olla podrida and yet of keeping a certain unity was one that the composer accepted with enjoyment. A hint of Chabrier creeps into some of the orchestration – that Chabrier whose ebullience is akin to Milhaud's – and there is something, too, of Bizet in the score. What is unique is the blend of Southerner and Jew which has always been a feature of Milhaud's own personality. Though Esther may at first sing in tones of seductive beauty, she ends her number with a lively maxixe. If we are amused at the Bishop's naïf idea that he can convert several thousand Jews at a stroke, we are touched by the ardour of his prayer at the end of the first act. And if the festival of Purim opens with a brisk South American dance, if the Jews dressed in carnival rig make their entrance to a fugue, then there are also unexpected moments when the bitterness of centuries of persecution colours the atmosphere. At the end of *Esther de Carpentras* the Bishop and his entourage move away singing loyalty to their faith while the Jews reply with an affirmation of their own beliefs. For a time, but only for a time, the religions have agreed to differ.

Esther de Capentras was not produced for more than ten years after it was written. The Opéra-Comique gave it six performances in 1938, since when, except for a radio broadcast, this unusual work has been neglected. By then the tireless Milhaud had composed over a hundred opus numbers, including ballets, concertos, film music, song cycles, quartets, and still more operas. Soon after he had finished *Esther de Carpentras* he was asked by Paul Hindemith to write something for a music festival. Hindemith was then in the enviable situation of being able to attempt any sort of experiment that appealed to him. 'Write an opera,' he told Milhaud in 1927, 'and make it as short as possible.' The reaction against Wagner and his long, excessively long epics was in full swing. Kurt Weill's *Mahagonny* lasted half an hour and Hindemith's own *Hin und Zurück* took precisely fourteen minutes to perform. Milhaud, already an old hand at the game, broke all records with an opera called *l'Enlèvement d'Europe*. It was nine minutes long.

His publisher was horrified. 'An opera lasting nine minutes!' he remonstrated. 'You could at least write a trilogy for me.' So Milhaud, who was always ready to accommodate his friends, added a brace of miniature operas. In their entirety the three works filled twenty-seven minutes. He called them his 'opéras-minute'. Each retells a classical legend in, as it were, fast motion, with quick dashes of irony. Europa is carried off by a taurine Zeus in a blessedly short space of time compared with the lengthy periods that have in the past been lavished on the story. *L'Abandon d'Ariane,* to which Massenet and Strauss devoted laborious hours, traces the plight of its forsaken heroine with a like celerity. Finally *la Délivrance de Thésée* encapsulates the myth of Poseidon's son. Each of these 'opéras-minute' has a cast of no more than five and an orchestra of small dimensions. The libretti by Henri Hoppenot have wit and allusiveness, qualities that the music reflects with an elegant concision which enables it to satirize, in passing, some of opera's more absurd conventions.

Another unusual venture to which Hindemith introduced Milhaud at this time was the composition of film music with the aid of a new synchronizing machine. Involved in a whirlwind of activity – besides teaching and composing, Hindemith was also the organizer of numerous festivals and events intended to put music within the reach of amateurs – he was insatiable for novelty. One of his festivals had film music as its theme, and at the last minute before it began he was to be seen composing with desperate haste and handing over the pages as soon as they were finished to his students, who there and then transcribed them on to player-piano rolls. An engineer had recently invented a device which was used for synchronizing

F

music with a cartoon featuring that legendary animal Felix the
Cat. While the film was projected the composer was able to
match his score, bar by bar which he wrote on tape, with the
action he saw in front of him. When the orchestra came to
record the music the conductor followed the composer's indica-
tions as the tape unrolled at his desk in time with the individual
frames of the film on the screen. In this way he achieved
perfect synchronization. Hindemith suggested that Milhaud play
with the new toy. Milhaud chose a newsreel for the experiment
and composed a suite for small orchestra which he later called
Actualités. Such was his introduction to the medium that Satie
and Honegger had already distinguished and which Auric was
to make especially his own. In the years to come Milhaud
wrote scores for over twenty-five films. Starting with the trans-
atlantic jocularity of *Hello Everybody,* his path in this new
field was to lead him by way of *Madame Bovary, Tartarin de
Tarascon* (a suitable commission for a son of the Midi), and
of cartoons and documentaries, to *The Private Affairs of Bel
Ami, Peron et Evita,* and *The Burma Road.* The note of
variety, as in everything to do with Milhaud, is insistent.

II

Milhaud's entry into the bizarre regions of the cinema was at
first greeted by its inhabitants with distrust and unease. Although, as cinéasts never tire of pointing out, the ranks of film
directors are rich with genius, their every production is an
epic, and their imaginative powers far outrank those of Tolstoy
and Dickens combined, these paragons, at least when Milhaud
came to know them, were singularly unappreciative of music
that had not been written by composers of foxtrots and commercial songs. Anything vaguely 'symphonic' aroused their
gravest suspicions. The serious composer who found his way
into their circle usually had the tact to cast his music in a style
that disarmed their misgiving. As Milhaud put it, he had to
disguise his music with a false nose.

When Auric wrote the score for René Clair's *A nous la
liberté* and won popular success, film makers realized that a
composer deemed avant-garde might serve their purpose as
well as any other. Even so, Milhaud's first steps in the medium

were taken under watchful eyes. Jean Renoir, the director of
Madame Bovary, called with his producer to hear the score
he had written. They listened in a silence that was inquisitorial.
They made their brief farewells and departed. Despite this
unfriendly reserve, Milhaud heard no more from them and
assumed that his music was accepted, however grudgingly. At
the time he was suffering from a bad attack of rheumatism
and had to be carried into the engineers' booth when he
supervised his recording. From the music he wrote he was
able to extract a suite for piano called *l'Album de Madame
Bovary.*

In collaboration with Honegger and Roger Désormière, Milhaud supplied the score of *Cavalcade d'amour,* a film treating
the same topic at different periods of time. Honegger was by
now well established in the film world. As a composer whose
music had a wide appeal and attracted audiences who would
not normally go to concerts, he was a natural choice for the
cinema. A benevolent cynicism enabled him to put up with
experiences that would have shattered men who lacked his
sturdiness. As he was fond of pointing out, people did not go
to the cinema for the sake of the music, and when they heard
it they did not listen to it. Writing for the films was an ungrateful task, he agreed. A documentary called for as much music
as went into the first movement of Beethoven's ninth symphony.
You had to be able to switch the mood at a moment's notice.
Your inspiration must be versatile enough to illustrate the techniques of growing rhododendrons or the packaging of synthetic
cheese. While you followed the promptings of your own ideas,
you had at the same time to submit melody, harmony and
rhythm to the strict discipline of what appeared on the screen.
Even then your music could not rely on a fair hearing, for as
soon as the credit titles faded there was usually a commentator
to engage in loquacious battle with your work. Why, then,
write film music? It was, replied Honegger, the only modern
form of composition that paid you enough to live on so that
you could spend the rest of your time writing the symphonies
which you hoped would bring you a reputation.

Another aspect of the cinema that stimulated Honegger's
sardonic humour was the way in which composers were shown
behaving in romantic film biographies. As one who knew something about the toil of composing, he had been fascinated to

see Bizet writing one of his famous melodies on the misted glass of a stage coach, and Beethoven, awkwardly crouched on a window ledge, scribbling a theme from the *Coriolanus* overture on a shutter with the aid of a piece of coal. None of the composers he knew, said Honegger, proceded in this way. Usually they took a piece of music paper and recorded their ideas on it in a disappointingly humdrum manner. Another idiocy he cherished was of seeing Johann Strauss riding in the woods and hearing three ascending notes played on a distant horn. A chorus of birds replied. With one hand grasping the waist of his girl friend, the accomplished Johann wrote down with the other the theme he had just heard. Two hours later, at dinner, the orchestra was playing the result of his 'inspiration', *The Blue Danube*. If only, said Honegger, film makers would spare the time to glance at a full orchestral score and to realize that, quite apart from matters of genius and inspiration, time and application were needed for the long, laborious process of writing it, not to mention a technique that was only to be acquired after lengthy studies. Perhaps, he surmised, it would make them a little less condescending towards the luckless musician they engaged to write their scores.

Through an irony that Honegger, for all his good nature, was the last to appreciate, one of his most popular compositions became also one of the most effective film scores he ever wrote. When *Pacific 231,* which had already triumphed at concerts, was chosen as incidental music to a film about an express train, it filled the purpose so admirably that many people thought it suited the medium better than the one for which it was intended. Honegger's original concept was totally different. He had to explain, a little wearily, that his music represented the working-out of an abstraction. His aim had been to create an impression of movement, not by obvious changes in tempo but by a progressive shortening of note values. The feeling of gradual acceleration was to be enhanced by the use of chorale themes and contrapuntal techniques. Having developed this purely musical idea to his own satisfaction, he gave it the title of *Mouvement symphonique*. He then found himself in the same situation as Liszt. The inventive Abbé, it will be recalled, once composed a rather striking orchestral piece for which he sought a name that would do justice to the romantic nature of the music. In the course of his reading he came across a Lamartine

poem, *les Préludes,* whose title and programme he calmly
tacked on to his work, thereby providing writers of concert
notes with an attractive but quite erroneous excuse for the
exercise of their fertile imaginations. Once Honegger had completed his *Mouvement symphonique,* a treacherous thought
came into his mind. Was there not something about the figuration that suggested the pistons of a railway-engine gradually
quickening their motion? Did not the prickly counterpoint hint
at a giant mass of machinery gathering speed? Was not the
whole thing a tone picture of 'the tranquil breathing of a
machine at rest, the effort of setting in motion, and then the
progressive increase in speed leading to the lyrical, exciting
mood of a 300-ton engine launched through the night at eighty
miles an hour'? So he re-titled his symphonic poem *Pacific 231*
after a certain type of engine then used for heavy express
trains. For what followed, one cannot help feeling, he was
himself largely to blame.

When Ansermet, to whom the work is dedicated, gave the
first performance in Paris, it enjoyed a success as immediate
as greeted *le Roi David.* Honegger was incautious enough to
tell a journalist: 'I have always loved railway engines passionately. For me they are living beings, and I love them in the
same way as other men love women or horses.' He was photo-
graphed wearing dungarees and expertly flourishing an oil can
beside the massive wheels of a locomotive. On a visit to London
he donned stoker's overalls at King's Cross station and rode
to Hitchin beside the driver in his cab. Visitors to his Paris
flat noticed one of the walls half-covered with picture postcards showing a wild variety of engines, including the homony-
mous *Pacific 231.* The legend was firmly planted, and no
amount of protest could subsequently change the image of
Honegger which the public insisted on preserving.

Much ingenuity was expended on literary interpretations of
Pacific 231. Brakes and cam shafts were enthusiastically evoked.
There was learned inquiry into the parallels between crank
arms and crotchets. One commentator improved on all these
glosses by reading the title as a reference to the Pacific Ocean
and by finding in the music an impression of wide, salty ex-
panses. Perhaps his theory was not so aburd after all, since in
this respect one man's opinion is quite as good as any other's,
and he only supplied another example of the dangers to be

found when programme music is discussed. As Constant
Lambert pointed out :

The objection to realism in music is not that it makes things too
easy for the listener, but that it makes them too difficult. Instead of receiving an immediate and incisive physical impression
he receives a vaguely visual one, which has to be related back to
early associations and personal experience before it produces the
emotional reaction which the music should have evoked directly.
It is for the composer, not the listener, to digest the raw material
of his inspiration.

And in a witty coupling of *Pacific 231* and Prokofiev's *le Pas
d'acier,* Lambert adds :

One feels they should have been written when railways and
factories really were beginning to alter our lives; that Prokofieff
should have written ballets about the spinning jenny and the
Luddite riots; that Honegger should have been there to celebrate
the opening of the Stockton and Darlington Railway and the
death of Huskisson with a *Symphonie Triomphale et Funèbre.*

A few years later, tempting Providence again, Honegger gave
the name *Rugby* to another of his pieces. He had since youth
been fond of tennis, football, running and basketball. He was
credited also with inventing a form of polo to be played on
bicycles. His interest in speed made him the dashing but erratic
driver of a blood-red Bugatti sports car. *Rugby* is in the form
of a rondo inspired by the matches Honegger saw at Colombes
Stadium, where he was a regular spectator in the public stand.
It was once given an open-air performance there, though the
reaction of the fans has not been recorded. He told an inter-
viewer that 'rugby is one of my favourite sports, and the impressions that a good rugby match awakens in my mind find
musical equivalents there.' Asked why he chose rugby instead
of football, he replied : 'Rugby says more to me. It seems to
me more spontaneous, more direct, closer to nature . . .' Whereas in *Pacific 231* the 'programme' was easily apparent, that of
Rugby was not so obvious. It sought to follow the evolution of
play, attack and defence. There were no convenient clues for
the unmusical listener to seize on. The crowds who had come
expecting another *Pacific 231* were disappointed. A little while
afterwards Honegger wrote a third piece in the same mould.
Simply called *Mouvement symphonique no. 3,* it lacked the

attraction of a novel title and for that reason did not achieve the popularity of *Pacific 231* nor even the modest reputation of *Rugby.*

Something similar occurred when Honegger thought to follow up the success of *le Roi David.* René Morax, his collaborator on that work, had gone to the Apocrypha for the piece he wanted to produce at his Théâtre du Jorat in 1925. His subject was the story of Judith, the widow of Bethulia. When Nebuchadnezzar and his army besiege her town she is divinely inspired to brave her way into the camp of the Assyrian general Holofernes. In his tent, while he sleeps, she cuts off his head and bears the trophy home as evidence that the warrior is no more. The town is saved and the heroine acclaimed by her people. The treatment devised by Morax and Honegger was a mixture of sung and spoken scenes calling both for singers and actors. *Judith,* finally described as an 'opéra biblique', was really, like *le Roi David,* the sort of work that is basically an oratorio. Again like the earlier piece, it is full of vigour and excitement, especially in the scene depicting the orgy in Holofernes' tent. Dramatic contrast is achieved by juxtaposing the barbarity of the Assyrians with the mystical aura of Judith and her divine mission. Another astute theatrical touch lies in the way Holofernes' death is presented. Instead of seeing the actual murder, which is carried out behind the tent, the spectator only realizes what has happened from the sudden expression of horror that passes over the face of the watching servant.

Painters, sculptors and dramatists, among them Jean Giraudoux, have all been inspired in their different ways by the story of Judith. Honegger's musical version brought to it a sense of mysticism. He is not so much interested in Judith the woman as in the play of opposition between barbarism and religion. Her personal character, and that of Holofernes, remains subordinate to the wider issues developed by the chorus. The audiences who applauded the first performance in Mézières had no doubt about the dramatic power of *Judith.* Parisian critics were less sure. Having overwhelmed *le Roi David* with praise they thought perhaps, as Honegger observed ironically, that they should redress the balance by rationing their enthusiasm for *Judith.* It was as if they felt a need to put him in his place and to remind him, like thoughtful schoolmasters, that effort, constant effort, was more important than a dazzling success.

Judith appeared at Monte Carlo the following year in a stage version. At one moment Wieland Wagner thought of mounting it at Bayreuth. It was, however, as an oratorio that *Judith* set off from its Protestant birthplace to travel the world, and that is the form in which it became best known. The title role is closely associated with Claire Croiza, who was the first to sing it. This exquisite mezzo-soprano, whose art can still be appreciated through the medium of rare gramophone records, distinguished herself in modern French song. She was born Claire Conelly, and under the name of Croiza became a noted singer of Debussy, Ravel and, above all, Fauré. She had a special tenderness for such shadowy figures as Gustave Samazeuilh and Pierre de Bréville, whose work she sang persuasively. Honegger and Poulenc were among the younger composers who, though flourishing after 1914, the year which marked the end of Croiza's triumph on the stage and the beginning of her dedication to song, were fortunate to have her as an interpreter. Before the war she had been a famous opera star in Brussels and Paris. After it, she started a new career with the intimate genre of the *mélodie* which she found more artistically rewarding than the stage.

Of the women in Honegger's life Claire Croiza was, with Andrée Vaurabourg, the most important. He met them both at about the same time in 1923. Andrée played his piano works. Claire sang his songs. He loved them both. The singer then was just over forty years old and Honegger ten years younger. When, in 1923, he married Andrée the liaison came to an end. Claire knew the double sorrow of emotional unhappiness and the decline of her vocal skill. To this was added her awareness of a vanished youth and the approach of age. Happily she was appointed teacher of singing at the Conservatoire, and though she may no longer have been able to enchant audiences as in the past, she was free to nurture the gift in others by drawing on the riches of her own unique experience. After the outbreak of the Second World War in 1939 she was careless enough to incur the charge of collaboration with the occupying German forces. She no longer sang in public, for her voice was quite gone, and she only emerged from her flat to give lessons. In 1944, at the Liberation, she was dismissed from the Conservatoire and threatened with arrest. Her failing intelligence could not grasp the nature of the accusations made against her, since by now she was suffering from the same illness, a tumour on the brain, that had stricken Ravel. Honegger took her to a specialist who pronounced her case incurable. On the very evening when a kindly examining magistrate, to impress on her that her problem was solved, tore up the arrest warrant in front of her, she lost her powers of speech. She died in 1946 at the age of sixty-four, leaving, said Marcel Delannoy, a close friend of the composer, 'a son who bears the name and face of Honegger'.

I I

THE WORLD OF MAURICE SACHS–*LES MATELOTS* AND ALCINA'S SPELLS–A RUSTIC CONCERTO

I

Paul Morand's chief impression of Maurice Sachs, he once told me, was of 'his extreme ugliness'. If Blaise Cendrars was a representative figure of the Twenties, Sachs was its remembrancer. He was the son of a bourgeois family whose wealth came from American investments. He aspired to be a writer, and his social connections enabled him, while still very young, to frequent the authors, artists and composers who then belonged to le Tout-Paris. His main problem, and one that confronts so many others of literary ambition, was to find something to write about. The novels he confected are only enjoyable if one knows the identity of the figures who inspired them. His autobiographical pieces are often tedious in their egocentricity. The best of his writing is to be found in his accounts of Parisian life during the Twenties. There he shines. He is unhampered by the need to construct plot and character, and his natural gift for observation is allowed full scope in recording the absurdity and extravagance of the age. Where Saint-Simon (a favourite author) had the court of Louis XIV as his province, Maurice Sachs had the drawing rooms of Chanel and of the vicomte de Noailles. He wrote of them with verve and malice.

It would be excessive to describe him as a scholar. He did, though, have some acquaintance with English literature. Among his permanent bedside books were the journals of Samuel Pepys and of Arnold Bennett. In the last days of his short life, which were spent in a Gestapo prison where he served his captors as an efficient stool-pigeon, he found distraction in reading the novels of Sir Walter Scott, whose dialogue, he surprisingly observed, struck him as 'rich and noble'. A translation which he undertook with the actor Pierre Fresnay of

Terence Rattigan's *French Without Tears* earned him much-needed royalties during the penurious 1930s. More in keeping with his real tastes were the translations he made of Daisy Ashford's *The Young Visiters* and of Ronald Firbank's *The Artificial Princess*. Throughout the Occupation he spent the occasional moments of peace and quiet with Arnold Bennett's *The Card*. It was, he said, 'one of the books that has amused me most'.

For Sachs himself was a card, a particularly Gallic type of card. Of course, Arnold Bennett's hero would never have allowed himself to be seduced, as did Sachs, by an elderly novelist who could be useful to him. Nor would he have insisted on sleeping, out of curiosity, with a peculiarly repellent Lesbian. But, like Bennett's Denry Machin, he had a steely eye for the main chance. However virulent the persecutions of his creditors, however outraged the protests of those whom he deceived and betrayed, he somehow turned up smiling again, ready as always to fascinate with his intriguing ugliness and his bewitching charm. Until, that is, he died in Holstein, aged thirty-eight, in 1944, with a German bullet in the back of his head.

The Twenties were a golden age for Sachs. He was young, he had money and he was determined to know everyone. Famous authors were touched by his flattery and invited him into their circle. Hostesses were amused by his conversation and put him on their guest lists. At Deauville he posed at the side of Gaby Deslys when she startled the crowds with her pink bathing suit, black satin lace, pink slippers, black turban and pink aigrettes. The photograph was one of his most treasured possessions. He went partridge shooting and felt a surge of heroism at the call of the horn in the woods, though by dinner time that evening he had lost his appetite for the dish put before him. He followed with tireless devotion a glittering round of party, ball and reception, and was rewarded by duchesses who said to him: 'My daughter is very literary. Are you, Monsieur?' It all went into his diary. After 1929 the entries stop. Life was no longer so amusing. He was reduced to literary hack-work, to shady deals in pictures and antiques, to intricate negotiations with money-lenders. Ten years later he was trafficking in gold and forged bank-notes. He showed a talent for double-crossing and was a skilled operator in the black market. The French authorities wanted him for currency offences. The Gestapo wanted him because he was a Jew. Nobody else much sought his company in those last dark days of the war.

For all that Sachs was cunning and amoral, an odd strain of innocence ran through him. He had a Boswellian readiness to display himself as a fool and a knave. He writes of the years between 1919 and 1929 with the naïveté of one who is trying to recapture the atmosphere of an Eden before the fall. Master Maurice makes his first appearance on a ladder set up by the kindly housekeeper and butler so that he may have a good sight of the Victory Parade. A few weeks later his adolescent face is glimpsed in the rue Huyghens at the first concert given by the Six. In a Paris deserted for the summer holidays, he un-typically ignores the fashionable exodus to Deauville and stays behind for a performance of *Socrate*. He gazes in dumb admiration at Gide, Claudel and Jammes. Cocteau he worships from afar. At last he is introduced: 'gay, charming, friendly and continually amusing', is his verdict on the man of whom he was to leave a portrait diverting in its spitefulness and irresistible in its cruel humour. *Le Gendarme incompris* finds him puzzled but bravely determined to understand the new movement. At *le Boeuf sur le toit* he feels the wind of change that will 'blow away the last fading shreds of Symbolism'. The names alone of contemporary ballets – *les Biches, les Fâcheux, le Train bleu, les Mariés de la Tour Eiffel* – fill him with a delicious emotion. He can no longer tell which notes belong to Auric or Milhaud, which curtains to Picasso or Matisse, which steps to Massine or Lifar. All he knows is that they blur happily into a haze of impressions. These include his memory of Barbette, the girl of dazzling beauty whose trapeze act thrilled everyone, and who, at the end, took off her wig to reveal that she was a man. Sachs went to visit him at his hotel. He was received by a naked figure in bed, its face covered with a thick plaster of black pomade. Among the books lying on a table was that definitive work known as *l'Onanisme seul et à deux*.

Sachs' pimply features were to be seen everywhere during the twenties. He was at the first ball to be given after the war in a private house. The mothers who had brought their daughters smiled tensely at the festivities. They did not want to show their enjoyment. So soon after the war, they thought, it would be indecent to give the impression of having a good time, and they concealed their pleasure with strained grimaces. The young people sat on the steps of the grand staircase, the girls looking especially attractive in the alluring poses they innocently adopted. Sachs was there with his Louise. He snatched a kiss over the champagne. He touched, greatly daring, a compliant knee. No one noticed. They were all too busy with their own explorations. (He was, we must remember, barely sixteen years old, and even he had to serve an apprenticeship, brief though it was.)

The arrival of broadcasting finds Sachs in wonderment. He reports that Sacha Guitry has acted a play in Melun and has been heard in Lille, Bordeaux and Marseille at one and the same time. With his wife Yvonne Printemps and his father Lucien, Sacha has nobly exiled himself to the provinces in the cause of modern science and has exerted his charm on a squat, black loudspeaker in the middle of an empty stage. Sachs' concierge believes it is an invention of the devil. She is little less disturbed by moving pictures. There are, Sachs records, forty-two cinemas in Paris. He goes to most of them in search of new films by Charlie Chaplin, now universally adopted throughout France as 'Charlot', and by Harold Lloyd. He admires the smiling heroics of Douglas Fairbanks. Will Rogers and Fatty Arbuckle make him laugh. Like all his friends, he is convinced that a new art has been born. There is no doubt that the theatre is doomed and that the film is killing the drama. A few more years and there will be no theatres left in Paris.

In 1924 he is astonished to find not a single horse-drawn cab the whole length of the avenue de l'Opéra. It is filled, now, with crawling motor-cars. How can people afford to drive? The tax has just been doubled and an extra five per cent levied on tyres. If the government goes on like this they'll put everyone off motoring. As for the traffic jams, they are appalling. His taxi takes twenty minutes one day to get round the place de l'Opéra. Another complaint he has to make reminds us that Paris has not changed at all in one respect : he spends over a quarter of an hour trying to put through a telephone call. Of course, there are people abroad who have worse problems. He sees photographs of German housewives setting off to market, their bags bulging with the two thousand million marks in bank notes they need for the morning's shopping. Perhaps even traffic hold-ups and an awful telephone service are preferable to inflation.

Young himself, Sachs was amused by his compatriots' admiration for antiquity, above all when it is embodied in actresses. The return of Sarah Bernhardt in 1920, a magnificent ruin seventy-five years old, was greeted with ecstasy. She had been away from the stage with a severe illness and had had to have a leg amputated. Her admirers wondered how she would triumph over this disability. Would she use crutches? Would she have a wooden leg? The noise of the 'trois coups' was heard, that series of sharp knocks on the floor made by a wooden stick that traditionally warns French audiences of curtain-rise. 'Here she comes!' murmured a cruel wit, who had opted for the second possibility.

If Maurice Sachs' journal sometimes takes on the quality of a yellowed newspaper cutting – as when he notes that Fatty Arbuckle comes to Paris and lays a wreath on the grave of the Unknown Warrior – this may be counted a part of its charm. His accounts of the Festival Dada suddenly catch the reader by surprise among a jumble of entries about Pearl White serials, Marshal Foch's presence at a rugby match, and the new vogue for cultured pearls. When André Breton and his anarchist friends appeared on the Festival platform they were hailed, Sachs notes, with a generously assorted shower of carrots, turnips, cabbages and rotten oranges. They were delighted. Was not their intention to *emmerder* the public? Anxious for truth, Sachs visited Francis Picabia, who, with his paintings, his poetry, his ballet *Relâche* and his magazine *391* was a leading propagandist for the theories of demolition represented by Dada. What, Sachs demanded earnestly, did it all mean? With a perceptibly twinkling eye, Picabia declaimed:

> Dada est insaisissable
> comme l'imperfection.
> Il n'y a pas de jolies femmes
> pas plus qu'il n'y a de vérités.

Max Jacob was more accessible. Sachs described him: '... a shining cranium, enormous nose, sensual lips, square chin, uniform complexion, comic, scandalmongering and poetical'. Max took to him – he always did to the young, however unattractive they might be. A princess had just written asking to buy one of his manuscripts. How flattered he was, said Max, that she should take an interest in an old and impoverished poet. (Here glancing around him victoriously and asking the universe to testify to his modesty.) She had sent him a large cheque. Knowing, she said, his charitable nature, knowing that he lived among the poor, would he please distribute the cash among them? He had replied: 'Princess, you are wonderfully kind, and since I consider myself to be, with good reason, the poorest of the poor in my parish, I will take the liberty of putting your cheque to my personal use.'

They met again, Max proudly wearing a pair of red socks knitted for him by yet another princess, and Maurice listening with greedy enjoyment to the stream of anecdote and libel that flowed from his new friend. Had he heard the one about Madame de Staël and Benjamin Constant? It dated from the time when she was at the height of her love for the novelist. They had been to the opera to see la Malibran. 'Ah!' cried Constant, 'Malibran was sublime in Act One!' 'Sublime?' sneered Madame de Staël. 'Well, she was wonderful in Act Two.' 'Wonderful? You're exaggerating,' was the cold and jealous reply. 'Well then, she was very beautiful in Act Three.' 'Very beautiful? How you go on, *mon cher ami*.' 'You must admit she showed delicacy in Act Four.' 'Delicacy ... delicacy ... pooh!' 'After all, *ma chère*, in Act Five the tones of her voice ...' 'Tones of her voice?' Constant admitted defeat. 'Oh well, what do you expect, Madame? The poor wench did what she could ...'

Before Max left Paris, that den of temptation which he periodically fled for the peace of Saint-Benoît, he inscribed Sachs' name in his missal, a plump black volume stuffed with religious pictures. 'So that I shall be able to pray for you every day at Mass,' he explained. It was about this time that Cocteau began a much advertised flirtation with religion. The sounds of theological argument were heard by startled customers at 'le Boeuf sur le toit', and the placid air of Maxim's was rent with pious self-questioning. Where Cocteau went, Sachs, the admiring disciple, was sure to go. He corresponded at length with his idol. He decided he would belong to God entirely. He exhorted Cocteau to join him at Holy Communion. He ended his letters: 'I embrace you in the love of Jesus', and drew the sign of the cross beside his signature. He wore the soutane with a special pleasure because, he said, when he gathered up the folds to climb stairs it made him feel like a woman. And anyway, black was such a flattering colour.

These aspirations to a higher life were not, we may be sure, of a lasting nature, and at no time was the church's canon in danger of being enriched by the addition of yet another Saint Maurice. Not long after his discussions with Cocteau of things holy, Sachs was taking his new girl friend on a tour of dance-halls. She had demure blue eyes and looked vaguely English, but when she danced the Charleston, Sachs observed admiringly, she was transformed. Their evening wanderings followed a litany of familiar names: the rue Pigalle, place Pigalle, rue Notre-Dame-de-Lorette, rue Blanche, rue de Clichy.... They would look in at le Perroquet, chez Florence, le Florida, le Jardin de ma tante, and, of course, the Boeuf sur le toit. There were 'dancings' everywhere that had sprung up in response to the raging Parisian fever for violent saltation. The most typical of them had red lacquered walls and were hung with lanterns both orange and blue that shed a dim, quavering light over the dancers shimmying ecstatically beneath them. At one side was the tango band. On the other was the jazz en-semble with its black piano, trombone, saxophone and per-cussion. In a tiny space, surging back and forth at a rate of perhaps three inches an hour, the dancers jerked to the rhythms of 'I wonder what's become of Sally?' They foxtrotted and one-stepped with grave pertinacity. The more ambitious of them introduced cunning variations on the usual steps: the 'rosalie', the 'allegro militaire', and the 'excentric'. And then the lights went even lower for tango time, when the tunes of *Flor de Ceibo* and *La Chirola* drifted through the room and Sachs' girl-friend reached the peak of excitement.

You were less likely to be annoyed by the nouveaux-riches and tourists who crowded the dance halls if you took your entertainment at private parties. There were many of these. Distinguished party-givers were the Faucigny-Lucinges, whose title dated from 1180. (The Faucigny branch went even further back to the tenth century.) They belonged to the oldest of the French nobility. They were kind enough to tolerate the dukes of the Empire who had come into existence only yesterday with Napoleon. There was true aristocratic condescension in the way they acknowledged creations of the Second Empire. They even had a gracious smile for those who bore a title conferred by the Vatican. Their speciality was fancy dress, a penchant which may have been inspired by dislike for the drabness of modern life and yearning for the colourful days when their ancestors went on Crusades or were authorized to attend Louis XIV at his defecations. At a ball give by the Faucigny-Lucinges the duchesse de Gramont (A.D. 1040) appeared dressed as a lioness, while her lover (very much of the twentieth century) was tricked out as a lion tamer. One enterprising lady contrived to portray Sodom and Gomorrah : at the front she wore the suit of a dashing young sportsman, vintage 1900, and at the back she wore a crinoline. Paul Morand was the baron de Charlus, and he was surrounded by friends impersonating Madame Verdurin, Oriane de Guermantes and the duc de Guermantes. In such a way did they combine perfect chic with literary awareness. One of the best fancy dresses of the season was that created by a Spanish artist. He came as Landru, the multiple murderer who disposed of his ladies by burning their corpses in a stove. The artist carried before him – and this, everyone agreed, was a masterly touch – a model stove with the leg of a victim sticking out of it.

At such parties Georges Auric was a frequent guest. He often dressed up as Balzac, and his plump, Bonze-like features smiled amiably out from above a splendiferous dressing gown. He would sometimes knock off a bit of music for his hostess and supervise the dance numbers. Or he would accompany a vocalist in some new songs he had just composed. He had come a long way from the days when, as a boy, he wrote his letters on paper headed with an effigy of Wagner. No one, except Cocteau, was now more articulate than he in the onslaught against Bayreuth. His notoriety as a propagandist was saluted by Picabia, in a reference to his friendship with Poulenc and Cocteau's *le Coq et l'Arlequin,* with the pun : 'Francis chante le Coq – Auric – haut.' In prefaces to books, in newspaper articles, in paragraphs for little magazines, he led the battle against German music and Debussy. 'I'd perhaps be happy for a moment if I could write music that would be played, between one and four o'clock in the morning, around the place Pigalle,' he told Picabia. 'But I can no longer go to bed late.'

Auric was, and is, a good man to have at a party. His

natural absent-mindedness added to his sociable charm. At a cocktail gathering assembled in honour of Edmond Jaloux, a then celebrated man of letters, Auric was confronted with the guest of honour himself.

'Je suis Jaloux,' announced the great man.

'Tiens,' replied Georges agreeably, 'de qui?'

Auric, like Francis Poulenc, chose to write at the piano. His first draft of an orchestral piece usually gave the impression of being a piano arrangement of some score as yet unwritten. Scribbled in four or five clefs instead of the usual two, it looked totally unplayable. He became a legend with his publishers through his habit of bringing with him his latest piece in this form and of massacring it at the piano in the attempt to give them a rough idea of how it sounded. (A publisher, rather unfairly, tape-recorded one of these sessions. He was forgiven by the kind-hearted composer.) On these monstrous piano scores Auric was able to indicate the orchestration he had in mind. He went in for sharp contrasts, for sudden switches between unexpected groups of instruments. This is the technique of the actor, of the public performer, who must keep the interest of the audience with a presentation that is always varied and, for the moment, stimulating. The composer who works for the theatre and the cinema needs a talent such as this, and Auric has it in full measure.

Apart from plays, films and ballets, he has written little for the concert hall. His most substantial writing has been for the piano, and even this has only been a sideline. The five *Bagatelles* for piano duet are taken from music which began life as an accompaniment to plays. They are well put together and lie easily under the fingers. The concert transcription of numbers from *les Fâcheux* has already been mentioned. The *Petite suite*, which is dedicated to Louis Laloy's wife, contains two neat adaptations of sixteenth-century Polish lute pieces. They are the sort of thing Saint-Saëns used to do so impeccably when his compulsive urge to write music was temporarily blocked for lack of an idea. The remaining items are embroideries on themes of a madrigal-like nature. The piano *Sonatine* of 1923 shows that Auric needs the stimulus of an extra-musical idea to do his best, for here, where there is no dramatic event to illustrate, he fumbles and is ill at ease.

Auric is much more at home in his natural place as a writer

of ballet. This branch of the theatre calls for a special sort of gift. The composer must adopt an approach quite different from the one required for writing 'pure' music. Instead of thinking in terms of symphonic development alone, he has to work to a scheme already laid down by the choreographer and he must produce music that underlines plot, rhythm and action. Writing ballet music is just as much a specialist technique as is the conducting of it. It is here that Auric finds his true métier. He has an instinctive feeling for the dance. Because he visualizes the music in a choreographic light he is able to adapt perfectly to the demands that are made on him.

Les Matelots was one of his notable ballets of the Twenties. It was the result of a commission from Diaghilev, who had quickly recognized and admired Auric's talent for the ballet. Auric was a favourite composer with the Russian impresario, who on this occasion helped Boris Kochno prepare the piece. While working on his score Auric stayed with friends near Cannes. His hosts went off one day to look at a château they wanted to buy and left him alone with a fellow guest who was none other than the omnipresent Nina Hamnett. She looked at her companion a little apprehensively and decided to take a stroll in the garden. As she admired the freesias which had just started to bloom she heard, from an open window, the strains of 'Je cherche Titine' being played on the gramophone. It stopped and then started all over again. She heard it not twice, not thrice, but thirty-five times in all. Georges, she decided, must either be a very interesting or a very mad person. She went back into the house and cocktails were served by the butler. In their attempts to open the shaker Nina and Georges became quite friendly. By lunch time they were on excellent terms. Georges revealed that he had just arrived from Monte Carlo and had completed the first two acts of *les Matelots*. 'It was,' said Nina Hamnett, who was something of an expert on this particular subject, 'all about sailors . . .'

Georges had hoped to complete his ballet while staying in the house. But ideas were stubborn in coming, he confessed, and he was worried about finishing his last act. At which the versatile Nina, drawing on the vast repertory of English sea songs with which she was accustomed to entertain her bar companions, whistled a choice of tunes to him. Soon he had devised accompaniments to them. The hosts returned next morning, and for the rest of the day everyone sang songs to him. Georges worked quickly, ignoring invitations to swim or take a walk, and spent all his time at the piano. *Les Matelots* was done, and Nina was charmed to hear the tune of *Nautical William* booming out in the finale. 'If you see Diaghilev don't say anything about the third act!' Georges warned her as he packed his bags. At one of the performances, however, Diaghilev came up to her and inquired, quoting from the song: 'And how is the fair young lady?'

Les Matelots, which appeared in 1925, was one of Diaghilev's most successful ballets. The plot is slight and is vaguely concerned with the comings and goings of three sailors and their two girl-friends. Instead of having to follow a complicated plot, all the audience had to do was sit back and enjoy a series of ingenious dance numbers exquisitely performed amid numerous changes of scenery. Serge Lifar as the French sailor danced Massine's choreography with elegance and brio. The part was one of his earliest triumphs and Diaghilev basked in the congratulations on his new 'discovery'. In Paris, which lately had been cold towards Diaghilev, or so he imagined, *les Matelots* revived the old admiration for the Ballet russe.

A year later Auric wrote *la Pastorale* for Diaghilev. Lifar again danced a leading role and Balanchine did the choreography. This time the ballet did not do so well, partly because the number of props required by the designer was a little excessive – there were rostrums and screens to be man-handled over the stage while the action was going on, and the bicycle which Lifar as a telegraph boy had such amusement in manipulating tended to steal the show. It even featured in a *pas de deux* with one of the other dancers, and the audience waited hopefully for some dreadful accident to happen. Twelve scene changes, moreover, were needed to tell the story which related, in some misty fashion, to the shooting of a film.

The last ballet Auric wrote during the twenties was *les Enchantements d'Alcine*. This was a full-scale piece for Ida Rubinstein, who produced it at the Opéra in a lavish and expensive setting. The plot, devised by Auric's old friend Louis Laloy, came from Ariosto. It was suitably exotic. In the gardens of a palace Roger the poet and Tancrède the warrior compete for the hand of Angélique. She is undecided and flirtatious. Alcine, the Rose Fairy, at this point falls in love with Roger and casts a spell over him. She changes the rocks into monsters and the flowers into Amazons so that they may keep him prisoner in her enchanted garden. Angélique comes to his rescue and breaks the spell with a magic rose. While Tancrède mopes in the background she bestows on Roger the favour he had sought.

This elaborate confection, which Auric dedicated to Ida Rubinstein, opens with a brisk and brilliant prelude later broadening out into processional grandeur. The mixture of styles is an intriguing one. The *pas de deux* of Roger and Tancrède recalls the 'Signes du Zodiaque' in Satie's *Mercure,* while the Amazons stamp out their hearty dance to music reminiscent of the finale in the first act of *Relâche.* The 'Nocturne' pays blatant tribute to Chopin. Yet another number, a pastel-coloured duo, would have disgraced neither Delibes nor Messager. The Flowers sway gracefully to a little melody like those sentimental songs that were to be heard at the tea dances in the Twenties, and Alcine's slow waltz is nothing more nor less than a popular café-concert tune. For a composer of ambitious symphonic works such remarks would be damaging. Here, though, we are speaking of ballet, where fleeting impressions are important and where music is only one of the elements. And that, so far as Auric is concerned, is all that matters.

II

Milhaud at this time was looking for wider horizons than those offered by Diaghilev and his troupe. He dreamed of epic compositions, of large-scale operas on big subjects. The adventure of Maximilian, the Hapsburg archduke whom Napoleon III had made Emperor of Mexico and whose short-lived reign ended in execution at the hands of Juarez, aroused Milhaud's interest when by chance he read an account of it on a long sea journey to America. He saw the timid and all too human Maximilian impelled into a tragic situation by the greedy ambition of his wife and by the plotting of Napoleon. It ended bleakly with the famous scene Manet depicted in his *Execution of Maximilian.*

No sooner had Milhaud started writing his opera than

Claudel summoned him to his holiday home at Brangues. There he proposed a new collaboration. This was to be a spectacle about Christopher Columbus that Max Reinhardt would produce as a film or as a play. In the library, where the sounds of his children playing outside and the click of croquet mallets could faintly be heard, the poet read his script to Milhaud. This, Milhaud decided, was the epic he had been looking for. Claudel returned to America and his diplomatic duties while Milhaud started composing. Soon after this Claudel fell out with Reinhardt, and the opera *Christophe Colomb* was accepted for the Berlin Staatsoper. It was given a magnificent production. The chorus alone were allowed the luxury of a hundred rehearsals and the orchestra twenty-five. All the great resources of the Staatsoper were freely deployed. The curtain was taken down and the stage extended on both sides the length of the theatre to make room for the large chorus. A cinema screen at the rear of the stage was used to project films illustrating the thoughts of the characters or commenting on the action. There were, in all, twenty-seven changes of scene.

Christophe Colomb was wildly successful and ran for two years. A concert version also was enthusiastically greeted in lands throughout Europe. Today it is possible to wonder at the reputation *Christophe Colomb* once enjoyed. Some of its success may have been due to the skilful stage techniques of the Staatsoper, to the sympathetic conducting of Erich Kleiber, and to the very boldness of the conception. There is no doubt that Claudel's verse is nobly equal to the subject. Yet Milhaud's genius does not run to the grandiose gesture. His score is full of ideas. It luxuriates in a wealth of happy discoveries and ready invention. What is lacking is a sustained breadth of imagination on a level with the exalted tone of Claudel's words. The best moments come not in the large-scale scenes but in the more intimate passages – such, for example, as when the solo soprano sings of the spirit of God descending on the waters: 'L'esprit de Dieu descendit sur les Eaux sous la forme d'une colombe.'

Milhaud next turned to a far less portentous matter. He, like many of his friends, often dined at the home of Jeanne Dubost. She was the hostess of a well-known salon where she liked to entertain musicians, artists, and politicians of the extreme left wing for whom she had a decided passion. A feature of the Paris season was the evenings she organized for famous visiting artists. One of them, a Russian bass of vibrant power, sang his piece so stridently that a crowd of alarmed passers-by stopped in the street and gazed anxiously up at the window from which the blasting decibels proceeded. Another memorable occasion took place when she invited a Red Indian chief to honour her drawing room with his presence. The Mohawk pranced frenetically back and forth across the carpet and shrieked a few well-chosen war cries. Then he went up to Jeanne and planted an immense feather in her hair. An obscure guest whom nobody knew discreetly waved to her to take it out. 'It's wonderful, mon cher,' sighed Jeanne, 'it's as if he'd decorated me with the Légion d'honneur.' The protesting unknown was her husband. He had come home late from the office, hoping to avoid what he called her 'mountebank friends'.

The 'mountebanks' decided one day to show their gratitude to Jeanne Dubost for her hospitality. This took the charming form of a ballet-divertissement which they called *l'Éventail de Jeanne* and which was danced at her house by girl ballerinas from the Opéra. Ravel contributed a delicious little Fanfare. It begins with elfin shyness and expands 'Wagneramente', as the direction runs, into a sonorous triple forte. A 'Marche' by Pierre Octave Ferroud is the opening number. (Ferroud was a young musician who had exchanged his early work in chemistry and physics for composition, music criticism and organizing a society which did important work in spreading the gospel of contemporary music.) He had been introduced to Jeanne Dubost by his teacher, Florent Schmitt, whose 'Kermesse-Valse' ended the programme in a mood of rumbling peasant jollity.

In between there came pieces by Jacques Ibert, Roland-Manuel, Marcel Delannoy and Roussel. The three members fo the Six who wrote for Jeanne were Milhaud, Poulenc and Auric. Ibert's 'Valse' was typical of the music he turned out when he chose to wear a jester's cap. It reads like a parody of Ravel's own *la Valse*. Since Ravel, to begin with, had created a Viennese pastiche, Ibert's little joke assumed an incestuous tinge. The next item was by Roland-Manuel, who, as composer, teacher, publisher and writer, was an all-pervading figure in modern French music. His 'Canarie', based on the ancient Spanish dance form that Lully used several times, had a cool restraint after Ibert's gaslit whirlings. Marcel Delannoy, Honegger's friend, also went back to earlier forms and wrote a 'Bourrée'. A repeat of Ravel's Fanfare was suceeded by Roussel's 'Sarabande'.

Then came the turn of the three representatives of the Six. Milhaud's 'Polka', danced by the eight-year-old Tamara Toumanova, was brief and pointed. There was humour in its prim rhythms and an engaging nonchalance in its harmonies. The 'Pastourelle' that Poulenc composed for the occasion was destined to achieve a fame which the musician himself thought disproportionate when he compared it with other works that he cherished more dearly. It was even used by unfriendly critics as ammunition when they attacked him for flippancy, as if he spent his time deliberately writing frivolous miniatures instead of the deeply felt songs and religious works. He classed it, regretfully, among his 'oeuvres maudites', that area of a composer's production to which Saint-Saëns relegated his *Samson et Dalila*, Ravel his *Boléro*, and Dukas his *Apprenti sorcier*. Finally, in the *Éventail de Jeanne*, Auric's 'Rondeau' added a touch of dry clarity contrasted with a smudgy episode not unrelated to a Satie *Gymnopédie*.

Among the audience at the private performance of *l'Éventail de Jeanne* was the director of the Opéra. He was so impressed by the spectacle, by Marie Laurencin's wispy décor and costumes, that he insisted on producing it in his own theatre. The situation was ironic, for Milhaud, who had written so many stage works that had never been seen at the Opéra, was understandably annoyed at the thought that he was at last to be represented in that hallowed place by a trifle he had dashed off in a few minutes one bright May morning. He pointedly stayed away from rehearsals. *L'Éventail de Jeanne* had a respectable run of twenty-three performances. And Milhaud's feelings were soothed when, shortly afterwards, the Opéra put on his *Maximilien*.

Poulenc's contribution to *l'Éventail de Jeanne* had been one of the piano pieces he was busy with during a time when Milhaud and Auric were concentrating on the theatre. The *Promenades*, written some years before, consisted of ten little sketches dedicated to Artur Rubinstein. (That high priest of Chopin had once joined Milhaud and Auric to play a piano arrangement of *le Boeuf sur le toit*. Though originally intended for four hands only, Rubinstein's impromptu assistance turned it into a thoroughly convincing arrangement for six.) 'A pied' ambles along in much the way Poulenc used to walk himself. There is, perhaps as a respectful gesture to the dedicatee, a snatch of Chopin embedded in the item called 'En auto', and it is carefully labelled as though to forestall unfriendly criticism. It seems that Poulenc's attitude towards the more speedy forms of mechanical transport was not unlike Rossini's when he set about writing the *Péchés de vieillesse*. A hint of timorous respect lies in the musical directions: 'très agité' for the motor-car, 'vif' for the railway, which is a brisk exercise in the style of Scarlatti, and for the bus, a shuddering succession of lurching chords, the single ominous word 'trépidant'. 'A cheval', by contrast, is another 'Mouvement perpétuel', and 'En avion' suggests the peaceful landscapes glimpsed from above. The *Promenades* did not wholly satisfy the composer and he withdrew them ten years later, reissuing them in 1952 with adjustments intended to improve the style of a suite which, if it is not a major work, at least contains effective passages.

Another work that Poulenc revised after publication was the *Cinq impromptus*. They are agreeable little pieces that flirt, lightly, with music-hall idiom and rely for their success on a stylized charm. The *Trois pièces* extend in time from 1917 too 1929. The 'Pastorale' which is of their number is the oldest of Poulenc's published items. He wrote it before *Mouvements perpétuels* and dedicated it to his teacher Ricardo Viñes. In 1929 Casella asked him what had become of the early 'Pastorale'. Poulenc refashioned it, added a 'Toccata' which Horowitz was to make into a tour de force, and tacked on a third number called 'Hymne'. Of these three it was the last-named for which he had most affection.

Chamber music was also a preoccupation during the Twenties. He wrote sonatas for clarinet and bassoon, and for horn, trumpet and trombone. They are unpretentious works. The second, as the combination of instruments implies, has about it a suggestion of Bastille day celebrations. In the *Trio* for piano, oboe and bassoon, however, Poulenc showed that he had come to grips with chamber music. He took Ravel's advice and based his first movement on a Haydn allegro. The rondo, again following in Ravel's footsteps, he modelled on the scherzo from Saint-Saëns' second piano concerto. The result, despite the careful and detailed planning that lies behind it, has an attractive spontaneity and freshness.

After the *Bestiaire* and *Cocardes,* Poulenc's vocal writing languished until he renewed acquaintance with Apollinaire's verse in the 1930s and went on to set the poems of Éluard. The *Poèmes de Ronsard* which he wrote in the mid-Twenties were an uneasy exercise. The influence of Stravinsky is a little too obvious in 'Attributs', and the complete set is generally uncharacteristic. It was necessary for Poulenc to feel in sympathy with a poet before he could set his verse, and, as Auric pointed out, Ronsard was not suited to him. Keep on with Apollinaire, Max Jacob, Éluard and Reverdy, Auric wisely counselled. Poulenc did not take the advice. The *Chanson gaillardes* which were his next offering went to seventeenth-century drinking choruses and love songs for their texts. They were boisterous and often crude. Refinement was the near-neighbour of coarseness, and a quatrain celebrating fidelity in love was abruptly followed by ribaldry. But the mixture, surprisingly enough, is successful. 'I'm very attached to this set, where I've tried to show that obscenity can settle down well with music,' Poulenc observed. 'I loathe dirty stories. The accompaniments are very difficult but well written, I think.' He was less fortunate in his choice of poet for the *Airs chantés*. Jean Moréas, the Greek-born writer of neo-classic verse, the specialist in marmoreal phrases and invocations to the gods, was far removed from the warmth and buoyancy of a Poulenc. Why the composer chose to set his poems is something of a mystery – unless he foresaw a perverse and childish delight in being able to tinker with the stately lines Moréas had chiselled. In fact, he admitted as much : 'I'm so little given to paradox – you need the mastery of a Ravel for it – that I'm still surprised at having written those four songs. I dislike the Moréas poems and I chose them precisely because I found them suitable for mutilation.'

In their time the songs Poulenc wrote at this point had success with audiences, and if today they are seen as not worthy of him at his best, they at least helped to confirm his reputation then. The *Chansons gaillardes* were given their first performance at a crowded concert where André Messager, who had known Poulenc since he conducted the première of *les Biches* and was interested to see what his young friend was doing now, found himself in danger of losing the seat that had been reserved for him because the crush was so great. Several hundred people were unable to get in and had to wait at the door. Those who succeeded in finding a place were rewarded by the début of a young and hitherto unknown singer called Pierre Bernac. His performance of the *Chansons gaillardes* brought him deserved recognition. It also earned him the friendship of Poulenc. Although they lost sight of each other for several years and did not meet again until a chance encounter in Salzburg, a collaboration of rare value soon grew up between them. After accompanying Bernac in some of his songs Poulenc realized that he had found the ideal interpreter. A concert tour followed. From then on the partnership flourished and became internationally known. They worked together so well, their artistic sympathies were so close, that they achieved an unusually perfect ensemble. Many of Poulenc's songs were written specially for Bernac, and he gave to them all a delicacy and lyricism that remain unique.

Poulenc always said that his meeting with Bernac was a turning point in his career. Another, he added, was his acquaintance with the harpsichordist Wanda Landowska. She was, like Bernac, to have a big influence on his work and also to inspire him to write one of his most substantial pieces, the *Concert champêtre*. The tiny figure of Landowska fluttered across his path in the mid-Twenties. She had been born nearly fifty years before in Warsaw, where she started playing the piano at the age of four. A visitor to the home once performed, for the little girl's delectation, some pieces at her little upright piano. As to be expected from a former pupil of Liszt, she dashed off a string of brilliant transcriptions. In between them was sandwiched a modest item that impressed Landowska far more than the bravura displays that succeeded it. She was struck by the purity and rhythm, and captivated by its melodic outline. Its title, she learned, was *le Tambourin* and its author was Rameau. However many times she played it in her later career – and she must have done so on hundreds of occasions – she never forgot the thrill of pleasure she felt on hearing for the first time a master of the old music which was to become her special province.

This moment of pleasure was brief. A new teacher disciplined her to play Kalkbrenner studies by the hour while she sighed for eighteenth-century music. Her secret ambition was to give a recital entirely of Rameau, Bach, Haydn and Mozart. She wrote out her programme and sealed it inside an envelope which she marked 'To be opened when I am grown up.' Subsequent teachers were Chopin specialists who put her through the Romantic repertory and only allowed her near Bach in transcriptions by Liszt, Bülow or Tausig. Gradually her real inclinations broke through. Nikisch heard the fourteen-year-old girl play pieces from *The Well-Tempered Clavier* and nicknamed her, with amused admiration, the 'Bacchante'.

In 1900, when she was twenty-one, she eloped to Paris with a journalist. There she found a growing, if often misguided, enthusiasm for seventeenth-and eighteenth-century music. The pianist Louis Diémer was attempting to revive works written for the harpsichord, and Saint-Saëns had joined in the scheme to publish the complete edition of Rameau. The early recital programmes in which Landowska took part are amusing evidence of musical taste at the time. Her own composition, a *Rapsodie orientale,* was followed by a Gounod duet. Daquin's eighteenth-century *le Coucou* was dwarfed on either side by a Schumann item and a Liszt Hungarian Rhapsody. There were several contributions by the dauntless but now forgotten Augusta Holmès, who attended in her own formidable person to play them. The names of Saint-Saëns and Diémer also figured as composers, and the recital closed with songs by Chaminade. Years later, as the result of Landowska's determined campaign on behalf of the older composers, her programmes were exclusively made up of the Bachs, Vivaldi, Couperin, Telemann and Rameau, which she played from scores whose accuracy she had established after long and minute research.

For, almost as soon as she had arrived in Paris, she was writing articles and books to champion the cause of old music undistorted by the modern piano. Even more important was the practical example she set. She made herself a virtuoso of the harpsichord. The notes she printed in her programmes showed an astonishing range of erudition in a subject which had up to then been relatively neglected. She travelled Europe lecturing and playing. And while she showed an unrivalled acquaintance with the topic she loved most, she was too versatile a musician to cut herself off from other aspects of her art. She had an instinctive sympathy with her compatriot Chopin, of

whom she wrote perceptively, and she showed as much skill in
her solutions of ornamentation problems in Mozart as she did
when discussing them in Bach.

Having completed what for many people would have been
the work of a lifetime, the tireless Wandowska now turned
her attention to modern music. When, in 1923, the first Paris
performance of Manuel de Falla's puppet show *El retablo de
Maese Pedro* was given at the home of the princesse de Polignac,
it was Landowska who played the harpsichord part written
into the score. For the first time the harpsichord took its place
in contemporary music. (The piece was dedicated to the princess, who had commissioned it, as she also commissioned
Socrate.) Poulenc was there, and his teacher Viñes, who had
helped work the puppets, introduced him to Landowska. He
was overwhelmed by the iron will, the patience, the bee-like
industry contained within her frail little body. 'Wanda
Landowska is one of the few women to give me the impression
of genius in its pure state,' he commented wonderingly.

She invited him to her home in Saint-Leu-la-Forêt. The
village lies fourteen miles to the north of Paris at the foot of
the forest of Montmorency. It once had, Proustians will be
pleased to note, a church dedicated to Saint-Loup. The present
church contains a depressing monument built to the memory
of the father of Napoleon. If the traveller ignores this he will
find much that is agreeable in Saint-Leu. The road that leads
through it is one of the main entry points into the forest where
Rousseau and Diderot took their promenades. An added charm
for Poulenc was the discovery that Couperin had stayed in
Saint-Leu many years before. Wandowska's house, transformed
by its owner into a place of beauty, looked out over a classical
French garden in which she had built a modest recital room.
Pianos there were, of course, and harpsichords too, as well as
the instruments she had been collecting for years : an eighteenth-
century organ, spinets, clavichords, pianofortes and violas. In
this place, on Sunday afternoons, she gave concerts where she
breathed new life into the music of centuries ago. It was here
that she founded her École de musique ancienne and gave
classes and lectures. The library she filled with innumerable
scores, manuscripts and books.

Some time after they had worked together on *El retablo,*
she asked Falla to write a harpsichord concerto for her. Her

enthusiasm inspired him to produce, after three years of work, one of his most important pieces. It was inevitable that by the time her friendship with Poulenc had ripened she should make the same request to him. Landowska, said Poulenc, had given him the key to Bach and taught him all he knew about the French harpsichordists. How could he refuse? He was, as we know, a slow and painstaking worker, especially when confronted with the many novel problems such an undertaking brought with it. By 1927, four years after their first meeting, she was kindly but firmly urging him on. She had just given the Falla concerto in New York and had interested Kussevitzky in Poulenc's forthcoming work. Would it be ready by next spring? She was anxious to rehearse it well in advance.

In August of the following year Poulenc had yielded up the first part of his concerto. 'I'm in a hurry to see you again,' wrote his gentle tormentor, 'because there are a thousand things on my mind and we shall have to spend whole days together at the harpsichord to discuss them.' Next month she was delighted to have portions of the finale: 'I throw myself hungrily on them, and I see they're very difficult! Mon Dieu! Mon Dieu! What shall I do? Why are you so far behind?' The thought of what devilish virtuosities Poulenc must be concocting for her made her horribly uneasy. After waiting three years for Manuel de Falla's concerto, she knew only too well the anxiety of having to un-learn whole passages discarded at the last minute, and of having to work out a completely new scheme of fingering.

At last the *Concert champêtre* was finished. One Sunday morning in the spring of 1929 Poulenc went out to Saint-Leu, and in the little recital hall, among the cherries and the peach trees of Wandowska's garden, he gave a private hearing of his work at the piano. A few days later Pierre Monteux conducted the first performance at the Salle Pleyel with Landowska playing the harpsichord. The collaboration between the tall young man and his diminutive mentor had produced music which was more than a pastiche and which revived the spirit of the French harpsichordists. A thorough study of the instrument's resources, aided by Landowska's practical knowledge, had enabled him to write a masterpiece of *art galant*. But while it evokes the rustic diversions of Watteau and Fragonard, it is also a uniquely personal work. Poulenc, the townsman born and bred, regarded Saint-Leu as the countryside, whereas in fact it is little more than suburbia. Up to the age of eighteen, and before he acquired his house in Touraine, he looked on the bois de Vincennes, the hillsides of Champigny, and all the immediate surroundings of Paris, as real country. For which reason he interpolated military fanfares at one point in his score and upset a critic who took them as evidence of frivolous incongruity. The intention was not to annoy. They were a reminiscence of bugle calls from the nearby fort of Vincennes, and for Poulenc 'they were as poetic as hunting horns heard in a vast forest had been for Weber.'

The orchestral writing is elaborate and includes a xylophone in the score. The first movement opens with some arresting Stravinskyan chords. Then it slips into an allegro molto with the harpsichord leading the chase in a gaily articulated staccato. The horns suddenly intervene with a tragic hunting call, introducing what is to be one of the most noticeable characteristics of the whole work : the sudden alternations between hectic gaiety and deep melancholy. Watteau's sad clown Gilles hovers again over Poulenc's music. The trumpet fanfare that so irritated the critic mentioned earlier now follows. The atmosphere softens with a flute solo that reminds us of *les Biches,* and the harpsichord in turn picks up the melody. After some freely arpeggiated chords from the solo instrument and a brief reflective passage, the brisk allegro of the opening movement returns.

The second movement is a delicately scored Sicilienne for strings and woodwind. The stars of this section are really the oboes and horns, who receive sympathetic assistance from the harpsichord. Even the basoon, usually fated to be the clown of the orchestra, has some thoughtful solos. The Sicilienne goes on its gently undulating way until the pace slows down for some ornamented reflections from the harpsichord. The mood of wistfulness becomes one of sorrow when the horns play the main theme in a black minor key. As the movement ends they repeat its first five notes in an upward motion of yearning unfulfilled.

The Handelian presto which launches the finale into orbit continues its speedy course for most of the movement. Halfway through it expands into a thumping jollity quite different from the febrile cheerfulness that coloured earlier sections of the concerto. The trumpets, unashamedly military now, cut in with

brittle interjections, and the harpsichord darts waywardly off
in figurations straight from *les Biches*. The full orchestra builds
up to a climax in which xylophone and big drum forcefully
emerge. There is a silence. The harpsichord plays a little fanfare that harks back to the opening phrases of the first movement. It ends the concerto with a long and lingering arpeggio
whose sound dies slowly away.

The autumnal crispness of the solo writing, the variety of
orchestration and the air of alacrity that runs through the
Concert champêtre give it an unusual distinction among
twentieth-century concertos. Naturally curious to see how his
friend had met the challenge he himself confronted earlier,
Manuel de Falla became one of the earliest musicians to recognize its value. After receiving a copy he wrote :

How splendid, my dear Poulenc, to have, at last !, your Concerto
which I'm reading with the lively enjoyment I've always had from
your music. Now I look forward to the happy time when I shall
hear it and talk with you about the plans you had for your use
of the harpsichord. You can just imagine how very interested I
shall be, especially after a good complete hearing of the work.

As for Landowska, in one way the 'onlie begetter' of the concerto, she took it everywhere on her concert tours, arguing
fiercely with timid impresarios afraid of novelty, sometimes playing at a reduced fee for the privilege of introducing a work
she so passionately believed in, and gradually making it known
throughout the world. The composer had become, for her,
'Mon Francis que j'aime' and 'Francis, mon enfant chéri'.
Why, she inquired, did she adore his *Concert champêtre*? It
was because, she said, giving a reason with which many listeners
would agree, it made her feel totally *insouciante et gaie*.

12

THE OX COMES DOWN FROM THE ROOF – *AUBADE*

I

WITH the year 1929 the 'années folles' began to merge stealthily into the 'années difficiles'. The Prime Minister Raymond Poincaré was sick and ageing. His fifth cabinet, haunted by the problem of reparations and war debts, gave up an ungrateful battle after eight months of existence. He was succeeded by Aristide Briand, who, for little more than three months, held the office of Prime Minister for the eleventh time. He, in turn, made way for an administration that lasted little longer and was followed by a new government which must, in one respect, hold something of a record : perhaps because its leader, Camille Chautemps, was a man of great charm and courtesy, it lasted four whole days.

But amid the rumours of financial crisis and the gloomy forecasts of ruin to come, there were gleams of light. No year could be wholly bad that witnessed the departure, after a long, devious life, of the grim and unscrupulous Clemenceau. Hemingway published *A Farewell to Arms*, and King Vidor, in Hollywood, produced *Halleluja*, an early sound film whose noise and exuberance have never ceased to impress French cinéasts. In Paris Sacha Guitry inaugurated the new théâtre Pigalle – an affair of revolving stages and electrical gadgets – with a delightfully misleading and wittily inaccurate history of France from the early Gauls down to Aristide Briand, whose luxuriant moustache provided a link with Childeric and his drooping Gaullish appendage. The theatre posters bore the names of the two Marcels, Pagnol and Achard, and of Jean Giraudoux. It was the year when Cocteau brought out one of his best books, *les Enfants terribles*, which was followed, with unintentional irony, by *l'Homme vierge* of that now forgotten novelist Marcel Prévost.

Maurice Sachs had a number of tricky problems on his mind. The affluence he saw all around had begun to weary him, as unbroken fine weather at the end of summer can weary. Sometimes he regretted not having fought in the war. If he had, he decided, he would have been able to stifle his feelings of guilt. Manfully, he faced up to his difficulties and spent half a day discussing with his tailor, the best in Paris, a question that caused him much anguish : should a double-breasted suit have four buttons or six? The matter was left unresolved, and Sachs comforted himself with the thought that it would also have given such dandies as Balzac and Baudelaire reason for agonized discussion. Another awesome task which called for all his energy and application was given him by Chanel. She planned a supper to mark the end of the 1929 Diaghilev season. She wished to invite eighty guests, no more, no less. Who were they to be? Sachs was recruited to help compile the list. He revelled, for some time, in a sense of power. It was not unpleasant to be courted by society figures who, though they normally cut him dead, were anxious to appear on the list. There was an ineffable sweetness in the pleasure he derived from a clamant telephone, from the kindnesses that people for once sought to do him, and from the humility they briefly adopted in their approaches to him.

Chanel was said to have spent two hundred thousand francs on the entertainment. Among her eighty hand-picked guests was Kiki, uproariously drunk and chanting songs so obscene that a government minister's wife stamped indignantly from the room. The Negro dancer 'Snaky' performed a more amusing number. As he glided over the floor he inadvertently dropped the contents of a cigar-box he had just raided. Without turning a hair, the versatile artiste improvised the steps of a dance that enabled him, in time with the music, to pick up one by one the twenty or so Corona-Coronas that lay scattered at his feet. When, with the utmost grace, he had pocketed the last, he made his exit to warm applause. Then there were fireworks in the garden. It was, noted Sachs, very beautiful and yet very melancholy.

The guest of honour at Chanel's party looked worn and sad. Diaghilev was in constant pain, but he had struggled conscientiously to her mansion in the rue du Faubourg Saint Honoré. He was seen to lean heavily on the shoulder of Igor Markevitch, the musician who was his latest protégé. Three

H

months later Diaghilev came to rest in Venice. He lay on his bed, shivering and sweating, despite the intense heat of the room. Lifar and Kochno hovered jealously beside him. During the night he dozed into a coma. A Catholic priest, annoyed at having to deal with a member of the Greek Orthodox religion, grudgingly administered absolution. At dawn the sun burst into the room and illumined the sallow forehead. While the sea glittered in the rays, a nurse closed Diaghilev's eyes. Lifar and Kochno, as if by a signal, flew violently at each other's throats and fought on the floor. Now that their master was gone there was no one to restrain the hatred they felt for each other. The body of the old enchanter was put into a gondola and taken over the water to the cemetery. A flickering taper lit the inscription on his tomb : 'Venise, l'Inspiratrice Eternelle de nos Apaisements.' One by one the lights of the Twenties were going out.

The preoccupation that absorbed Maurice Sachs after Chanel's party was what to wear at the fancy-dress ball given by the vicomte and vicomtesse de Noailles. It would, he at last resolved, be a costume made of pebbles. The Noailles deserved the compliment of a well thought out dress, for they were among the most seasoned party-givers of the twenties. The vicomtesse, born Marie-Laure Bischoffsheim, was a granddaughter of the noblewoman whom Proust made into the duchesse de Guermantes. As a little girl she had horrified her grandmother by declaring an ambition to marry Jean Cocteau, her childhood playmate, when she reached the precise age of fifteen years and three months. Happily she kept her scutcheon unblemished in the years of discretion by espousing instead the vicomte Charles de Noailles, who belonged to the same family as that into which the Roumanian poetess Anna de Noailles had entered by a different branch.

Marie-Laure, whose complaisant husband sympathized with her arty inclinations, was an admirer of the avant-garde. She entertained lavishly in her splendid Paris home, in a country house near Fontainebleau, and in her villa at Hyères. Her portrait was drawn by Picasso and she had a wide acquaintnce among artists, musicians and writers. Inspired by the Surrealist film *Un Chien andalou* which Salvador Dali and Luis Buñuel had just made, she and her husband commissioned them to produce another. The result, *l'Age d'or*, shocked them and even brought about a dreadful incident for Charles : he was expelled from the Jockey Club, that most exclusive of Paris institutions. At about the same time they gave Cocteau a million francs to make *le Sang d'un poète* with a score by Auric. When they saw what they had brought into existence, they were almost as dismayed as they had been by the Dali-Buñuel collaboration. What was worse, their dear friends the Faucigny-Lucinges, who had among others agreed to take part in the film as a lark, found themselves involved, by ingenious cross-cutting, in scenes which were of a decidedly ignoble nature. But the Noailles, undaunted by threats of excommunication and by Charles' exclusion from the Jockey Club, smiled bravely and made a gift of all rights in the film to Cocteau.

The party to which they invited Sachs was one of their best. His pebble costume was acutely uncomfortable and inflicted horrible injuries on his dancing partners. It looked, moreover, dirty. 'I ought to have made it with shells,' he reflected sadly, 'but I didn't think of it at the time.' Marie-Laure was resplendent in holly – which must have been as dangerous to everyone concerned as Sachs' pebbles – and gleamed red and green in the light like a fire-fly. Charles wore a suit perfectly cut in oil cloth. One of the guests came as a mirror, and Paul Morand was dressed in the magazine covers of the *Nouvelle Revue Française*. Several hundred people, feathered and spangled, crowded into the garden which had been covered over for the evening. Max Jacob was to be seen wearing a black domino and leaning on a balustrade. He looked, someone said, like Pontius Pilate washing his hands of all the sins he saw being committed. After the Rocky Twins opened the spectacle with a dance number, there was a musical interlude by Georges Auric. The Étienne de Beaumonts then put on a *Divertissement gothique,* in which a countess wore a wimple and others paraded as angels. Sitting in agony on his pebbles, Sachs cursed the moment that had given him the ill-conceived idea for his costume.

The climax of the evening was a first performance of a new work by Poulenc. With their usual generosity the Noailles had commissioned from him a ballet and engaged both an orchestra and a troupe to perform it. The spectacle was called *Aubade.* Poulenc described it as 'amphibie', an epithet which nicely qualifies a Janus-faced composition that can be played either as a ballet or as a concerto for piano and eighteen instruments. The construction is episodic and the various items are linked by extended recitatives that introduce yet another element : that of opera. Horns and trumpets, 'lento e pesante', intone a rustic fanfare that recalls the *Concert champêtre*. The piano breaks out into an urgent, almost violent allegro which lasts until the curtain rises on a woodland glade at dawn. The companions of Diana the huntress awake one by one. Their vague presentiment of sadness is expressed by a repeat of the fanfare already heard in the overture, heavy and lagging. Diana herself appears. Consumed by a burning passion, she is yet condemned to eternal chastity, and for her each day that dawns is a reminder of her gloomy fate. She dances a Rondeau whose tune makes its wistful appearance on the piano, to be taken up softly by an oboe and developed by the woodwind – an enchanting touch. The gentle mood becomes one of anguished despair as the horns bellow the theme fortissimo. She passes, wild-eyed and distraught, among her retinue while the music shatters into brief syncopated phrases. She leans against a tree, her back to the audience, and various solo instruments again play the earlier theme to a soft accompaniment from the piano.

Diana's friends press round her and she allows herself, with a sulky grace, to be made up. Her toilette is the excuse for a mercurial presto clipped out by the piano against a background of swooping phrases contributed by, among others, woodwind and 'cellos. A larghetto, introduced by gulping grace notes from the bassoon, is heard while Diana accepts her bow and presses it to her heart. Then she dances her Variation. This is a delightfully Mozartian piece – as, indeed, it ought to be, since the melody is taken direct from one of the divertimentos. (Not the least of Poulenc's affinities with eighteenth-century composers was the habit he shared with them of putting to his own use a tune that happened to catch his fancy.) The Variation starts tranquilly and works up to a forceful climax before subsiding again. But the peacefulness is only an interlude. Diana's despair bursts out once more into an allegro feroce. She throws away her bow and vanishes into the wood, only to reappear and fall to the ground. An Adagio concludes the action. The woodwind play a misty phrase and the youngest of Diana's retinue hands the bow back to her. No one moves as she walks away and is suddenly hidden by the trees. The piano starts on a slow succession of chords. Her arm is glimpsed between the branches waving a last farewell. The melody moves forward to the steady beat of drum and plucked strings, and then circles endlessly in a revolving figure while Diana's retinue stay motionless in their surprise. The sun comes out. A sharp staccato octave brings down the curtain.

Poulenc wrote *Aubade* in a surprisingly short time for one who was usually a laborious worker. He did not begin until a month or so before the first performance at the Noailles' ball on 19 June 1929. His instructions for the playing of the work were clear and explicit. If *Aubade* were to be given in its concert version he insisted that it be described as a 'Concerto pour piano et 18 instruments' and not as a 'Concerto chorégraphique'. There was, further, to be no mention of the ballet plot in the programme, and the different movements were listed simply as Toccata, Recitative, Rondo, and so forth. He also had firm ideas about it as a ballet. At the Noailles performance all his directions were observed by Nijinska, who devised the choreography, while Poulenc himself took the piano part. It was a different matter at the first public production a year later in the Théâtre des Champs-Élysées. For this, Georges Balanchine drew on the myth of Diana and Actaeon and added to the scenario a male dancer. The innovation, as Poulenc rightly claimed, altered completely what he had conceived as a 'ballet de femmes'. During his lifetime the whims of choreographers and producers were to irritate him in the numerous productions *Aubade* received throughout the world. The one that came nearest to his original idea was given at the Opéra-Comique in 1952, where again he was at the piano.

It is often dangerous to look for a self-portrait of a composer in his music. Yet with *Aubade,* even more than with the *Concert champêtre,* one feels that Poulenc is in a revealing mood. The 'galant' manner conceals a strain of entrenched pessimisim. However impertinent the wit, however frisky the rhythms, the feeling of sadness persists. The inspiration, that of Diana condemned to a life of chastity, leads Poulenc to write passages suggestive of a longing that will never be assuaged. This, in turn, may well reflect his own experience of life. We know that even Cocteau, the prince of love à la grecque, had one or two flirtations with women that verged on reality.

There are no such events recorded in Poulenc's history. He was aware that his emotional make-up precluded marriage and a family. Like Diana, he sublimated his great reserves of warmth and affection. These he lavished on a wide circle of friends instead of on the children for whom he would have made an endearing father. If *Aubade* purports to be the story of Diana, it also tells us something about Poulenc.

I I

Aubade brought to its end a flamboyant evening that Maurice Sachs believed would mark an epoch. He crouched awkwardly among his pebbles in the taxi on the way home and thought about what he had seen. The Tout-Paris had flaunted themselves before him, people of talent, wealth, reputation and title, who in their absurd costumes summed up the madness of the age. Though was that age, he wondered, at all different from any other? Things did not really change a bit. 'Elegance is elegance : it will not alter its setting, any more than talent does. Those lovely women, those slim men with their little moustaches, they are France herself as one imagines her to be and as she really is on an evening in spring.' They represented, those men and women, a world that was little different from the Balzacian society that Rastignac had challenged and conquered.

Sachs was tired. That summer he felt a malaise settling on him. He went on holiday to Quiberville, near Dieppe. The crowds of people there were mostly unknown to him. He was bored by the grossness of the mothers and disappointed by the plainness of the girls. Was he getting old? It was more likely that the time of the Twenties was running out. Diaghilev, he noted in his journal, had taken the spirit of the age with him to his grave. And when summer was over, the restless Sachs debated whether he should spend winter in Paris or whether he should go to Morocco. In the meantime he bought a new motor car and toyed with the idea of investing money in a film project. 'Change your life. Do something!' said his mother, who had carefully brought him up to do nothing. (The energetic matron had recently had to spend a hurried vacation in England to avoid prosecution for passing dud cheques.)

Music-hall entertainers still sang about the Twenties woman,
though with a certain lassitude :

> Elles jouent du banjo
> Prennent des cocktails, mènent des autos
> Eh eh ! oh oh !
> V'là qu'ell' font beaucoup mieux
> Non contentes de se couper les cheveux
> Elles nous font voir leur mollets
> Jusqu'en haut, jusqu'en haut, s'il vous plaît !

Still you saw the flat-chested, short-haired ephebes at Nice
and Deauville, in Paris and Dieppe. From shoulder to waist
they formed a rectangle. From waist to knees they took the
shape of an irregular quadrilateral. A couturier once mingled
boys with his models at a fashion show and no one noticed
the difference. But the rectangular women now wore their
cloche hats with less assurance. They no longer bothered to
quote Joan of Arc in defence of their short hair. It did not
seem necessary when husbands and lovers were more concerned
with the news from Wall Street than with the performance of
the latest Isotta-Franchini, and when they anxiously scanned
the stock-exchange bulletins rather than their mistresses to see
if armpits had been shaved after the latest fashion.

On 'Black Thursday', 24 October 1929, share quotations on
Wall Street tumbled vertiginously. Many fell at a rate of twenty
points an hour. The source of all French economic problems
during the next ten years had begun to flow. Some were
affected much more quickly than others. Among them was
Maurice Sachs, whose family had all their money in American
stocks. His uncle committed suicide. His mother took to her
bed with a heart attack. Sachs telephoned New York and
found there was nothing left. All that remained in their Paris
bank account was ten thousand francs. Madame Sachs would
have to sell her jewels. Maurice would have to find a job.
He did so, and launched with varying success throughout the
following decade on his career as writer, petty thief, swindler,
and finally, as Gestapo nark.

On 11 December that year the Six met to celebrate their
anniversary. It was ten years since they had given their first
concert together in the cramped premises of the rue Huyghens
and a journalist had given them the label that made them

notorious. The age which had seen the birth of the group was dead. Indeed, no sooner had the group come to life than its various members were each going off on their own different ways. The situation was somehow typical of the ambiguity that characterizes the Twenties. The existence of the Six as a movement was an amusing legend dextrously fostered by Jean Cocteau, the arch-creator of myth. He, of course, was in the Théâtre des Champs-Élysées that day to weave more spells around the audience and to enchant them with his talk. The programme included Milhaud's *2ᵉ suite symphonique* which he had drawn from the incidental music composed for Claudel's *Protée*. Of the original satire which Aeschylus wrote only the title remained, and Claudel, with a boldness that could either be regarded as admirable or foolhardy, had written a full-length play which mingled clowning and poetic seriousness in full Claudelian measure. *Protée*, suitably enough for a work of that name, underwent four transformations. At first it took the shape of music for Claudel's play when given an amateur performance by Dutch students. Then it was enlarged to accompany a circus version . . . which never materialized. Finally Milhaud adapted and added to it for a full-scale theatre. This again came to nothing. At last, he turned it into a suite. It was *Protée* which, at its first public performance in 1920, caused the riotous scenes which have been mentioned earlier and which caused Saint-Saëns to write his furious letter of protest. In 1929 its controversial fugue was heard in respectful silence.

Germaine Tailleferre succeeded Milhaud on the programme and played the solo part in her piano concerto. Next to be heard were an extract from Honegger's incidental music for d'Annunzio's *Phaedra* and his symphonic poem *Rugby*. Louis Durey came out from exile at Saint-Tropez to hear a performance of his *Sonatine* for flute and piano. Deliberately written within a limited compass, and only allowing the flute a brief cadenza in the slow movement, the work satisfied its composer by achieving the sober tone and clarity he had sought. Then he conducted orchestral versions of his two lively piano pieces *Carillons* and *Neige*. The elusive Auric, probably busy in some film studio or other, does not seem to have been present.

The other work that figured at this anniversary concert was Poulenc's *Aubade*. Honegger conducted and Poulenc was the soloist. It was fitting that the Théâtre des Champs-Élysées, which had seen the first performance of *les Mariés de la Tour Eiffel*, should now be the the place where *Aubade* sounded the knell of a period that was over. For anniversaries commemorate something that is past. The febrility of *Aubade*, its *galanterie* and its playfulness, its humour and its hurt, contained within itself the disappointed hopes and wounded sensibilities of a youth that vanished with the epoch. In the earnest times that were to follow there was little room for the gay informalities of the band that once was known as the Six.

13

ENVOI

I

HONEGGER was the first to leave the scene. He died in 1955 at the age of sixty-three. Some of the works that made him a celebrity in the Twenties – *Pacific 231, Rugby* – seem faded now. Others have survived, and *le Roi David* continues to move its hearers. In the same vein he went on to write *Jeanne d'Arc au bûcher,* where Claudel's text inspired from him a fresco that worthily extended his gifts. Here he worked on a larger scale than in *le Roi David,* handling with assurance the big vocal forces – they included a children's chorus as well – and an orchestra augmented with saxophones and 'ondes Martenot'. *Les Cris du monde,* which took as its point of departure a poem by Keats, was another ambitious venture, though its limited success may have been due to the lack of such a universally known heroine as Joan of Arc. Again with Claudel as his librettist, he wrote *la Danse des morts,* one of his most affirmative declarations of faith. Towards the end of his life, when he was struggling against the ravages of heart disease, he managed to complete the *Cantate de Noël* of 1953. It is based on the carols of various European countries interwoven with liturgical texts and folk song. After this he was to write no more music, and the *Cantate de Noël,* in its austere grace, stands as a testament to the fundamental simplicity and honesty of its composer.

Honegger did not really find himself as a symphonic composer until after the Twenties. *Pacific 231* and *Rugby* were deliberate show pieces. His first symphony, written in 1930, shows him groping awkwardly for expression. With the second, which belongs to 1941, he arrives at mastery. Although it is conceived for chamber orchestra, the inspiration transcends the limitations of the form : in the last movement, with its trumpet solo outlined against the strings, the symphony becomes directly expressive of the composer's belief in the future of a Europe devastated at the time by war and misery. His third symphony he called a 'symphonie liturgique', not because it relates to plainchant but because his reading had given him the idea for the layout he adopted : a 'Dies irae' which is an explosion of ruinous anger, an adagio 'De profundis' of supplication, ending with a brief flute song, and a 'Dona nobis pacem' where anguish is transformed into hope. The fourth symphony, the 'Deliciae Basiliensis', returns to Honegger's Swiss origins, for it was written under the influence of a holiday near Basle. It has, as Poulenc remarked, a 'feeling of freshness, of the mountain, of pure air and edelweiss'. The last symphony of all was sub-titled 'di Tre Re'. Honegger good-humouredly explained that after Beethoven it was impossible for any other composer to talk about a fifth symphony, and so he had given his own the nickname as a reference to the 'ré' (D) which ends each of the three movements. It is not a peaceful work. Commissioned by the Boston Symphony Orchestra, it was expressly designed to show off the talents of virtuoso players, notably in the monumental finale. Personal anxiety and physical suffering provided the background to which the composer worked, and these influenced the tragic mood which pervades the whole symphony. Soon afterwards the *Cantate de Noël* was to restore Honegger's spiritual balance.

There were other aspects to Honegger's character. That he could write with Gallic lightness is shown by the *Concerto da Camera* for flute, cor anglais and strings. His operetta *les Aventures du Roi Pausole* is a diverting entertainment based on Pierre Loüys' hedonistic tale. *Les petites Cardinal* was another light-hearted excursion into the world of easy sentiment and last-act curtains when everyone lives happily ever after.

Like many of his fellow composers, Honegger was an articulate writer of prose. He himself did not see the necessity for music critics, and he observed that those whose names are still remembered owe their posthumous and unenviable fame to the stupid things they said. It was the public who made the final verdict, he claimed, and it did so for mysterious reasons that no critic could ever fathom. Writing about music only became necessary, in Honegger's view, when the need to champion new works arose. For a time he contributed regular articles to *Comoedia*. In them he attacked the hackneyed programmes which comprised the bulk of Paris music-making – the permanent Beethoven seasons, the piano recitals where Chopin's works gave 'star' performers an excuse for running a sort of relay race, and the insipid monotony induced by endless repetitions of the same small handful of works. He welcomed, with relief, the arrival on the scene of a young composer called Olivier Messiaen.

Honegger also broadened his scope to call public attention to the tribulations that faced the modern composer. He quoted figures to show that the four hundred copies of Debussy's *Première Arabesque*, which were printed in 1891, took twelve years to sell. A piano piece by Messiaen had a print order of five hundred in 1930 and was still not exhausted in 1951. The hundred copies of Milhaud's *2ᵉ Suite symphonique* remained unsold thirty years later. He contrasted this with the lot of an author, no more meritorious in his art than a composer, who sold many thousands of his novel, or with the young artist whose first exhibition might easily bring cash as well as reputation. How, asked Honegger, was the composer to make his way in economic conditions like these? What should he reply to the publisher who, when offered a new manuscript, said : 'Get yourself known and I will publish you'?

Of course, this was something peculiar to the musical life, and the literary man, by the very nature of his medium, was better placed than the unhappy composer. Honegger realized that he had been one of the lucky ones. Performing rights and conductor's fees had helped him to lead a reasonably comfortable existence. There was little to be done about the unsold works of aspiring Debussys and Messiaens that languished on the shelf. But when, at last, the composer had achieved a measure of fame, why should the unjust laws of copyright deprive his heirs, fifty years after his death, of their entitlement to what had been created? The public was legally allowed in this way to despoil another man's property. If you tried to obtain a free copy of the *Bachgesellschaft* or of Victor Hugo's works you would be unsuccessful. 'The argument will be that paper and ink cost money. Agreed. The thoughts of Bach and Victor Hugo are worth nothing, but paper and ink keep their value, don't they?'

The daughter of Johann Strauss died of an illness brought on by starvation. An operetta made up of tunes strung together from her father's work made a fortune for its exploiters. When Gounod's *Faust* became public property his family were automatically robbed of their heritage. Yet the price of seats at the Opéra remained the same, the singers and players received the same fee, the charge for programmes did not alter, and the usherette's tip was unchanged. 'The scholar, the artistic or intellectual creator, is, however, the only person who does not enrich himself by exploiting his neighbour. On the contrary, he makes a gift to humanity often by renouncing many material satisfactions. We know that he is rarely rewarded during his lifetime. He has the right to incomprehension, discouragement, contempt and sometimes poverty. Talent and genius are rewarded by the seizure of property.'

As time went by Honegger's pessimism increased. His fame brought him many letters from ambitious young people who wanted to write music. Grocery, he warned them, would be a better choice of occupation. The public would always need soap and noodles. The one thing they certainly did not desire was new music. Composing was neither a profession nor a career. It was a kind of intellectual malformation that was unforgivable. The first condition of indulgence was not to seek a hearing for your music and to talk about it as little as possible. After working hard on twenty or so works you might be lucky enough to obtain a performance of one of them. Don't think yet that you deserve the title of composer, Honegger warned. This only comes when you have painfully acquired the right to demand payment for your work. Sometimes the opportunity never happens. Rest assured that no one thought of Schubert as a 'great composer' in his lifetime.

Even so, Honegger gave the lie to this gloomy advice by working with even greater intensity as the end of his life approached. In 1947 a violent heart attack laid him low. Despite pain and discomfort, he insisted on composing and fulfilling rigorous concert engagements throughout the world. It may be that his pessimism was encouraged by his physical state. The handsome, energetic young man who had charmed his fellow-students at the Conservatoire became a gaunt, ashen-faced spectre who climbed stairs with agonizing effort and who lost all desire for the meals he once enjoyed with a gourmet's relish. On 27

November 1955, while awaiting his doctor's visit, he made to get up from his chair, fainted, and suddenly died in the arms of his wife. 'Arthur,' said Cocteau at his funeral, 'you were a charming friend : today is the first time you have caused us sorrow. Not the least of your merits was to have earned the respect of a disrespectful age.'

Only in the last two years of Honegger's life did Poulenc come to know him well. Until then the two composers had been friendly but not close. Their tastes and personalities were entirely different. The one was a Protestant, the other a Catholic. Honegger admired Beethoven, Wagner, Fauré and van Gogh. When Poulenc happened to hear some Wagner on his radio, he would afterwards put on a gramophone record of *Don Giovanni* 'to cleanse the ears and mind', he used to say. He worshipped Mozart and Chabrier. Erik Satie, whom he venerated, was for Honegger bereft of all creative power. Honegger shut himself up in his room to work, switched off the telephone, ignored the door bell and refused to answer letters. Poulenc rang up his friends every day for long conversations and loved to entertain crowded rooms with impersonations at the piano.

For Poulenc, the 1930s were a time when the two contrasting sides of his character, buffoonery and high seriousness, established themselves once and for all as the dominant qualities of his music. Two incidents served to remind him that the carefree days of the Twenties were over. The first was a decline in the family fortunes. He was assailed by financial problems which he had never, cushioned till then by shrewd investment, thought to meet. The second was the death of his close friend Pierre-Octave Ferroud, who, with Poulenc, was a fellow contributor to *l'Éventail de Jeanne*. At the age of thirty-six Ferroud was beheaded in an appalling car accident. When the news came through Poulenc was about to visit the shrine of Rocamadour and its black wooden statue of the Virgin. Soon afterwards he started work on the *Litanies à la Vierge Noire* for women's voices and organ. It is the first of his important religious works. Mourning for his lost friend inspired him to write with the simplicity and directness that characterized his religious beliefs. Then came a setting of the Mass and a number of motets that show how carefully this most eclectic composer had studied Monteverdi. The *Quatre petites prières* use texts by Saint Francis of Assisi, a man for whom Poulenc – and it is not difficult to see why – felt an admiring affection.

Poulenc's writing in this genre attains a high point in the *Stabat Mater* which he dedicated to the memory of Christian Bérard, the artist and stage designer. Technically it achieves a fine balance between the soprano solo, mixed chorus and orchestra. Aesthetically it is a rich experience, leading from the heartfelt 'Cujus animam' to a radiant 'Paradisi gloria'. There is no attempt at grandeur, and unity of tone is preserved by keeping the dimensions to those of a private but ardent prayer. The *Gloria*, written nearly ten years later, is by contrast exuberant in mood and attracted to Poulenc the same reproaches that were made about Haydn when he was charged with the high spirits of his religious music. If, Haydn was said to reply, as Poulenc might well have done, his oratorios were happy, that was because the thought of God made him so. In any case, Poulenc's final work, the *Sept répons des ténèbres*, which are settings of Holy Week texts, contain enough sublime gravity to disarm the most sober Catholic.

Poulenc's religious inspiration takes its most spectacular form in the opera *les Dialogues des Carmélites*. Originally a short story by a German author, it was turned into a film scenario for which Georges Bernanos was commissioned to write the dialogue. The film was never made. After Bernanos' death his work was adapted for the theatre. The suggestion to make an opera out of it came from Poulenc's Italian publisher. The composer needed no encouragement. In the *Dialogues des Carmélites* he set to music an exploration into the workings of grace. Though the period is that of the French Revolution, the background is only incidental and is a convenient setting for the main thesis of the work : we die not for ourselves but for each other, or even in the place of others. The mastery Poulenc showed in his songs is here deployed on a wider canvas. Although the orchestra is a large one, it is used sparingly and always in a manner that complements the vocal line. On the title page of the score Poulenc wrote a significant dedication : 'To the memory of my mother, who revealed music to me; of Claude Debussy, who gave me the urge to write it; and of Claudio Monteverdi, Guiseppe Verdi, Modeste Mussorgsky, who have served me here as models.'

Poulenc was to write only one more ballet after the Twenties.

During the sombre days of the Occupation he produced *les Animaux modèles*, in which he 'transposed' six fables of La Fontaine. It was not surprising that he should capture the worldly humour of 'l'Ours et ses deux compagnons' whose moral was to do with counting chickens before they are hatched. Neither was it unexpected that into 'les Deux coqs', a bustling tone painting like an item from Mussorgsky's *Tableaux d'une exposition*, he should introduce the tune of 'Non, non, vous n'aurez pas notre Alsace Lorraine' by way of cocking a snook at the German occupant. Just as typical of the 'Twenties' Poulenc are the grasshopper's twinkling dance in 'la Cigale et la fourmi' and the Java he incorporates into 'le Lion amoureux'. What is most impressive of all is his version of 'la Mort et le bûcheron'. The miserable woodcutter, dirty and sweating from the great pile of logs he carries on his bent shoulders, drops his load and reflects on his misfortune :

> Quel plaisir a-t-il eu depuis qu'il est au monde?
> En est-il un plus pauvre en la machine ronde?

Horribly poor, starving, taxed to the bone, he solicits Death, who comes to him in the shape of a beautiful and seductive woman. (This may be an idea borrowed from Cocteau, with whom it was a favourite – though, of course, the French word for death has always belonged to the feminine gender.) Despite his infinite wretchedness, the woodcutter changes his mind at the prospect of death and asks the lady to help him load up his wood again :

> Le trépas vient tout guérir;
> Mais ne bougeons d'où nous sommes.
> Plutôt souffrir que mourir,
> C'est la devise des hommes.

This grim evocation of the misery that lay behind the sumptuous age of Louis XIV led Poulenc to write some of his finest music. He contrasts the sinister charms of Death with the woodcutter's despair in several pages of intense but restrained emotion. No mere parlour clown could have done this.

The concertos he wrote after the *Concert champêtre* and *Aubade* proved once again that he followed no preconceived system. He openly avowed that he did not have a cut-and-dried formula. 'Inspiration is such a mysterious thing that it is better not to explain it,' he once said. The Concerto for two pianos flashes with a silvery smoothness. The initial haze of Balinese inspiration – a memory of the 1931 Colonial Exhibition – is dispelled by a crystalline Mozartean larghetto. The finale is a eupeptic saltarello tapped out by the pianists in turn. For the Organ concerto, as for the harpsichord, Poulenc carefully studied the instrument before writing music that utilized all its resources. While giving the virtuoso every opportunity to show his mettle, the piece happily combines passages of majestic thunder with others of gossamer delicacy, all the while preserving a neat equilibrium between the various elements involved. The last work Poulenc wrote in this form was the piano concerto of 1950. After the graver tones of much of his post-war music, the reappearance of his urchin side in this concerto upset many of his listeners. It is more of a 'divertissement' than anything else, and mingles the rhythm of a maxixe with the tune of *Way Down Upon the Swanee River,* a pleasantry he included for the benefit of the Bostonian audience who were the first to hear it. They were not very amused by what Poulenc gaily described as 'ce shake-hand'.

However much argument may simmer about the quality of Poulenc's other work, it cannot be contested that he is one of the greatest French song writers. He had an innate feeling for poetry and a hypersensitive gift for bringing out its musical qualities. Apollinaire, as we have seen, was a favourite with him, and he set no less than thirty-four of his poems. He never knew Apollinaire well, but :

The important thing was that I heard the sound of his voice. I think this is vital for a musician who is anxious not to betray the poet's intention. Apollinaire's tone, like the whole of his work, was both melancholy and gay. Sometimes there was a shade of irony in his talk, but never the tongue-in-cheek quality of a Jules Renard. That is why my Apollinaire songs should be sung without emphasizing the drollness of certain words.

The *Quatre poèmes* of 1931 evoke a turn-of-the-century atmosphere where the cinematograph is observed with an ironical eye, where Toulouse-Lautrec women play at cards, and where ornate Edwardian hotel bedrooms are the scene of weekend romps. As with the *Quatre poèmes*, many of the other items Poulenc was to choose came from the collection to which

I

Apollinaire gave the title *Il y a*. They include experiments in typographical layout ('Bleuet'), a lament for the vanished glories of Sunday boating on the Seine ('La grenouillère'), and baroque fancies like 'Dans le jardin d'Anna' and 'Allons plus vite'. In the cycle *Banalités* the Parisian tone of 'Hôtel', a poem that immediately represented for Poulenc a room in Montparnasse, and of 'Voyage à Paris', a naïf little jingle, is offset by the 'Chanson d'Orkenise' and the 'Fagnes de Wallonie'. 'Chanson d'Orkenise' is Poulenc's title for a song contained in the strange mixture of prose and poetry which Apollinaire called 'Onirocritique'. The narrator sings of the tramp who sets out from Autun by the Orkenise gate. To the authorities who ask what he is taking away with him, he replies : 'J'y laisse mon coeur entier.' 'Fagnes de Wallonie' speaks of the doleful uplands of the Ardennes and of the sadness they inspire in the poet's heart. The cycle ends with 'Sanglots', one of Apollinaire's finest poems on the universality of lost love, a theme that Poulenc matches with exquisite modulations in a setting which embodies the essence of the words. In *Calligrammes*, the last of Poulenc's songs from Apollinaire, he takes his leave of the poet with seven numbers which, if they do not better 'Sanglots' – an impossible task anyway – are as craftsmanlike as any of his earlier settings.*

The other poet whose writing excited Poulenc was Paul Éluard. They had met in Adrienne Monnier's famous bookshop towards the end of the 1914–18 war, when Poulenc heard him read his poems 'in a warm voice, by turn gentle and violent, soft and metallic'. It was necessary for Poulenc to have a personal contact with the writers whose verse he set, as otherwise he did not feel at ease when he attempted the musical transposition of their words. Even so, it was another fifteen years before he was ready for Éluard. In 1935 he wrote the *Cinq poèmes* as an experiment after a long period of getting to grips with the poetry. (Often some of Poulenc's shortest songs took him years before they came to fruition. An opening line here, a phrase there, would lie for an eternity at the back of his mind until one day, by an inexplicable process, he suddenly 'found' the complete work.) Three major cycles were to have Éluard

---

* Poulenc himself thought 'Voyage', the concluding song, to be superior to 'Sanglots'. Two isolated songs, 'Rosemonde' and 'la Souris', were set later as a sort of postscript to the Apollinaire canon.

as their poet: *Tel jour, telle nuit, la Fraîcheur et le feu,* and *le Travail du peintre.* The last of these celebrates Poulenc's twin loves, poetry and painting, for each of the seven poems has as its subject an artist. Among them are Picasso, Chagall, Braque and Klee. In *le Travail du peintre* voice and piano form a miraculous whole. Poulenc's own preference was for the 'Juan Gris', where a grave melody, to be pedalled with care, accompanies

> Table guitare et verre vide
> Table devait se soutenir.

His only regret about this cycle was that Éluard had never been able to write a 'Matisse', whom Poulenc adored but whom Éluard did not like. So, instead of the sunshine ending of a Matisse, *le Travail du peintre* closes with the sombre shades of a 'Jacques Villon'. The cantata, *Figure humaine,* is also to words by Éluard. It is an imposing, and difficult, *a capella* work written in 1943 when so many of Poulenc's fellow countrymen were being imprisoned, deported and shot. 'Finding in Éluard's poems the exact equivalent of what I felt, I set to work in complete faith,' said Poulenc, 'not without having commended my task to our Lady of Rocamadour.' The treatment is sober, and the mood, triumphant over sorrow and violence, is one of dignity.

In all, Poulenc set the same number of poems by Éluard as by Apollinaire. 'If,' he once said, 'the words: "Here lies Francis Poulenc, the musician of Apollinaire and Éluard" were to be put on my gravestone, I should feel that they were my finest claim to fame.' Apollinaire was also to provide him with the libretto of *les Mamelles de Tirésias.* This 'drame surréaliste', which Apollinaire completed in 1917, is a mad burlesque on the legend of the man-woman Tiresias. (Different versions of the legend had Tiresias, the Theban soothsayer, change his sex with bewildering speed. When asked by the gods which sex had more pleasure in love, he opted for the woman, thus annoying a goddess who struck him blind.) The heroine, who is dissatisfied with being a woman, turns into a man, her metamorphosis being the signal for a pair of shapely bosoms to fly up into the wings. Now she can have a career! Now she can be a soldier, an artist, a lawyer, a senator, a doctor, a philosopher, a chemist, a mathematician! It is her husband who is left to wash up the dishes and bear children... at a rate of forty thousand a day. In the end his wife returns to him, and they both exhort the audience to go forth and produce as many children as possible. Several earnest commentators have read into this farrago a serious plea by the author for re-population. It is, of course, nothing more than a zany joke into which Apollinaire shovelled ineptitudes characteristic of boulevard plays of the time. He wrapped up the mixture in a parody of the government mentality which awarded, and still awards, shiny medals and cash to 'mères de familles nombreuses', it being one of the highest patriotic achievements to possess a womb copiously fruitful of Frenchmen.*

Both Satie and Auric had been invited by Apollinaire to write incidental music for his play. Daunted by the mitsch-matsch put before them, they declined. It was left to Poulenc to write the Opéra-bouffe which so annoyed patrons of the Opéra-Comique in 1947, accustomed as they were to the more conventional suavities of Massenet and Puccini. The prologue to the *Mamelles de Tirésias* is eminently solemn. It is succeeded immediately by outright burlesque. An airy waltz accompanies the flight of the heroine's charms. From then onwards a kaleido-scope of different styles alternately surprises and amuses. Snatches from the café-concert are followed by Twenties tunes. Chabrier jostles Offenbach and musical comedy gives way to straight-faced chorale. In the middle of the broadest clowning a sudden word, an unexpected modulation, will change the mood abruptly to one of tenderness. The presence of a notorious pun in the lines 'Puisque la scène se passe à Zanzibar, autant que la Seine passe à Paris' does not conflict with the gentle, appealing nostalgia of the music. Satire and pastiche abound in *les Mamelles de Tirésias*, but so, too, does a lyricism that comes from the heart. 'If,' Poulenc once told a friend, 'you want to get an idea of my complex musical personality, you will find me exactly as I am as much in *les Mamelles de Tirésias* as in my *Stabat Mater.*'

Poulenc wrote two more works for the stage, both of them one-act monologues and both taken from original plays by

---

* Another explanation came from the painter André Derain, who loathed Apollinaire ('c'était un con'): 'He suffered from an ailment of the mammary glands, and when he squeezed them milk came out. That's why he wrote *les Mamelles de Tirésias.*'

Jean Cocteau. The first of them was *la Voix humaine*, Cocteau's
most widely performed piece. A woman deserted by her lover
speaks to him on the telephone for the last time. The audience
only hears her side of the conversation, and as the minutes
pass her despair intensifies. For it becomes clear that he is not
speaking to her from his own home and that perhaps there
is someone else with him. She cannot accept that she no longer
has a place in his heart. Through a maze of crossed lines,
wrong numbers and crackling interruptions, she tries, without
success, to reawaken a spark of their dead romance. The conversation ends. She prepares to strangle herself with the telephone cord. Cocteau's achievement was to take a situation as
old as the world itself and to exploit it cleverly in a novel setting.
In Poulenc's musical version the short phrases of the text are
paralleled by the orchestra. Passages where the woman reflects
sentimentally on the past come over with a Massenetic fullness.
Moments of sudden tension are heightened by acrid harmonies.
Both for the composer and for the singer, *la Voix humaine* is a
tour de force. The second of Poulenc's one-act monologues was
la Dame de Monte Carlo. Here the note is tragic also. One of
those aged, faded women who haunt the casino at Monte Carlo
reflects with disillusionment on her life. Convinced that she
alone has the secret formula to break the bank, she lives in
squalid lodgings she cannot afford and exists from day to day
in the tenacious hope that any moment now she will hit on a
winning run. More static than *la Voix humaine, la Dame de
Monte Carlo* is a 'complainte' in greyish tints, desolate and
wintry.

From *les Mamelles de Tirésias* of 1944 to *la Dame de Monte
Carlo* of 1961, the singer who created the leading roles in each
of Poulenc's operas was Denise Duval, an artist as beautiful
as she is gifted. In January 1963, Poulenc gave a concert with
her in Holland. When it was over he sent some flowers to her
room with the message :

> Ma Denise
> Je te dois ma dernière joie.
> > > Ton pauvre Fr.

On 28 January Poulenc returned to Paris. Next day he telephoned to make a lunch appointment with her. On the 30th
he rang to cancel it. His voice was hoarse and he thought it best

not to go out in the icy weather. At one o'clock that day, alone in his flat, he died with brutal suddenness from a heart attack. He was sixty-four. Jean Cocteau wrote :

A man so alive, so in love with life, and suddenly, in that room, a statue of wax, a face inscrutable as if it had been double-locked. It seemed to me that an irreparable quarrel had sprung up between us and I was almost tempted to cry out to the corpse : 'What have I done to you?' . . .

Eight months later Cocteau himself was to vanish, also of a heart attack. Both he and Poulenc, so often accused of heartlessness, seemed in the last resort to have proved their critics wrong.

I I

And then there were four.

Louis Durey, the eldest of the Six, was forced in 1930 to desert his home in Saint-Tropez for a time. The allowance his family made him did not keep up with the increased cost of living that the crash of 1929 brought with it. Most of the time he spent in Paris on tasks that enabled him to earn enough to keep a growing family. He worked mostly in libraries and museums researching for new editions of eighteenth-century French composers. During the Occupation, his thickly mittened hands trembling with the cold, he laboured in chilly rooms on the transcription of madrigals by Marenzio and of chansons by Josquin des Prés and Lassus. He resurrected, with affectionate care, nearly half the total output of Janequin.

The creative work he really wanted to do was limited to holidays in Saint-Tropez. Very little of what he has written is available in published form. The incidental music for radio plays has been heard once or twice, never to surface again. Songs and chamber works have had their brief hour at provincial festivals and concerts given by the Fédération Musicale Populaire, the organization of which Durey was an enthusiastic and unselfish member. From 1945 onwards he became engrossed in the composition of songs which could be quickly learned by choirs for performance at trade union rallies and mass demonstrations. There was no room for serial or concrete music in his philosophy :

I believe that art (and music in particular) should remain closely linked to the realities of life and the defence of the most basic moral and cultural values. I am a Communist because Communism represents the ideal of justice and brotherhood to which I aspire and because it aims to abolish the inhuman division of society into classes.

This interest has led him to specialize in amateur choral activities and the restoration of French folk song. His settings of verse to the greater glory of Mao Tse Tung and of Algerian guerrillas have been accompanied by a lengthy series of traditional songs drawn from nearly every province of France. He has found his niche in life. It is one that he occupies with grace and attractive modesty. At Saint-Tropez, where he still lives with his family and grandchildren, the eldest member of the Six continues his chosen work in an atmosphere of contentment.

No one could be more different in his way of life from Durey than Georges Auric, the sociable Parisian. Yet the friendship that bound them more than fifty years ago is powerful still. With the introduction of the sound film Auric came into his own. He had written ballets and other incidental pieces since the Twenties, but it is the cinema that had benefited most from his fluent and adaptable talent. The number of films with a score by Auric is unknown even to the composer himself, but it must run to close on a hundred. He provided the music for all but one of Cocteau's major films. His most famous success was the theme song from John Houston's production of *Moulin Rouge*. Whereas the Six had looked to popular music for their inspiration, here was one of their number actually writing it. The situation of the Twenties was pleasantly reversed. Then, like Cocteau who found respectability and the Académie Française towards the end of his life, Auric became a member of the Académie des Beaux Arts. From 1962 to 1968 he was director of the Opéra and the Opéra-Comique, where he showed himself to be a hard-working administrator with a scrupulous aversion to putting on his own works. It may be a symbol of his recent identification with authority that he and his Russian wife Nora live in the palatial avenue Matignon close by the official home of the President of France.

In 1931 Germaine Tailleferre gave birth to a daughter. Family preoccupations now usurped the time she had given to composing. For some years afterwards she lived with her husband and daughter at Grasse, where she made the acquaintance of Paul Valéry. He suggested that she set his new version of the *Cantate du Narcisse*. Flattered but dismayed, she protested that the task was beyond her. Then she remembered something Picasso had once said to her: 'When you start work don't try to write every morning a "piece by Germaine Tailleferre". Try to find something else, to renew yourself. Avoid using the formulas you've already discovered.' Bearing Picasso's advice in mind, she sought for a style of greater purity, and as Valéry brought her the various sections of *Narcisse* she gradually achieved the simplicity she was looking for. 'I'd never have imagined it,' she said. 'Me, writing a work in rigorous and classical form. When I was twenty I had a passion for "wrong" notes and polytonality . . . all that's over now.'

A flavour of the Six clings to the ballets she wrote – *Paris-Magie* and *Parisiana* – and her comic opera *Il était un petit navire* recalled for older members of the audience her youthful vivacity. Her incidental music for Eugène Ionesco's *le Maître* represented the same sort of commission she undertook for *les Mariés de la Tour Eiffel*. Apart from scores for the cinema, radio and theatre, she has written five concertos. The piano concerto, which has already been discussed, was later followed by a *Concertino* for harp, and then by one for flute, piano and chamber orchestra. This taste for unusual combinations was to be indulged by a concerto for baritone, piano and orchestra, and, eventually, one for soprano. The piano has always been important to her. Like her master Ravel, she finds her ideas by improvising at the piano. These she scribbles down as a first draft. Then follows revision after revision, so that in the end she writes, as she says, with a rubber. Her attitude to her own work is modest. 'My music no longer interests me, and concrete and twelve-tone music, which attract me, call for such hard labour that I haven't the strength to cope with them. It's rather as if I wanted to express myself in Chinese! It's a bit late to start learning!'

It is impossible yet to say the last word on Milhaud's huge output. A man who has been composing for seventy years, and who continues to write music with all the keenness and enjoyment of youth, does not fit easily into pigeonholes. He has been the target of virulent critical attacks. He has been dismissed as frivolous and crude. He remains supremely indifferent. All that interests him is the practice of his craft.

In 1940, confined to bed with one of his periodic attacks of rheumatism, he wrote his first symphony while listening to the radio announcement of France's collapse. He knew what a German occupation would mean. With his wife and small son he made a nightmare journey to Lisbon by way of Spain. On the boat sailing to America he received a telegram from Mills College in California. It invited him to become a teacher there. The journey to Mills took him through the limitless wheatfields of the Middle West, past the mountains of Wyoming and across desert landscapes that resembled, he thought, a picture by Dali. After the stifling heat of the desert, the crystal dazzle of the Mormon country, and the tragically contorted rocks stretching for hundreds of ochreous miles, he saw at last the fertile plains of California. The 'Boeuf sur le toit' and Montmartre were a long way away.

From 1940 to 1947 the exile found a new life at Mills College. His house was surrounded by mimosas and palm trees, camellias and magnolias. Across the yard ran partridges, squirrels and hares. In the distance he could glimpse the bay of San Francisco. Vivid blue jays haunted the woodland, and there were humming birds with flickering wings and throats of a brilliant metallic red that glinted in the sun like flashes of lightning. In this oasis of peace, shadowed only by the ominous reports that came from Europe, Milhaud taught harmony, counterpoint and orchestration to girl students. His wife Madeleine organized lectures and produced plays in French. They were joined from time to time by other distinguished exiles such as André Maurois, Fernand Léger and Julien Green, whom the college invited to lecture there. San Francisco, where the conductor Pierre Monteux lived, was only a half-hour drive away. The Stravinskys were settled in Los Angeles. At one time, in the jungle of Hollywood, René Clair strove to implant a touch of Gallic fantasy. There were friends all around.

In 1942 Milhaud's father died at the age of eighty-nine. A year later, driven into hiding by Nazi persecution, his mother followed, alone except for the devoted couple of servants who had saved her from the Gestapo. On a train journey from Laramie to Oakland Milhaud heard about the end of the war. His nephew and more than twenty cousins had been murdered in German extermination camps. He came back to Paris to find his flat in the boulevard de Clichy plundered and wrecked.

New generations were growing up. Milhaud's son, Daniel, showed a talent for painting. Just as Milhaud's own father had subsidized his son's early steps in an artistic career, so Milhaud in turn helped Daniel. A fresh pattern of life began to evolve. Milhaud now divides his time between Paris and California. In Paris, where social life is demanding, he composes little but teaches at the Conservatoire and keeps up with his innumerable friends. At Mills College he finds the peace necessary for sustained composition. His zest for travel and new experience is insatiable. It has triumphed over a state of permanent invalidism and has taken him across continents. It has inspired his interest in the Beatles' orchestration and has led him to experiment with electronic music.

The Twenties were only a brief period in the life of a musician who had composed his first opera by the time Debussy brought out the preludes for piano. So far as Milhaud is willing to go back into the past, he will admit to a preference for *l'Homme et son désir* among the things he wrote as a member of the Six. In the years that have followed he has written something like four hundred opus numbers. These include twelve symphonies and fourteen string quartets which bring his work in the genre up to a total of eighteen.

'I have been very lucky,' he remarks in the soft voice that even keen-eared orchestral players must strain to hear from the back row. 'I have had a happy life,' he adds, eager to disprove those who believe that a creator's existence should be one of torment and sorrow. Surrounded in his Paris flat by reminders of the past – a large beaming portrait of his old friend Erik Satie, a Dufy stage design for *le Boeuf sur le toit,* a yellowing photograph of Verlaine at a café table – Milhaud lives ardently in the present and in the future.

The last occasion when the Six came to the public's attention was in 1961. This was the fortieth anniversary of *les Mariés de la Tour Eiffel.* There was a ceremony at the Hôtel de Ville, and the chairman of the Paris town council, no less, invited the five surviving members and Jean Cocteau to receive the medal of 'la Ville de Paris'. For the time of the thesis had arrived, the voice of the researcher was heard in the land, and the scandals of the Twenties were now fit for embalming by civic dignitaries.

GENERAL BIBLIOGRAPHY

L'Approdo musicale, nos. 19–20, 1965 : 'Il gruppo dei Sei'.

Beach, Sylvia : *Shakespeare and Company*, Faber & Faber, 1960

Brown, Frederick : *An Impersonation of Angels*, Longmans, 1968

Cendrars, Blaise : *Blaise Cendrars vous parle*, Denoël, 1965
   Trop c'est trop, Denoël, 1965
   Ferragus (préface), Denoël, 1965

Chanel, Pierre : *Album Cocteau*, Tchou, 1970

Charters, James : *This Must Be the Place*, Lee Furman Inc., N.Y., 1927

Chastenet, Jacques : *Quand le boeuf montait sur le toit*, Fayard, 1958

Clair, René : *Entr'acte*, Poligono Società editrice in Milano, 1945
   Entr'acte, in *l'Avant-Scène, Cinéma*, no. 86, November 1968

Cocteau, Jean : *Cahiers Jean Cocteau*, vol. 1, Gallimard, 1969
   Les mariés de la Tour Eiffel, in *l'Avant-Scène*, special Cocteau number, nos. 365–6, October 1966
   Le rappel à l'ordre (including *le Coq et l'Arlequin, Carte Blanche, le Secret professionnel*, etc.), Stock, 1948

Collaer, Paul : *La musique moderne, 1905–1955*, Elsevier, 1955

Cooper, Martin : *French Music from the Death of Berlioz to the Death of Fauré*, O.U.P., 1951

Crespelle, J-P : *La folle époque*, Hachette, 1968

Drew, David : 'Modern French Music', in *European Music of the Twentieth Century*, ed. Hartog, Routledge, 1957

Fay, Bernard : *Les précieux*, Librairie académique Perrin, 1966

Georges-Michel, Michel : *De Renoir à Picasso*, Fayard, 1954

Grigoriev, S. L. : *The Diaghilev Ballet, 1909–1929*, Constable, 1953

Guilleminault, Gilbert (ed.) : *Les années folles*, Denoël, 1956
   La France de la Madelon, Denoël, 1966

Hamnett, Nina : *Laughing Torso*, Constable, 1932

Kohner, Frederick : *Kiki of Montparnasse*, Cassell, 1968

Jacob, Max : *Correspondance* (ed. F. Garnier), vol. 1, Editions de Paris, 1953

Lettres, 1920–1941 (ed. S. J. Collier), Blackwell, 1966

Lambert, Constant : *Music Ho!*, Faber & Faber, 1934

Laurencin, Marie : *Le carnet des nuits,* Pierre Cailler, 1956

Meylan, Pierre : *Les écrivains et la musique,* Editions du Cervin, Lausanne, 1952

Morand, Paul : *Journal d'un attaché d'ambassade,* Table ronde, 1949

Myers, Rollo : *Erik Satie,* Dennis Dobson, 1948

Picabia, Francis : *391* (reprint of magazine, ed. M. Sanouillet), Terrain vague, 1960

Poiret, Paul : *En habillant l'époque,* Grasset, 1930

Radiguet, Raymond : *Gli inediti* (ed. L. Garuti delli Ponti), Guanda, Parma, 1967

Regamey, Constantin : *Musiques du vingtième siècle,* Editions du Cervin, Lausanne, 1966

Roy, Jean : *Présences contemporaines,* Nouvelles Editions, Debresse, 1962

Sachs, Maurice : *La décade de l'illusion,* Gallimard, 1932
Alias, Gallimard, 1935
Au temps du Boeuf sur le toit, Editions de la Nouvelle Revue Critique, 1939
La chasse à courre, Gallimard, 1949
Chronique joyeuse et scandaleuse, Corréa, 1950

Salmon, André : *Souvenirs sans fin, 2e époque, 1908–1920,* Gallimard, 1956

Samuel, Claude : *Panorama de la musique contemporaine,* Gallimard, 1962

Sert, Misia : *Two or Three Muses* (trans. M. Budberg), Museum Press, 1953

Shattuck, Roger : *The Banquet Years,* Faber & Faber, 1959

Sokolova, Lydia : *Dancing for Diaghilev* (ed. R. Buckle), John Murray, 1960

Steegmuller, Francis : *Cocteau: A Biography,* Macmillan, 1970

Templier, P. D. : *Erik Satie,* Riéder, 1932

Thomson, Virgil : *Virgil Thomson,* Weidenfeld & Nicolson, 1967

Van Parys, Georges : *Les jours comme ils viennent,* Plon, 1969

Warnod, André : *Fils de Montmartre,* Fayard, 1955

INDIVIDUAL BIBLIOGRAPHY

[Musical works are listed separately under the composer's name in the Index]

GEORGES AURIC

Own Writings:

Many prefaces to books, and articles on music in *Marianne, Paris-Soir* and *les Nouvelles littéraires*

Bruyr, José : *L'écran des musiciens,* Corti, 1930

Cortot, Alfred : *La musique française de piano,* vol. 3, P.U.F., 1948

Goléa, Antoine : *Georges Auric,* Ventadour, 1958

Myers, Rollo : 'Georges Auric' in *Grove,* 5th edition, vol. 1, Macmillan, 1954

Poulenc, Francis : *Moi et mes amis* (with S. Audel), Palatine, 1963

Rostand, Claude : *La musique française contemporaine,* P.U.F., 1952

Schaeffner, André : *Georges Auric,* Paris, 1928

LOUIS DUREY

Own writings:

Text of a lecture on the Six; radio talk on Janequin; article on the Debussy centenary; various pronouncements on the harmonization of folk-songs, etc. (All the above reproduced in the biography by F. Robert, see below.)

Bruyr, José : *L'écran des musiciens,* Corti, 1930

Catalogue de l'Exposition Louis Durey, Fédération Musicale Populaire, 2, rue de Louvois, Paris, 2

Cortot, Alfred : *La musique française de piano,* vol. 3, P.U.F., 1948

Dumesnil, René : *Le monde des musiciens,* Crès, 1924

Milhaud, Darius : *Entretiens avec Claude Rostand,* Julliard, 1952

Notes sans musique, Julliard, 1949 and 1963

Poulenc, Francis : *Entretiens avec Claude Rostand,* Julliard, 1954

Journal de mes mélodies, Grasset, 1964

247

Robert, Frédéric : *Louis Durey, l'aîné des Six,* Éditeurs Français Réunis, 1968

ARTHUR HONEGGER
Own writings:
  'Collaboration avec Claudel', *Nouvelle Revue Française,* September 1955
  Honegger vous parle, Disque Festival F.L.D.–50, 1955
  Incantation aux fossiles, Ouchy, Lausanne, 1948
  Je suis compositeur (with B. Gavoty), Conquistador, 1951
Ansermet, Ernest : 'Un génie classique', *Journal Musical Français,* 15 December 1955
Auric, Georges : 'Judith', *Le Ménestrel,* 5 March 1926
Bruyr, José : *Honegger et son oeuvre,* Corréa, 1947
Claudel, Paul : *L'oeil écoute,* Gallimard, 1947
Cortot, Alfred : *La musique française de piano,* vol. 3, P.U.F., 1948
Delannoy, Marcel : *Honegger,* Horay, 1953
Feschotte, Jacques : *Arthur Honegger,* Seghers, 1966
Gauthier, André : *Arthur Honegger,* Eise, 1957
George, André : *Arthur Honegger,* Aveline, 1926
Gérard, Claude : *Honegger,* Editions de la Nouvelle Revue Belge, 1945
Guilbert, Yves : *Arthur Honegger,* Apostolat de la Presse, 1959
Landowski, Marcel : *Arthur Honegger,* Seuil, 1957
Matter, Jean : *Honegger, ou la Quête de Joie,* Foetisch, 1956
Meylan, Pierre : *René Morax et Arthur Honegger au Théâtre du Jorat,* Editions du Cervin, Lausanne, 1966
Milhaud, Darius : 'Arthur Honegger', *The Chesterian,* December 1921
  'Honegger, mon ami', *Figaro littéraire,* 3 December 1955
Roland-Manuel : *Arthur Honegger,* Sénart, 1924
Tappolet, Willy : *Arthur Honegger,* Hug., Zurich, 1933
Special numbers of periodicals :
  Comoedia, Charpentier, 1943
  Feuilles Musicales Suisses, Lausanne, September 1952
  Journal Musical Français, 15 December 1955

DARIUS MILHAUD
Own writings:
  'Arthur Honegger', *The Chesterian,* December 1921
  Correspondance Claudel-Milhaud, Gallimard, 1961

Darius Milhaud vous parle, Disque Festival F.L.D.–76, 1957
Entretiens avec Claude Rostand, Julliard, 1952
Etudes, Aveline, 1927
'Hommage à Bela Bartok', *Revue musicale,* 1955
'Hommage à André Gédalge', *Revue musicale,* March 1926
'La musique au Brésil', *Revue musicale,* November 1920
Notes sans musique, Julliard, 1949 and 1963
Notes sur Erik Satie, Oeuvres nouvelles, New York, 1946
'Polytonalité et atonalité', *Revue musicale,* February 1923
'Quelques souvenirs sur Paul Claudel', *Nouvelle Revue Française,* 1 September 1955
'Roland-Manuel', *Revue musicale,* 15 May 1937
Film:
Une visite à Darius Milhaud, Rolf Swickard, Hollywood
Beck, Georges: *Darius Milhaud,* Heugel, 1949 and 1956
Braga, Antonio: *Darius Milhaud,* Ardia, Naples, 1969
Collaer, Paul: *Darius Milhaud,* Richard-Masse, 1947
Cortot, Alfred: *La musique française de piano,* vol. 3, P.U.F., 1948
'Hommage à Darius Milhaud': Special number of the *Bulletin des Amis du Festival d'Aix-en-Provence,* June 1962
Poulenc, Francis: 'Oeuvres récentes de Darius Milhaud', *Contrepoints,* January 1946
Roy, Jean: *Darius Milhaud,* Seghers, 1968

FRANCIS POULENC
Own writings:
Correspondance 1915–1963 (ed. H. de Wendel), Seuil, 1967
Emmanuel Chabrier, Palatine, 1961
Entretiens avec Claude Rostand, Julliard, 1954
'Feuilles américaines', *Table Ronde,* June 1950
'Hommage à Bela Bartok', *Revue musicale,* 1955
Journal de mes mélodies, Grasset, 1964
'La musique de piano d'Erik Satie', *Revue musicale,* June 1952
'Mes mélodies et leurs poètes', *Les Annales,* 1947
Moi et mes amis (with S. Audel), Palatine, 1963
'Oeuvres récentes de Darius Milhaud', *Contrepoints,* January 1946
Cortot, Alfred: *La musique française de piano,* vol. 3, P.U.F., 1948

Davies, Laurence : *The Gallic Muse,* Dent, 1967

Hell, Henri : Francis Poulenc, Plon, 1958

Milhaud, Darius : *Etudes,* Aveline, 1927

Myers, Rollo : 'Hommage à Poulenc', *Music and Musicians,* March 1963

'Poulenc' in *Grove,* 5th edition, vol. VI, Macmillan, 1954

Roy, Jean : *Francis Poulenc,* Seghers, 1964

GERMAINE TAILLEFERRE

Cortot, Alfred : *La musique française de piano,* vol. 3, P.U.F., 1948

Jourdan-Morhange, Hélène : *Mes amis musiciens,* Editeurs Français Réunis, 1955

INDEX